New Trends in Blockchain

Editors

Kanchan Naithani

Department of Computer Science and Engineering
GL Bajaj Institute of Technology and Management
Uttar Pradesh, India

Shrikant Tiwari

Department of Computer Science and Engineering
School of Computing Science and Engineering (SCSE)
Galgotias University
Uttar Pradesh, India

Abhishek Danu

Department of Business Management
Hemvati Nandan Bahuguna Garhwal University (A Central University)
Uttarakhand, India

CRC Press
Taylor & Francis Group
Boca Raton London New York

CRC Press is an imprint of the
Taylor & Francis Group, an **informa** business
A SCIENCE PUBLISHERS BOOK

Cover credit: Image reproduced by kind courtesy of the editors.

First edition published 2026
by CRC Press
2385 NW Executive Center Drive, Suite 320, Boca Raton FL 33431

and by CRC Press
4 Park Square, Milton Park, Abingdon, Oxon, OX14 4RN

CRC Press is an imprint of Taylor & Francis Group, LLC

Library of Congress Cataloging-in-Publication Data (applied for)

ISBN: 978-1-032-86260-6 (hbk)
ISBN: 978-1-032-88914-6 (pbk)
ISBN: 978-1-003-54032-8 (ebk)

DOI: 10.1201/9781003540328

Typeset in Times New Roman
by Prime Publishing Services

Preface

Blockchain is more than a new and emerging technology—it's a metamorphosis, an innovation, a revolution that is changing the way of trusting a person in the era of tech. Blockchain will revolutionize not only financial transactions, but also supply chains, and healthcare, education and even Artificial Intelligence. *New Trends in Blockchain* presents a rich representation of recent research and insights to give an overview of how this technology continues to evolve and unlock new opportunities across a range of domains.

With blockchain fundamentals under your belts, this book covers in-depth detail on further critical areas like scalability, privacy and security. It discusses the use of the different blockchain-based solutions, which focus on privacy to ensure private transactions and their application in IoT intrusion detection for healthcare, in automated land registry through smart contracts and to protect academic credentials. The book also cites blockchain's potential for detecting anomalies in food supply chains, optimizing energy storage in solar microgrids and improving transparency in global underregulated markets.

In addition to its technological developments, blockchain is an exciting opportunity with incredible real-world applications. It allows companies to boost data security, immutability, enhance data security, reduce dependency on intermediaries, and increase transparency within any industry. Blockchain can benefit businesses by encouraging greater operational efficiencies, lowering the opportunities for fraud and encouraging more participatory ecosystems based on trust. Read regime-type, researchers and policymakers can explore its regulatory implications while developers can create solutions that solve real-world problems.

Written with an eye towards the future, this book delves into the opportunities at the crossroads of Artificial General Intelligence and blockchain, painting an aspirational picture of our world, one in which these technologies join forces to deliver intelligent, secure, and autonomous systems. This book will be of great value to researchers, industry professionals, and technology enthusiasts alike, providing the latest scholarly insights and real-world applications of blockchain technology.

Given the diversity of topics, New Trends in Blockchain has a little bit for everyone from beginners to experts who want to keep up to date in the dynamic blockchain ecosystem. From cross-border remittance to early-stage financing, it is evident that the possibilities presented by blockchain are endless, and the world has merely scratched the surface of its true potential. We hope you will explore this book for new ideas, innovations, and that you will feel inspired to play your part in the next wave of digital transformation.

The time to explore, experiment and shape the future of blockchain is now!

Content

CHAPTER 1

Introduction to Blockchain

Vaibhavi Ajay Bansode,[1,2] *Pradeep Kumar Tiwari*[1,2,*] and *Mangesh Bedekar*[2,3]

1.1 Introduction

As a revolutionary approach to data and transaction management, blockchain is increasingly relevant in today's digital world. Understanding blockchain is crucial for grasping how it can enhance security, transparency, and efficiency in numerous applications (Nakamoto 2008; Swan 2015). Understanding blockchain technology is vital because it represents a significant shift from traditional centralized systems. Its transparency provides a more secure and clear way to record and verify transactions, reducing the risk of fraud and increasing participants' trust. Additionally, blockchain's ability to create immutable data ensures data integrity, which is important for many industries such as finance, supply chain management, healthcare, and governance (Pilkington 2016).

Blockchain technology, initially developed as the foundation for Bitcoin, has rapidly evolved into a transformative framework impacting various sectors beyond finance. As a d distributed ledger, blockchain provides immutability and transparency by recording transactions across multiple computers. By eliminating intermediaries, it enhances transaction efficiency and speed while reducing costs and fraud risk. Each transaction is time-stamped, grouped into blocks, and linked securely using cryptographic techniques. Operating on a peer-to-peer network, blockchain fosters transparency and trust, with consensus mechanisms ensuring data accuracy and integrity (Swan 2015).

As blockchain technology continues to evolve, staying informed about its advancements and applications becomes increasingly important. This chapter aims

[1] Department of Computer Science and Applications.
Emails: vaibhavibansode143@gmail.com
[2] Dr. Vishwanath Karad MIT World Peace University, Pune, India, 411038.
[3] Department of Computer Science and Engineering.
Emails: mangesh.bedekar@mitwpu.edu.in
* Corresponding author: Pradeeptiwari.mca@gmail.com

DOI: 10.1201/9781003540328-1

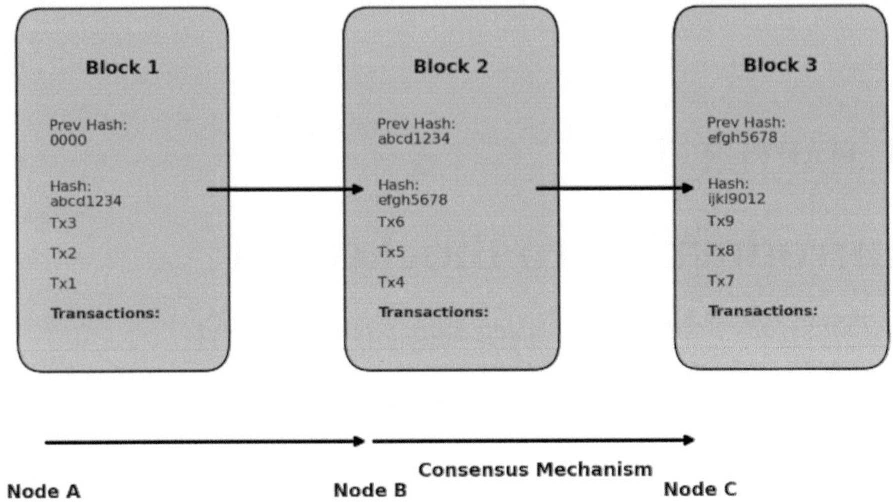

Figure 1.1. Blockchain Consensus Mechanism.

to provide readers with the information needed to navigate the rapidly changing blockchain technology landscape and realize the potential for change. This Figure 1.1 depicts the connection and continuity of blocks in a blockchain. It illustrates how each block is linked to the next through cryptographic hashing, where each block contains the hash of the previous block, ensuring data integrity and security

1.2 Historical Context

1.2.1 Origins of Blockchain Technology

Blockchain technology traces its origins to the early 1980s when cryptographer David Chaum proposed a protocol resembling today's blockchain in his dissertation. It aimed to establish secure computer systems among distrustful groups (Chaum 1982). Building on this concept, Stuart Haber and W. Scott Stornetta created the cryptographically secure blockchain aimed at tamper-proof timestamping of data in 1991 (Haber and Stornetta 1991). The addition of Merkle trees in 1992 by Haber, Stornetta, and Dave Bayer further enhanced efficiency by consolidating multiple document certificates into single blocks. Their company, Surety, showcased practical blockchain applications by publishing document certificate hashes weekly in *The New York Times* starting from 1995 (Bayer et al. 1993).

The pivotal moment came in 2008 with Satoshi Nakamoto's invention of the first decentralized blockchain for Bitcoin. Nakamoto introduced innovations such as a Hashcash-like method for timestamping blocks and a difficulty parameter for stabilizing block creation rates, revolutionizing digital trust and currency (Nakamoto 2008). By 2016, the term "blockchain" became ubiquitous as adoption within financial services reached 13.5%, signaling its entry into the early adopters' phase (Iansiti and Lakhani 2017). Despite initial enthusiasm, widespread adoption faced challenges, with only a small percentage of Chief Information Officers (CIOs) implementing

Table 1.1. Blockchain Technology Timeline.

Year	Events
1982	David Chaum introduced a blockchain-like system in his article focusing on computer security for mutually suspicious groups (Chaum 1982).
1991	Stuart Haber and W. Scott Stornetta developed a cryptographically secure blockchain for tamper-proof information timestamping (Haber and Stornetta 1991).
1992	Haber, Stornetta, and Dave Bayer improved the performance of their design by using Merkle trees to organize the evidence into blocks (Bayer et al. 1993).
1995	Their company, Surety, began publishing proof-of-concept hashes in The New York Times every week, showing how blockchain technology works (Haber and Stornetta 1995).
2008	Satoshi Nakamoto conceptualized the first decentralized blockchain for Bitcoin, introducing a Hashcash-like method for block timestamping and a difficulty parameter to regulate block creation (Nakamoto 2008).
2014	The Bitcoin blockchain reached 20 GB in size, containing all transaction records since its inception (Blockchain.com 2014).
2016	Blockchain technology gained popularity, with "block" and "chain" combined into "blockchain." Adoption within financial services reached 13.5%, marking the early adopters' phase (Iansiti and Lakhani 2017).
2018	Gartner reported that only 1% of CIOs had implemented blockchain in their organizations, with 8% actively experimenting or planning to do so (Gartner 2018).
2019	5% of CIOs believed blockchain was a 'game-changer' for their businesses, reflecting cautious optimism and ongoing exploration of its potential (Gartner 2019).

blockchain by 2018, though perceptions improved slightly by 2019 with 5% of CIOs viewing blockchain as a potential game-changer for business (Gartner 2019). Thus, blockchain technology has evolved from theoretical foundations to practical applications, reshaping industries while navigating challenges on its path to broader adoption shown in the Table 1.1.

1.2.2 Development and Significance of Bitcoin

Bitcoin, abbreviated as BTC and symbolized by ₿, emerged in 2008 as the pioneering decentralized cryptocurrency. Its creation by an anonymous figure known as Satoshi Nakamoto was rooted in a free-market ideology, aiming to establish a digital cash system independent of centralized control (Nakamoto 2008). Announced as open-source software in January 2009, Bitcoin operates on a peer-to-peer network where nodes cryptographically verify transactions and record them on a public ledger called the blockchain. This ledger ensures transparency and security without the need for a central authority, achieving consensus through a computationally intensive process known as mining (Antonopoulos 2017). Mining, however, has drawn criticism for its significant energy consumption and environmental impact (Stoll et al. 2019).

Originally conceived as electronic cash, Bitcoin has gained traction primarily as a store of value rather than being widely used as a centralized unit of exchange or account (Yermack 2015). Its adoption has sparked regulatory scrutiny due to concerns over its pseudonymous nature facilitating illicit activities, prompting bans in several countries by 2021 (Foley et al. 2019). Despite these challenges, Bitcoin continues to grow, attracting large investors and supporting advances in technology such as the integration of non-fungible tokens (NFTs) and the launch of exchange-traded funds such as Bitcoin ETFs, indicating that it is moving towards a broader milestone of recognition and financial innovation (Hougan and Lawant 2021).

1.2.2.1 Bitcoin Historical Timeline

Pre–2008

- Digital cash technologies were explored, including ecash by David Chaum in the 1980s and Hashcash by Adam Back in 1997 (Chaum 1982; Back 2002).
- Cryptographers proposed the idea of computational puzzles having value in 1992 (Dwork and Naor 1992).
- In 1998, Cypherpunks Wei Dai and Nick Szabo introduced the concept of decentralized digital scarcity cryptocurrencies, including b-money and Bit gold (Dai 1998; Sazabo 1997).
- In 2004, Hal Finney produced the first results based on reproducible data (Finney 2004).

2008–2009

- August 18, 2008: The domain name bitcoin.org was registered (Whois 2008).
- October 31, 2008: Satoshi Nakamoto published the Bitcoin whitepaper titled *Bitcoin: A Peer-to-Peer Electronic Cash System* (Nakamoto 2008).
- January 3, 2009: The Bitcoin network was created when Satoshi Nakamoto mined the genesis block, embedding it with a headline from *The Times* newspaper (Nakamoto 2009).
- January 2009: Bitcoin software was released as open source (Nakamoto 2009).
- January 12, 2009: Hal Finney received the first Bitcoin transaction of 10 BTC from Satoshi Nakamoto (Nakamoto et al. 2009).
- May 22, 2010: The first commercial transaction using Bitcoin occurred on the day now known as 'Bitcoin Pizza Day' when Laszlo Hanyecz purchased two pizzas for 10,000 Bitcoins (Hanyecz 2010).

2010–2012

- Satoshi Nakamoto mined an estimated one million bitcoins before disappearing in 2010, transferring control to Gavin Andresen (Andresen 2011).
- February 2011: The dark web Silk Road began exclusively accepting bitcoins as payment (Christin 2013).
- September 2012: The Bitcoin Foundation was founded to promote Bitcoin, with Gavin Andresen becoming lead developer (Bitcoin Foundation 2012).

2013–2014

- March 2013: The U.S. Financial Crimes Enforcement Network (FinCEN) issued regulatory guidelines for decentralized virtual currencies like Bitcoin (FinCEN 2013).

- May 2013: American authorities seized anonymous trading platform Mt. Gox (Vigna and Casey 2015).
- June 2013: The U.S. DEA seized Bitcoin in a drug-related case; this was the first time Bitcoin was seized by the government (United States DEA 2013).
- October 2013: Following the arrest of Silk Road founder Ross Ulbricht, the FBI seized the Bitcoin platform (Greenberg 2013).
- December 2013: The People's Bank of China banned accounting firms from using Bitcoin (Yao 2013).

2015–2019

- 2017: Research estimated that 2.9 to 5.8 million unique users owned cryptocurrency wallets, mostly Bitcoin (Cambridge Centre for Alternative Finance 2017).
- August 2017: The SegWit software upgrade launched to increase scalability (Bitcoin Core 2017).
- December 2017: The Chicago Mercantile Exchange introduced the first futures on Bitcoin (CME Group 2017).
- February 2018: Bitcoin prices declined after China banned Bitcoin trading and following hacks on cryptocurrency exchanges (Hougan and Lawant 2021).

2020–Present

- 2020: Major companies like MicroStrategy and Square began acquiring Bitcoin as a treasury reserve asset (MicroStrategy 2020).
- November 2020: PayPal expanded Bitcoin support in the U.S. (PayPal 2020).
- February 2021: Bitcoin's market cap reached $1 trillion for the first time (CoinMarketCap 2021).
- September 2021: Bitcoin joined the U.S. dollar as legal tender in El Salvador (Bukele 2021).
- October 2021: The SEC approved BITO, the first Bitcoin futures ETF to list on CME (SEC 2021).
- May-June 2022: Bitcoin prices crashed after the collapse of TerraUSD and Celsius Network (Bloomberg 2022).
- 2023: Non-fungible tokens (NFTs) on Bitcoin went live, and U.S. spot Bitcoin ETFs began trading (Messari 2023).
- June 2023: Bitcoin had an estimated 81.7 million users globally (Chainalysis 2023).

1.2.3 Bitcoin Holds Significant Implications Across Several Domains

- **Decentralization and Financial Sovereignty:** Bitcoin works on a decentralized network by eliminating the need for intermediaries such as banks or governments in transactions. Decentralization empowers individuals by granting greater control over their finances and reducing dependence on conventional financial systems.

- **Security and Transparency:** Transactions on the blockchain are cryptographically protected to ensure that they are secure and recorded on a public ledger which serves as a transparent and distributed record of all transactions. This ensures transparency and reduces the risk of fraud or manipulation, enhancing trust among users.
- **Scarcity and Store of Value:** Bitcoin is limited to 21 million coins, making it similar to precious metals like gold in terms of scarcity. These features, combined with its nature, ensure that Bitcoin has the ability to retain its value and resist inflation.
- **Global Accessibility and Financial Inclusion:** Bitcoin enables cross-border transactions without traditional banking infrastructure, providing financial services to unbanked populations worldwide. This participation empowers people in developing countries who do not have access to traditional banking services.
- **Innovation and Technological Advancement:** The blockchain technology underlying Bitcoin has fueled innovation in many sectors beyond finance, including supply chain management, voting elections, and business applications (dApps).
- **Investment and Diversification:** Bitcoin has evolved into a recognized investment asset, attracting institutional investors and serving as a diversification tool in investment portfolios. Its potential for high returns, albeit with volatility, has made it appealing to investors seeking alternative assets.
- **Economic and Regulatory Impact:** Bitcoin's rise has prompted discussions on regulatory frameworks for cryptocurrencies globally. It challenges traditional monetary policies and raises questions about governance, taxation, and financial stability.
- **Cultural and Social Influence:** Bitcoin has fostered a community of enthusiasts, developers, and innovators dedicated to advancing blockchain technology and promoting financial sovereignty. It has also influenced popular culture and mainstream media coverage, shaping public perception of digital currencies.

Bitcoin's significance lies in its potential to redefine finance by promoting decentralization, security, and financial inclusion while driving technological innovation and challenging existing economic paradigms. Its journey continues to unfold amid evolving regulatory landscapes and technological advancements in the broader cryptocurrency ecosystem.

1.2.4 Evolution of Blockchain beyond Cryptocurrency

Blockchain technology, initially developed to support cryptocurrencies, holds significant promise beyond financial transactions. Unlike traditional centralized systems, blockchain operates on a peer-to-peer network where each participant, or node, maintains a copy of the ledger. Transactions are grouped into blocks, which are cryptographically linked to form a chain, ensuring transparency, security, and immutability (Nakamoto 2008).

Cryptocurrencies, such as Bitcoin, revolutionized digital currency by utilizing cryptography for secure transactions and decentralized networks to operate independently of central authorities (Antonopoulos 2017). These networks employ consensus mechanisms like proof-of-work (PoW) or proof-of-stake (PoS) to validate transactions and maintain blockchain integrity. Users store their cryptocurrency in digital wallets, and transactions involve transferring currency between pseudonymous addresses on the blockchain.

Beyond digital currencies, blockchain technology is transforming various industries. In supply chain management, blockchain provides transparency and traceability from raw material sourcing to retail, reducing fraud, counterfeiting, and inefficiencies (Kshetri 2018). The healthcare industry leverages blockchain to securely store and share patient records, ensuring data integrity and privacy. Additionally, blockchain helpsauthenticate pharmaceuticals, tracking them from manufacturer to patient to combat counterfeit drugs (Agbo et al. 2019).

Identity management is another area where blockchain excels. Traditional systems are vulnerable to breaches and identity theft, but blockchain enables individuals to control their digital identities securely. This decentralized solution has significant implications for secure access to services, voting systems, and refugee management (Zyskind et al. 2015). Furthermore, smart contracts, which are self-executing contracts with terms written into code, automate and enforce agreements without intermediaries, reducing transaction costs in industries such as real estate, insurance, and legal services (Szabo 1997).

Content creators are also turning to blockchain for digital rights management. By recording ownership and usage rights on a decentralized ledger, artists, musicians, and writers can ensure fair compensation and streamline licensing processes (De Filippi 2018). The benefits of blockchain technology are vast, offering transparency that enhances trust and accountability. It also provides security by ensuring transactions are tamper-proof, while improving efficiency by streamlining operations, reducing costs, and enabling automation through smart contracts. Additionally, its decentralized nature removes single points of failure, making systems more resilient to censorship and data breaches.

Despite its promise, blockchain faces challenges such as scalability, interoperability, and regulatory concerns. However, ongoing innovation and collaboration within the blockchain ecosystem are addressing these issues, paving the way for broader adoption and integration into diverse industries. As blockchain technology continues to evolve, it presents exciting possibilities that extend far beyond its origins in cryptocurrency, offering transformative solutions across multiple sectors.

1.3 Fundamental Principles of Blockchain

1.3.1 Definition and Basic Concept of Blockchain

Blockchain is a record is a record of transactions that anyone can view and verify. Blockchain is the underlying technology that enables the distribution and security of information and transactions. At its core, a blockchain is a data record that stores incremental data (called blocks). These blocks are linked and protected using cryptography techniques, ensuring the integrity and immutability of the data they contain. Figure 1.2 shows that at its core, a blockchain is a data record that stores incremental data (called blocks). These blocks are linked and protected using cryptographic techniques, ensuring the integrity and immutability of the data they contain.

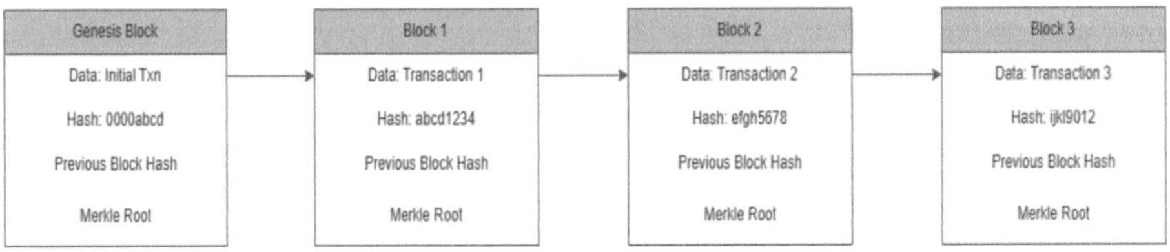

Figure 1.2. Concept of Blockchain

1.3.2 Blockchain Properties

Decentralization: Traditional storage facilities are centralized and managed by a single organization, such as a bank or company. In contrast, blockchain operates on a decentralized network of computers (nodes), with each node storing a copy of the entire blockchain. This decentralized structure makes the system resilient to faults and tampering of data (Nakamoto 2008).

Transparency: Every transaction or data entry in the blockchain is recorded in a block and is visible to all participants in the network. This transparency enhances users' trust and accountability (Pilkington 2016).

Immutability: Once data is recorded in a block and added to the blockchain, it is difficult to change or delete it. This is because each block contains a unique cryptographic hash of the previous block, thereby forming a chain. Changing one block requires altering all subsequent blocks, which is both impractical and easily detectable (Yaga et al. 2018).

Consensus Mechanisms: A consensus mechanism is necessary for adding new blocks to the blockchain. This ensures that all nodes agree on the validity of the transaction or a specific decision. For example, Bitcoin uses **Proof of Work (PoW),** while other platforms like Ethereum also utilize **Proof of Stake (PoS)** (Bonneau et al. 2015).

Security: Cryptography plays a crucial role in blockchain security. TransaActions are secured using cryptographic techniques, and participants in the network have cryptographic keys that enable them to interact with the blockchain (Zheng et al. 2017).

Smart Contracts: Some blockchain platforms (such as Ethereum) support smart contracts. These contracts are self-executing, where the terms are directly written into the code. They automatically execute tasks when predefined conditions are met, enabling decentralized applications (**DApps**) and programmable operations (Buterin 2014).

1.3.3 Structure of a Block

Linked list: The fundamental structure of a blockchain is a linked list of hashes. In a regular connection, there are nodes. The two aspects of a node are indicators and data. The next node is indicated by a pointer. Just replace normal pointers in the blockchain with hash pointers.

Merkle tree: The Merkle tree is named after its inventor Ralph Merkle. It is a binary tree constructed using pointers.

- **Structure of a Block:** Each Block in the Blockchain consists of a Block Header and a Merkle Tree.
- **Block Header:** The block header file contains the block's metadata, i.e. information about the block itself. The contents of the block header are as follows:
  - The hash of the previous block header.
  - The hash of the current block.
  - A Timestamp.
  - Cryptographic nonce.
  - Merkle root.

Figure 1.3 Showing Block Structure: A Block contains a Header, Metadata, and Transactions. The Header includes a Timestamp, Nonce, and Merkle Root.

The Merkle Tree

A **Merkle tree** is a binary tree constructed using hash pointers. Each block in a blockchain is designed to store a specific number of transactions. The challenge lies in efficiently organizing and verifying these transactions within a block (Merkle 1987).

One approach is to create a linked list of transactions using hash pointers and store the entire list within a block. However, this method becomes impractical as the number of transactions increases. Searching for a specific transaction would require iterating through each block separately, leading to significant computational overhead and degrading blockchain performance (Nakamoto 2008).

This is where the **Merkle tree** provides an efficient solution. A Merkle tree is a single-block structure that groups all transactions within that block into a hierarchical,

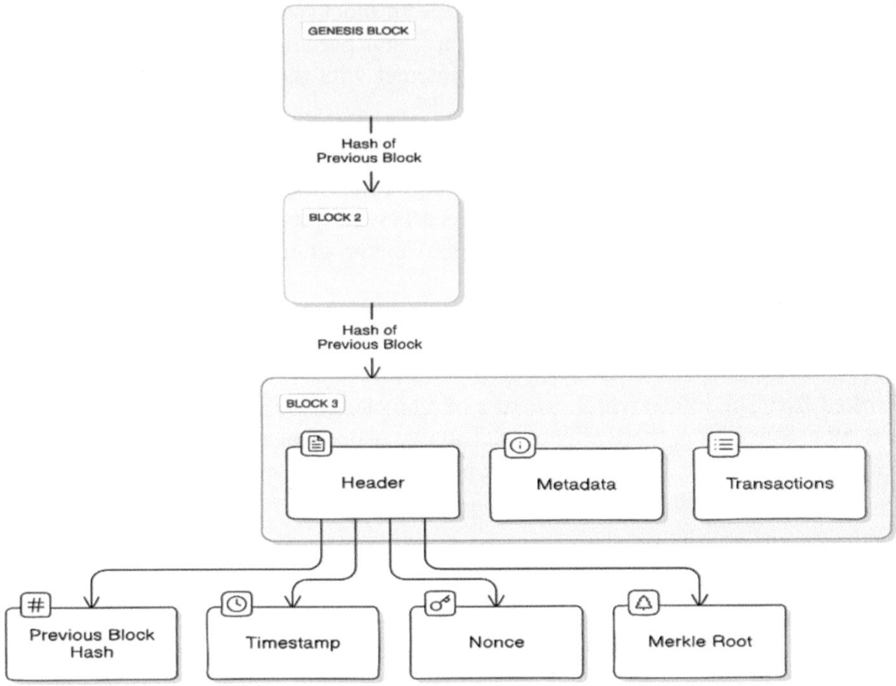

Figure 1.3. Block Structure.

hash-based tree. Instead of storing individual transactions sequentially, it allows for hashing and summarizing transactions, enabling quick verification of ownership and inclusion (Zheng et al. 2017).

Since a **blockchain** is a hash-based linked list of blocks, where each block consists of transactions and a header, the **Merkle tree** is a crucial component in the organization of transactions. It enhances security, scalability, and verification efficiency in blockchain networks (Narayanan et al. 2016).

Figure 1.4 Depicting how the Merkle Tree mechanism works and how blocks are connected in the form of a Merkle Tree.

The different types of nodes in a Merkle tree:

Root node: The block header includes the Merkle root, which serves as the root of the Merkle tree. It is the upper part of the tree structure. The hashes of all child nodes (which can be other nodes or leaves) are recursively combined until only hash remains (the root hash).

Leaf node: Transaction data hashes are stored in this node. The data for each transaction in the block is hashed, and the leaf nodes store the hash value (also known as the identification number).

Non-leaf node: The hash value of each child is included in the non-leaf nodes. Because the hashing process continues from these intermediate nodes to the root of the tree, which also holds intermediate hash results, they are also called intermediate nodes.

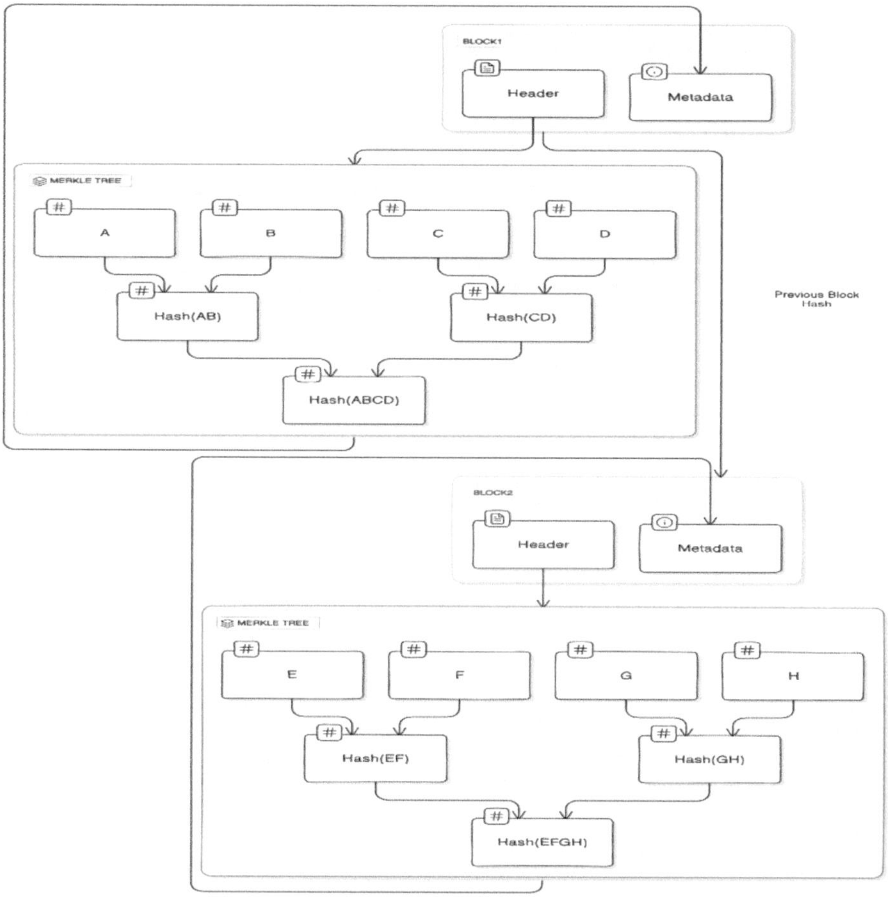

Figure 1.4. Blockchain Block Structure with Merkle Tree.

Figure 1.5 depicting the Root Node, Leaf Nodes, and Non-Leaf Nodes, along with their connections and working mechanism

1.3.4 How Does a Transaction Take Place in Blockchain?

Figure 1.6 Showing how transactions take place in the blockchain mechanism. This diagram illustrates Transaction Initiation, Verification, Grouping of Transactions, Block Addition, Ledger Update, and Completion of the Transaction.

1.3.4.1 How Blockchain Works

1. **Transaction Initiation:** A user initiates a transaction involving the transfer of information or assets from one party to another. The transaction is represented as digital data and includes essential details such as sender, receiver, and amount (Nakamoto 2008).

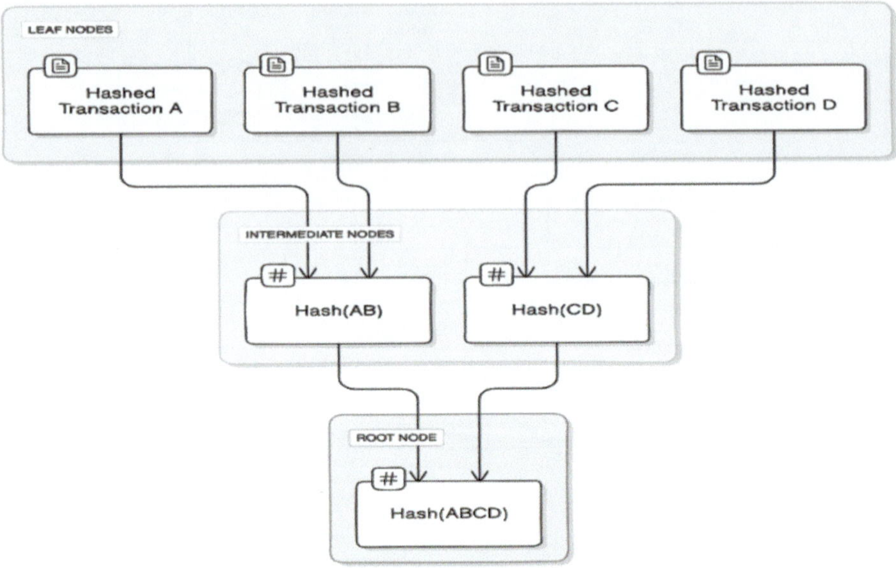

Figure 1.5. Nodes in Merkle Root.

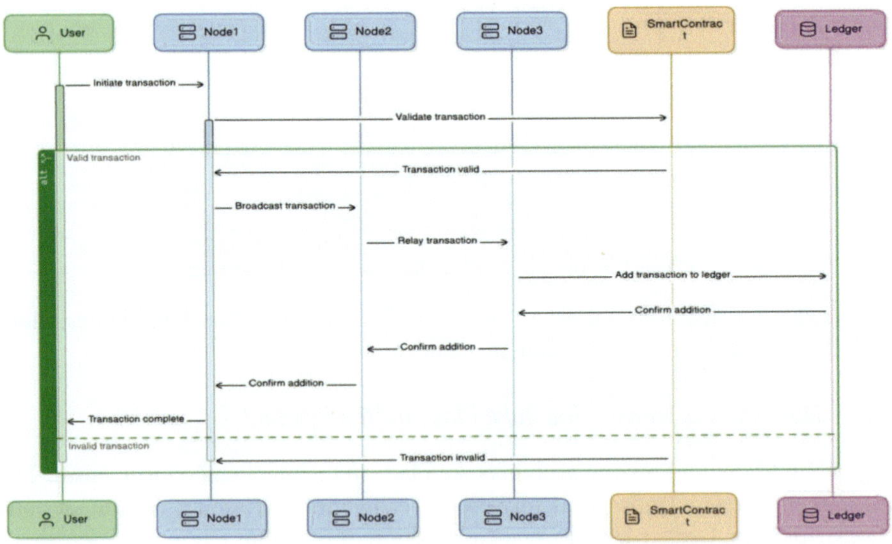

Figure 1.6. Blockchain Transaction Process.

2. **Transaction Verification:** The transaction is broadcast to a network of peer-to-peer computers (nodes). These nodes use cryptographic algorithms to verify the validity of the transaction by checking the sender's balance, digital signature, and other criteria (Pilkington 2016).

3. **Transaction Grouping:** Verified transactions are grouped into blocks. Each block contains:
   - o A list of transactions
   - o A timestamp
   - o A reference to the previous block (the hash)
   - o A unique identifier of the current block (the hash) (Zheng et al. 2017).
4. **Consensus Mechanism:** Nodes must reach an agreement on the validity of new blocks before they are added to the blockchain. This is done through different consensus mechanisms:
   - o **Proof-of-Work (PoW):** Miners use computational power to solve complex mathematical puzzles, securing the network and adding blocks (Bonneau et al. 2015).
   - o **Proof-of-Stake (PoS):** Validators are chosen based on the amount of cryptocurrency they hold and their willingness to "stake" their coins to participate in block validation (Buterin 2014).
5. **Block Addition:** Once consensus is reached, the validated block is added to the existing blockchain, linking it to the previous block. This ensures data integrity and immutability (Narayanan et al. 2016).
6. **Ledger Update:** The updated blockchain is distributed across the entire network. Each node updates its copy to reflect the latest changes, ensuring consistency and security (Yaga et al. 2018).
7. **Transaction Completion:** The transaction is considered finalized once it is included in a block and confirmed by the network. It is now permanently recorded on the blockchain and cannot be altered (Merkle 1987).

1.3.5 Types of Blockchain

1.3.5.1 Public Blockchain

It is the first type of blockchain technology. Its permissionless and borderless nature allows anyone with an internet connection to join the blockchain platform and become an authorized entity. In this blockchain the user has access to historical and current data in addition to the mining process (such as transaction analysis and adding to inventory) (Nakamoto 2008). Since most policies are publicly available and cannot be altered by legal documents or network changes. Anyone can verify transactions, report errors and flag changes (Swan 2015).

Advantages: Public blockchains offer the advantage of decentralized governance. This ensures that even if the organization that created them shuts down, public blockchains will continue to operate as long as there are computers connected to the network (Buterin 2014).

Disadvantages: Public blockchains are not very scalable either. When more nodes join the network, its speed decreases. Businesses cannot restrict access or usage and the network becomes slow. Godefroy (2020) says hackers could replace the public blockchain network if they get at least 51% of the work.

Use Cases: Mining and trading cryptocurrencies such Bitcoin are the most popular users of public blockchain. On the other hand, it can also be used to create a permanent record through audit analysis, such as public records of members and electronic written evidence. This blockchain is perfect for organizations that rely on transparency and trust, such as NGOs or community groups. Given that the network is public, private companies should not use it (Antonopoulos 2017).

1.3.5.2 Private Blockchain

Private blockchains are controlled by an organization or operated within a controlled environment (such as a closed network). Although this blockchain operates on a smaller scale, it operates similarly to the public blockchain network in that it provides peer-to-peer connectivity and decentralization. Private blockchains typically operate on restricted networks within a company or organization and are not accessible to everyone who wants to join and contribute. These are also called enterprise blockchains or permissioned blockchains (Pilkington 2016).

Advantages: Appropriate levels are determined by the security, permissions, and access governing body. For example, an organization creating a private blockchain network can decide which nodes have permission to view, contribute, or modify information. It may also provide information that is not accessible to third parties. Private blockchains can run faster than public blockchains due to size limitations (Yaga et al. 2018).

Disadvantages: One of the disadvantages of private blockchains is that they are not true blockchains because distribution is at the heart of the blockchain concept. Furthermore, private blockchains frequently have closed-source, proprietary source code. There may be less security if users are unable to independently audit or validate it. On a private blockchain, anonymity does not exist either (Zheng et al. 2017).

Use Cases: Because of their speed, private blockchains are the best option when cryptographical security is required for the blockchain but the governing entity does not want the public to have access to the data. In addition to private blockchain technology, internal voting, asset ownership and chain management are also used (Tapscott and Tapscott 2016).

1.3.5.3 Hybrid Blockchain

Organizations looking to get the best of both worlds sometimes adopt hybrid blockchains, or blockchain systems that combine public and private blockchain. It allows companies to create non-public permissions in addition to privacy-based permissions, allowing them to control what information is public and who can access certain information stored on the blockchain. In a hybrid blockchain, data and transactions are mostly private but can be verified when necessary, for example by authorization via smart contract. Although the blockchain secures the contract, confidential information can still be discerned. Hybrid blockchains may be owned by private organizations but are not transferable (Xu et al. 2019).

Advantages: The main advantages of hybrid blockchain is that external hackers cannot perform a 51% attack on the network because the network operates in a closed environment. In addition to protecting privacy, it also allows communication with outsiders. Has greater scalability than public blockchain networks and enables cheap, fast transactions (Crosby et al. 2016).

Disadvantages: This type of blockchain allows information to be hidden, so it is not completely transparent. Users have no incentive to join or contribute to the network and development can be difficult (Swan 2015).

Use Cases: Real estate is among the numerous use cases of hybrid blockchain technology. Hybrid blockchain allows companies to keep their operations private while making certain information (like inventory) publicly available. Hybrid blockchain technology can help businesses such as financial services and retail run efficient operations. This kind of blockchain can also be used to store medical records (Zheng et al. 2017).

1.3.5.4 Consortium Blockchain

Hybrid blockchains share the same characteristics as four forms of blockchains combined into chains, often referred to as federated blockchains (consortium blockchains). However, it is different in that it is a joint venture where many members of the organization work together. By restricting access to specific groups, shared blockchains essentially eliminate the dangers associated with an organization running a private blockchain network. Default nodes control the consensus process. Validator nodes are responsible for initialling, accepting and verifying transactions. Transactions can be initiated or received by number nodes (Buterin 2014).

Advantages: Consortium Blockchain is more scalable, secure and efficient than public blockchain networks. Provides control like private and hybrid blockchains (Yaga et al. 2018).

Disadvantages: Compared to public blockchains, consortium blockchains are less transparent. However, if one member of the community is affected, the network's ability to function will still be affected by the blockchain's own rules (Pilkington 2016).

Use Cases: There are mainly two applications of consortium blockchain: payments and banking. An association of banks can decide which nodes will verify the transaction. Research centers and groups that want to monitor nutrition can also create similar models. Ideals for supply chains, especially applications involving food and pharmaceuticals (Crosby et al. 2016).

1.4 Core Components of Blockchain

1.4.1 Decentralized Ledgers

Blockchain technology provides a solution to the problem of electronic decentralization (sometimes called a public ledger) to record transactions and assets in a business network without the need to use a trusted intermediary (Nakamoto 2008). Anything with material or moral value can be tracked and traded on the blockchain network (Swan 2015). This is a data blockchain because blocks of digital data are protected and interconnected by a chain and data (Pilkington 2016). It forms the basis of many cryptocurrencies such as Bitcoin and Ethereum and provides a list of data collected over computer networks (Tapscott and Tapscott 2016). Table 1.2 shows the difference between decentralized and centralized systems across various parameters. It highlights how decentralized systems differ from centralized one.

1.4.1.1 Process

Figure 1.7 presents a flowchart of the Consensus Process, starting with the Consensus Algorithm, followed by the Decentralized System, Validation by Miners, Block Creation, Proof of Work, and Distributed Ledger.

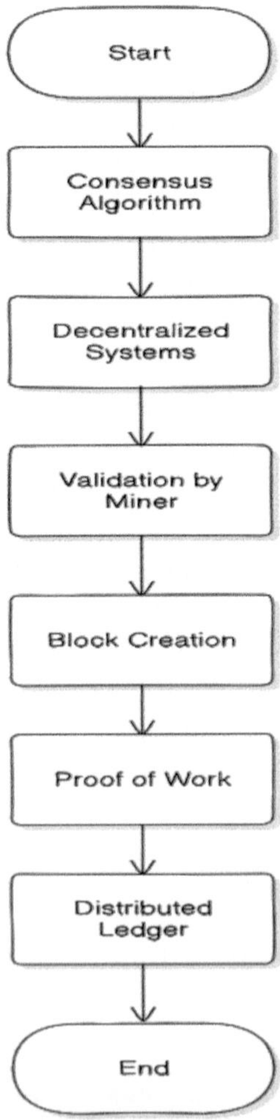

Figure 1.7. Blockchain Consensus Process.

1.4.1.2 Decentralized vs Centralized Systems

Table 1.2. Decentralized vs Centralized Systems.

Aspect	Decentralized Systems	Centralized Systems
Control	Control is distributed across multiple parts of the network (Nakamoto 2008).	Control is carried out by a central authority or several organizations (Tapscott and Tapscott 2016).
Data Storage	Data is stored on multiple nodes, each having a copy of the entire ledger (Swan 2015).	Data resides in a centralized location or database overseen by a single authority (Pilkington 2016).
Security	High security due to distributed nature and cryptographic techniques; resistant to single points of failure (Narayanan et al. 2016).	Lower security; a single point of failure makes it more vulnerable to attacks and data breaches (Zheng et al. 2017).
Trust	In a non-secure environment, participants do not need to rely on trust between each other; instead, they rely on trust in the system and its approval mechanisms (Buterin 2014).	Trust-based environment; participants must trust the central authority to manage and secure the data (Pilkington 2016).
Transparency	High transparency; all transactions are publicly visible and verifiable by any node in the network (Tapscott and Tapscott 2016).	Lower transparency; data access and visibility are controlled by the central authority (Zheng et al. 2017).
Immutability	Transactions, once recorded, cannot be easily altered or deleted, ensuring data integrity (Narayanan et al. 2016).	Data can be altered or deleted by the central authority, risking data integrity (Pilkington 2016).
Consensus Mechanism	It uses consensus mechanisms like Proof-of-Work (PoW), Proof-of-Stake (PoS), etc., to validate transactions and uphold the ledger (Nakamoto 2008).	No need for consensus mechanisms; the central authority validates and manages transactions (Zheng et al. 2017).
Scalability	Often faces scalability challenges due to the need for consensus across many nodes; slower transaction speeds (Buterin 2014).	Generally, more scalable and faster transaction speeds, as the central authority can optimize for efficiency (Zheng et al. 2017).
Cost	Can be more cost-effective in the long run by eliminating intermediaries; however, high initial setup and maintenance costs (Pilkington 2016).	May involve high costs due to central management, maintenance, and potential intermediaries (Swan 2015).
Resilience	High resilience; the failure of one or a few nodes does not affect the overall system (Narayanan et al. 2016).	Lower resilience; failure or attack on the central authority can disrupt the entire system (Zheng et al. 2017).
Examples	Bitcoin, Ethereum, Decentralized Finance (DeFi) platforms (Nakamoto 2008).	Traditional banking systems, centralized databases, social media platforms (Tapscott and Tapscott 2016).
Overall	Offer distributed control, high security, transparency, and resilience but face challenges in scalability and can have higher initial costs (Buterin 2014).	Provide centralized control, potentially higher scalability, and efficiency but have lower security, transparency, and resilience due to a single point of failure (Zheng et al. 2017).

1.4.2 Consensus Mechanisms

1.4.2.1 Consensus in Decentralized Systems

Consensus is the process of reaching an agreement among a group of participants (Lamport et al. 1982). In the context of decentralized systems, consensus ensures that all nodes in the system agree on a single decision or single value (Narayanan et al. 2016).

1.4.2.2 Challenges in Distributed Systems

In distributed systems, achieving consensus faces challenges such as network delays, node failures, and communication issues. These challenges make it difficult to determine whether all nodes have the same view of the system (Fischer et al. 1985).

Use Cases: *Consensus methods are employed in various applications, including blockchain technology (e.g., achieving agreement on a single valid block), distributed databases, cloud computing, and collaborative decision-making processes (Pilkington 2016).*

1.4.2.3 Properties of Consensus

- **Termination:** The process eventually reaches a decision (Lamport 2001).
- **Agreement:** All correct nodes agree on the same value (Nakamoto 2008).
- **Validity:** The agreed-upon value is a valid input from one of the nodes (Castro and Liskov 1999).

1.4.2.4 Challenges in Achieving Consensus

- Achieving consensus often involves trade-offs between fault tolerance, latency, and scalability (Zheng et al. 2017).
- Different algorithms prioritize these factors differently, and the selection of the most appropriate algorithm depends on the specific requirements of the system (Buterin 2014).

1.4.2.5 Types of Consensus Mechanisms

1.4.2.5.1 Proof-of-Work (PoW)

The idea behind PoW is that it requires a large computational investment to find a valid solution, making it expensive and time-consuming (Nakamoto 2008). Security is ensured because altering a previous block necessitates redoing the proof of work for that block and all subsequent blocks (Narayanan et al. 2016).

1.4.2.5.2 Working of PoW

- **Transaction Initiation:** Users initiate transactions on the blockchain.
- **Verification:** Transactions are cryptographically verified by network nodes.
- **Block Formation:** Verified transactions are grouped to form a block.

- **Hashing**: Miners compete to solve a complex mathematical problem known as "proof of work."
- **Difficulty Adjustment**: The network adjusts difficulty to maintain consistent block creation time.
- **Mining**: Miners use computational power to find a solution.
- **Verification of Solution**: Other nodes verify the correctness of the solution.
- **Block Addition**: A new block is added, and the miner receives a cryptocurrency reward.

1.4.2.5.3 Proof-of-Stake (PoS)

In PoS, staking functions similarly to PoW's mining but replaces energy-intensive computation with financial commitment (King and Nadal 2012). Network validators stake cryptocurrency to gain selection rights for confirming new transactions.

Working of PoS

1. **Staking Coins:** Users lock up coins to validate transactions.
2. **Choosing Validators:** A validator is randomly selected to verify transactions.
3. **Adding Blocks and Earning Rewards:** Validators earn cryptocurrency for validating transactions.
4. **Mining Power and Random Selection:** The probability of selection increases with staked cryptocurrency.
5. **Staking Pools:** Users combine their stakes in pools for better selection chances.

1.4.2.5.4 Proof-of-Authority (PoA)

Relies on a limited number of trusted validators instead of computational power or staking (De Angelis et al. 2018). Validators maintain reputations and follow strict criteria to participate.

1.4.2.5.5 Proof-of-Burn (PoB)

Requires miners to destroy coins by sending them to an unusable address to earn mining rights, reducing coin supply and ensuring commitment to network security (Ittay and Eyal 2014).

1.4.2.5.6 Proof-of-Elapsed-Time (PoET)

Ensures fair mining by making each node wait for a random time before block selection, mimicking a lottery system (Intel Corporation 2016).

1.4.2.6 Byzantine Fault Tolerance (BFT) and Its Variants

1.4.2.6.1 Byzantine Fault Tolerance (BFT)

Allows decentralized systems to function even if some nodes fail or act maliciously (Lamport et al. 1982).

1.4.2.6.2 Classic Byzantine Generals Problem

This problem illustrates the difficulty of reaching consensus in untrusted networks, where false messages can lead to failures (Lamport et al. 1982).

1.4.2.6.3 Practical Byzantine Fault Tolerance (PBFT)

Achieves consensus by allowing a leader node to propose transactions, which are verified by two-thirds of the network (Castro and Liskov 1999).

1.4.2.6.4 Federated Byzantine Agreement (FBA)

Divides nodes into sub-networks that reach local consensus before agreeing globally, reducing communication overhead (Mazieres 2015).

1.4.3 Cryptographic Hashing

Figure 1.8 illustrates the flowchart of the cryptographic mechanism, showing the role of encryption and decryption and how plaintext is converted into ciphertext and vice versa.

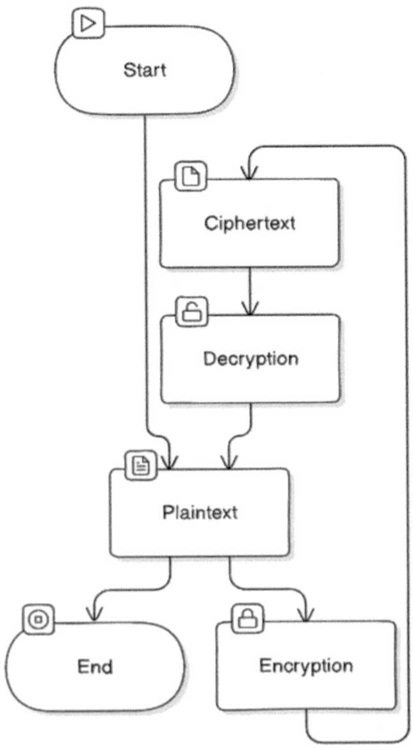

Figure 1.8. Cryptography in Blockchain.

1.4.3.1 Importance of Cryptography in Blockchain

Cryptography is crucial for ensuring the security and integrity of blockchain networks (Narayanan et al. 2016). Blockchain technology, which underpins cryptocurrencies like Bitcoin, depends on cryptographic techniques to achieve various goals such as secure transactions, data integrity, and decentralized consensus (Nakamoto 2008).

Encryption and decryption ciphers are fundamental components of cryptography, the science of secure communication. These ciphers are algorithms that transform plaintext (readable data) into ciphertext (encoded data) during encryption and reverse the process during decryption (Stallings 2020).

1.4.3.1.1 Symmetric-key (Private-key) Ciphers

A single key for both encryption and decryption processes. The challenge of symmetric-key cryptography is to securely share keys between communicators (Schneier 1996).

Examples:

- **DES (Data Encryption Standard):** An early symmetric-key algorithm with a fixed key size, now considered insecure (Menezes et al. 1996).
- **AES (Advanced Encryption Standard):** A widely adopted symmetric-key algorithm with key sizes of 128, 192, or 256 bits (Daemen and Rijmen 2002).

1.4.3.1.2 Asymmetric-key (Public-key) Ciphers

Utilize both a public and a private key pair. Data encrypted with the public key can only be decrypted with the corresponding private key, and vice versa. This eliminates the need for secure key exchange (Diffie and Hellman 1976).

Examples:

- **RSA (Rivest–Shamir–Adleman):** A widely utilized asymmetric algorithm for secure data transmission and digital signatures (Rivest et al. 1978).
- **Elliptic Curve Cryptography (ECC):** An asymmetric algorithm based on elliptic curves, known for its efficiency and security (Miller 1986).

1.4.3.1.3 Hash Functions

Although the hash function is not an encryption cipher, it plays an important role in cryptography. It generates fixed-size output hashes from inputs of different sizes and is used to verify data integrity (Schneier 1996).

Examples:

- **SHA-256 (Secure Hash Algorithm 256-bit):** Frequently employed in blockchain and cryptocurrencies to generate secure and unique hashes (NIST 2015).

1.4.3.1.4 Block Ciphers

These ciphers process fixed-size blocks of data at a time. Different modes of operation determine how these blocks are processed and combined (Stallings 2020).

Examples:

- **AES:** Operates on blocks of data, and various modes define how these blocks are encrypted (Daemen and Rijmen 2002).

1.4.3.1.5 Stream Ciphers

These ciphers usually encrypt data in a continuous stream, one bit or byte at a time, making them suitable for real-time applications (Schneier 1996).

Examples:

- **RC4:** A widely used stream cipher, but now considered insecure and not recommended for use (Paul and Maitra 2007).

1.4.3.1.6 Transposition Ciphers

These ciphers rearrange the sequence of characters in the plaintext without altering the characters themselves (Stallings 2020).

Example:

- **Rail Fence Cipher:** Involves writing characters in a zigzag pattern across multiple lines.

1.4.3.1.7 Substitution Ciphers

These ciphers replace each character in the plaintext with another character or symbol (Kahn 1996).

Example:

- **Caesar Cipher:** Each letter is shifted by a fixed number in the alphabet.

1.4.3.1.8 Cryptography Using Arithmetic Modulo Primes

Purpose: Essential for public-key cryptography, ensuring secure communication over insecure channels (Diffie and Hellman 1976).

- **Diffie-Hellman Key Exchange:** Allows two parties to reach a mutual agreement via private and public keys derived from the original password.
- **RSA Encryption:** Relies on the difficulty of factoring large primes, using modulo arithmetic for secure encryption and decryption (Rivest et al. 1978).

1.4.3.1.9 SHA-256

SHA-256 (Secure Hash Algorithm 256-bit) is a widely adopted cryptographic hash function that belongs to the SHA-2 family of hash functions (NIST 2015).

Hash Function: A hash function like SHA-256 converts the input (or message) into a fixed-size output of 256 bits, irrespective of the size or length of the input. It is often used to create digital signatures, store passwords, and ensure data integrity (Schneier 1996).

- **Fixed Output Size:** The resulting hash, also known as the hash value or hash digest, is consistently 256 bits in size. This fixed-size output is a crucial property for cryptographic hash functions as it allows for consistent representation of variable-length inputs (NIST 2015).
- **Collision Resistance:** SHA-256 is designed to be collision-resistant, implying that it is computationally infeasible to find two different inputs that produce the same hash value. It is an important tool for securing hash functions in various applications (NIST 2015).
- **Common Usage:** SHA-256 is commonly used in blockchain and cryptocurrency technologies, where it serves as the basis for creating digital signatures and hash functions for data integrity. It is also used to enable data transmission or storage in many security protocols and applications (Narayanan et al. 2016).

1.4.4 Smart Contract

Smart contract is a self-executing contract. The code written on top of the blockchain contains the criteria that nodes agree on to interact with each other. They automatically check and enforce the terms of the contract when prerequisites are met. This eliminates the need for intermediaries and ensures transparency and stability of the business.

Figure 1.9 depicts the flowchart of the agreement process between the buyer and seller in the blockchain mechanism. It shows how transactions are executed and how ownership and payment are transferred.

➢ **Characteristics:**

- Simplest form of decentralization
- Automatic agreement enforcement
- Higher degree of security
- Turns legal obligations into automated processes
- Eliminates the need for third-party
- Lowers transaction cost
- It is a self-verifying, self-executing Contract
- It is resistant to tampering

1.5 Real-World Applications

Finance Blockchain technology has transformed the financial industry by offering a secure, transparent, and efficient method for handling transactions and data (Nakamoto 2008). Here's an overview of how blockchain is used in finance.

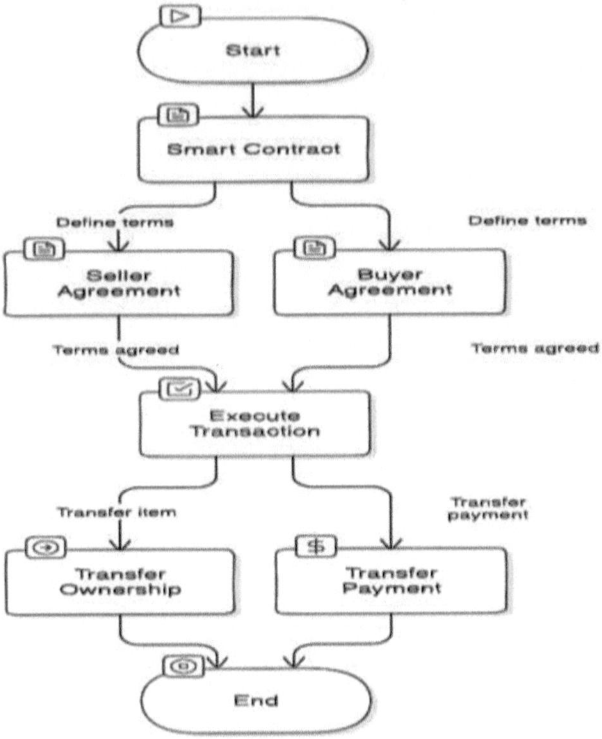

Figure 1.9. Smart Contract: Seller and Buyer Transection.

1.5.1 Cryptocurrency

- **Definition:** Cryptocurrency is a digital or virtual currency that utilizes encryption technology to ensure security and operates on a decentralized network (usually blockchain) (Antonopoulos 2017).
- **Application:** It is primarily utilized for peer-to-peer transactions, investments, and as a store of value, without relying on traditional financial intermediaries like banks.
- **Benefits:** Offers global accessibility, reduced transaction costs, faster settlement times, and potential for financial inclusion (Tapscott and Tapscott 2016).
- **Examples:** Bitcoin (BTC), Ethereum (ETH), Litecoin (LTC).

1.5.2 Decentralized Finance (DeFi)

DeFi refers to the ecosystem of decentralized financial applications (such as lending, borrowing, trading) built on the blockchain platform (Schär 2021).

- **Application:** Utilizes smart contracts to automate processes traditionally handled by banks and other financial institutions.
- **Benefits:** Provides open access to financial services, transparency, lower fees, and enables peer-to-peer transactions without centralized control.

1.5.3 Supply Chain Management

Blockchain technology transforms supply chain management by enabling transparent, secure, and efficient tracking of goods from their origin to their destination. It ensures immutable record-keeping, enhancing traceability and reducing fraud by creating a permanent audit trail (Casino et al. 2019). Decentralization boosts data security, while smart contracts automate processes, cutting administrative costs and errors. By fostering trust among participants through transparent, verifiable data, blockchain improves collaboration and compliance with regulatory standards, streamlining operations and enhancing overall supply chain integrity.

Tracking and verifying goods:

- **Definition:** Blockchain facilitates tracking products throughout the supply chain, from manufacturing to delivery.
- **Application:** Every transaction or movement of goods gets recorded on the blockchain, ensuring transparency and traceability (Helo and Hao 2019).
- **Benefits:** Reduces fraudulent activities, verifies authenticity, improves efficiency in logistics and inventory management, and enhances trust between parties.

1.5.4 Healthcare

Blockchain can transform healthcare by providing a secure, transparent, and efficient way to manage medical records and transactions. It ensures that patient data is stored immutably and accessed only by authorized parties, enhancing data security and privacy (Kuo et al. 2017). Blockchain facilitates seamless sharing of patient information among healthcare providers, improving care coordination and reducing errors. It also supports the verification of pharmaceutical supply chains, ensuring the authenticity of drugs and preventing counterfeiting (Mettler 2016). Additionally, blockchain can streamline administrative processes and billing, reducing costs and improving the overall efficiency of healthcare delivery.

1.5.4.1 Secure patient records

Blockchain securely stores and manages patient health records.

- **Application:** Ensures data integrity, enhances privacy through encryption, and enables patients to control access to their medical information.
- **Benefits:** Facilitates interoperability among healthcare providers, reduces administrative costs, mitigates data breaches, and supports medical research.

1.5.5 Transparent Pharmaceutical Supply Chains

Blockchain verifies the authenticity and integrity of pharmaceutical products as they move through the supply chain.

- **Application:** Records each transaction, ensuring drugs' origin, handling, and storage conditions are transparent and compliant with regulatory standards (Mackey and Nayyar 2017).

- **Benefits:** Combats counterfeit drugs, improves drug safety, enhances supply chain efficiency, and builds trust among consumers and stakeholders.

1.5.6 Governance

Blockchain can enhance governance by providing transparent, secure, and efficient mechanisms for public administration and citizen engagement. It makes data immutable and transparent, reduces corruption and fraud by making government processes auditable and verifiable (Olnes et al. 2017). Blockchain can streamline voting systems with secure, tamper-proof electronic voting, ensuring integrity and trust in electoral processes. Additionally, it can improve the management of public services and resources by enabling transparent tracking of government expenditures and delivery of services. By fostering greater transparency and accountability, blockchain strengthens trust between citizens and their governments, ultimately enhancing the effectiveness of governance.

Transparent Voting Systems

Blockchain provides a secure and transparent platform for elections and voting.

- **Application:** All votes are recorded as a transaction on the blockchain to ensure anonymity, non-interference, and ensure verifiability and immutability.
- **Benefits:** Reduces fraud, enhances voter trust, enables remote and secure voting, and potentially increases voter turnout.

Public record keeping

Blockchain maintains transparent and tamper-proof records of public information and transactions.

- **Application:** Used for land registries, legal documents, identity verification, and more, ensuring authenticity and reducing disputes (Graglia and Mellon 2018).
- **Benefits:** Increases transparency, reduces bureaucracy, minimizes fraud, and improves efficiency in public administration

1.6 Challenges and Limitations

Despite its transformative potential, blockchain technology faces several challenges and limitations that hinder its widespread adoption and implementation. These include scalability issues, as blockchain networks can struggle to handle large volumes of transactions efficiently (Zheng et al. 2018). High energy consumption, particularly in proof-of-work-based systems, raises environmental concerns (Sedlmeir et al. 2020). The lack of interoperability between different blockchain platforms creates integration difficulties (Casino et al. 2019). Regulatory uncertainty and the need for clear legal frameworks pose significant obstacles (Cong and He 2019).

1.6.1 Scalability Issues

Transaction speed and network capacity

- Public blockchain networks like Bitcoin and Ethereum often encounter challenges with transaction speed and scalability (Zohar 2015).
- **Impact**: High transaction fees and slower confirmation times during peak usage periods limit scalability for mainstream adoption.
- **Examples**: Bitcoin exchange rates are only around 7 transactions per second (TPS), while Ethereum aims to increase its TPS with new updates such as Ethereum 2.0 (Buterin 2020).

1.6.2 Energy Consumption

Environmental impact of PoW

- **Issue:** Proof-of-Work (PoW) serves as a consensus mechanism widely adopted by Bitcoin and other cryptocurrencies, demanding considerable computational power and consequently leading to high energy consumption (Sedlmeir et al. 2020).
- **Impact:** Environmental concerns arise from the carbon footprint created by mining operations.
- **Examples:** Bitcoin's energy consumption has been likened to that of small countries, raising sustainability concerns (Krause and Tolaymat 2018).

Efforts to develop more energy-efficient solutions

- **Efforts:** Transitioning to alternative consensus methods like Proof-of-Stake (PoS) aims to reduce energy consumption by eliminating the need for energy-intensive mining (Bonneau et al. 2015).
- **Advantages:** PoS and other energy-efficient models offer potential solutions to mitigate blockchain's environmental impact while maintaining network security.
- **Examples:** Ethereum plans to move to Ethereum 2.0, including switching from PoW to PoS to address energy concerns (Buterin 2020).

1.6.3 Regulatory Concerns

Legal and compliance issues

- **Issue:** Blockchain and cryptocurrencies face varied regulatory frameworks globally, posing challenges for compliance and legal clarity (Cong and He 2019).
- **Impact:** Uncertainty around taxation, money laundering, and consumer protection hinders mainstream adoption and development.
- **Examples:** Differences in regulatory approaches between countries like the US, EU, and Asian markets create compliance complexities for blockchain projects and businesses (Zhang and Xue 2020).

Global regulatory landscape

- **Concerns:** Navigating diverse regulatory environments requires global coordination and alignment to facilitate innovation and adoption (Casino et al. 2019).
- **Efforts:** Industry collaboration, regulatory sandboxes, and international standards development aim to harmonize regulations and foster responsible blockchain innovation.
- **Examples:** Initiatives by international organizations like the FATF (Financial Action Task Force) to develop guidelines for cryptocurrency regulations (FATF 2019).

1.7 Future of Blockchain

The future of blockchain technology holds immense promise, with the potential to revolutionize various industries through enhanced transparency, security, and efficiency. As the technology matures, we can expect greater scalability and energy-efficient consensus mechanisms, addressing current limitations. Increased interoperability between different blockchain platforms will facilitate broader adoption and integration. Regulatory frameworks will likely evolve, providing clearer guidelines and fostering trust in blockchain applications. Innovations such as decentralized finance (DeFi), smart contracts, and digital identities will continue to expand, transforming financial systems, supply chains, healthcare, and governance (Nakamoto 2008; Swan 2015). Overall, blockchain is poised to become a foundational technology, driving significant advancements and efficiencies across numerous sectors.

1.7.1 Emerging Trends and Innovations

Emerging trends and innovations in blockchain technology are shaping its future development and application across various industries. Here are some key trends:

Transition to Proof-of-Stake (PoS):

PoS is a consensus concept where validators create and validate new blocks based on the number of coins they choose to stake.

- **Significance**: It aims to replace the energy-intensive Proof-of-Work (PoW) mechanism employed by Bitcoin and other cryptocurrencies. It promises lower energy consumption, reduced environmental impact, and potentially higher transaction throughput.
- **Example**: Ethereum transitions from PoW to PoS with Ethereum 2.0, aiming to enhance scalability and sustainability (Buterin 2020).

Interoperability Between Blockchains:

Interoperability in the context of blockchain refers to the capacity of diverse blockchain networks to communicate and exchange information smoothly.

- **Significance:** It enhances the ease and efficiency of using blockchain by allowing assets and data to move between different blockchains without intermediaries.
- **Example:** Projects like Polkadot and Cosmos are building infrastructure for cross-chain interoperability, enabling decentralized applications (dApps) to operate across multiple blockchains (Wood 2016).

Decentralized Finance (DeFi):

DeFi encompasses financial services and applications constructed on blockchain technology. Its goal is to revolutionize traditional finance by eliminating intermediaries.

- **Significance:** Provides access to financial services like lending, borrowing, trading, and earning interest through decentralized protocols and smart contracts.
- **Example:** Platforms like Uniswap (decentralized exchange), Compound (lending protocol), and Aave (liquidity protocol) are leading the DeFi ecosystem, offering users new ways to interact with digital assets (Schär 2021).

Non-Fungible Tokens (NFTs):

NFTs are singular digital assets stored on the blockchain, serving as proof of ownership or authenticity for a specific item (usually a graphic or writable item).

- **Significance:** NFTs enable new forms of ownership and monetization for digital creators, providing provenance, and scarcity in the digital realm.
- **Example:** CryptoKitties (digital collectibles), NBA Top Shot (digital basketball highlights), and Beeple's artwork (sold for millions as NFTs) illustrate the diverse applications of NFTs (Wang et al. 2021).

Enterprise Blockchain Solutions:

Blockchain solutions tailored for enterprise use, focusing on scalability, privacy, and integration with existing IT systems.

- **Significance:** Addressing the needs of businesses in sectors like supply chain management, healthcare, and finance by providing secure, transparent, and efficient solutions.
- **Example:** Hyperledger Fabric (permissioned blockchain for enterprises), IBM Food Trust (supply chain transparency), and Ripple (cross-border payments) are deploying blockchain solutions for enterprise applications (Hyperledger 2017).

1.7.2 Potential Future Applications

Looking ahead, blockchain technology holds vast potential for disruptive applications across diverse sectors. In supply chain management, blockchain's ability to provide transparent and immutable records can revolutionize logistics, ensuring traceability and authenticity throughout the supply chain. Moreover, blockchain's role in enhancing data security and interoperability makes it promising for transforming healthcare systems (Kuo et al. 2017). Secure management of patient records, streamlined medical supply chains, and efficient healthcare data sharing are just a few potential applications that could improve patient care and operational efficiency. Additionally, blockchain's impact on governance is increasingly significant, with potential applications in transparent voting systems, public record keeping, and ensuring accountability in public administration. Furthermore, advancements in blockchain technology are expected to drive innovation in fields such as identity verification, intellectual property management, and digital rights management (Zyskind et al. 2015). As blockchain continues to mature, its integration with emerging technologies like artificial intelligence (AI) and the Internet of Things (IoT) is likely to unlock even more transformative applications, paving the way for a decentralized and interconnected digital economy.

1.7.3 The Ongoing Development of Blockchain Technology

The ongoing development of blockchain technology is characterized by continuous innovation and evolution aimed at addressing current limitations and expanding its practical applications (Swan 2015). Highlights of this development are as follows:

- **Scalability Solutions:** Blockchain networks are actively seeking scalability solutions to increase the number of transactions without compromising decentralization or security. This involves optimizing consensus algorithms (such as transitioning from Proof-of-Work to Proof-of-Stake), implementing sharding (dividing the network into smaller segments), and employing Layer 2 solutions (e.g., sidechains or state channels) for data transmission (Buterin 2020).
- **Privacy Enhancements:** Improving the privacy of the blockchain network is important for industries such as finance and healthcare. Technologies such as zero-knowledge proofs (ZKPs), ring signatures, and cryptographic techniques such as homomorphic encryption have been developed to ensure transaction confidentiality and data sharing while controlling the transparency and integrity of the blockchain (Ben-Sasson et al. 2014).
- **Interoperability Standards:** Interoperability of different blockchain networks is a significant focus area for developers. Standardization efforts, protocols like Polkadot's parachains, Cosmos' Inter-Blockchain Communication (IBC), and interoperability frameworks are being developed to facilitate seamless data and asset transfer across multiple blockchains (Wood 2016).
- **Governance and Consensus Mechanisms:** Innovations in governance models are exploring decentralized decision-making processes to improve network management and protocol upgrades. DAOs (Decentralized Autonomous Organizations) and new consensus mechanisms beyond PoW and PoS are being researched and implemented to enhance network security, fairness, and scalability (Wright and De Filippi 2015).
- **Integration with New Technologies:** Blockchain technology is progressively integrated with other new technologies such as artificial intelligence (AI), Internet of Things (IoT), and big data analytics. These integrations are designed to improve data management, automate processes, and create new data usage

across the business, providing an optimized supply chain for healthcare (Christidis and Devetsikiotis 2016).

- **Regulatory Clarity and Compliance:** As blockchain adoption grows, there is a parallel focus on regulatory frameworks and compliance standards. Governments and international organizations are actively developing guidelines for cryptocurrencies, tokenization, and blockchain-based applications to foster innovation while addressing concerns around security, consumer protection, and financial stability (FATF 2021).

1.8 Conclusion

The exploration of blockchain technology has illuminated its profound impact across various sectors and its transformative potential in reshaping traditional paradigms. Beginning with its humble origins rooted in Bitcoin's creation, blockchain has evolved into a robust ecosystem with diverse applications beyond cryptocurrencies. This chapter has provided a foundational understanding of blockchain's fundamental principles, core components, real-world applications, challenges, and future prospects.

Blockchain's defining characteristics of decentralization, transparency, and immutability form the bedrock of its appeal and utility. Decentralized ledgers offer a paradigm shift from centralized control, fostering trust and reducing dependency on intermediaries in transactions and data management. Consensus mechanisms like Proof-of-Work (PoW) and Proof-of-Stake (PoS) ensure the integrity and security of the network, while cryptographic hashing technologies protects data from tampering.

Real-world applications of blockchain span across industries. In finance, cryptocurrencies have emerged as digital assets reshaping financial transactions and decentralized finance (DeFi) is revolutionizing traditional banking services. Blockchain enhances supply chain management by improving transparency and traceability, increasing accuracy and reducing fraud. Healthcare leverages blockchain for secure patient data management and transparent pharmaceutical supply chains, enhancing efficiency and accountability. Additionally, blockchain offers transparent and tamper-proof solutions for governance, including voting systems and public record keeping.

Despite its revolutionary potential, blockchain still encounters significant challenges. Issues such as scalability and energy consumption, particularly with the PoW algorithm, remain crucial for its advancement. Regulatory landscapes worldwide present varied challenges, necessitating thoughtful navigation to ensure compliance while fostering innovation.

References

Agbo, C. C., Mahmoud, Q. H., and Eklund, J. M. (2019). Blockchain technology in healthcare: A systematic review. *Healthcare*, *7*(2), 56. https://doi.org/10.3390/healthcare7020056.

Andresen, G. (2011). *Bitcoin: Decentralized digital currency*. Bitcoin Foundation.

Antonopoulos, A. (2017). Mastering Bitcoin. O'Reilly Media.

Antonopoulos, A. M. (2017). Mastering Bitcoin: Unlocking digital cryptocurrencies (2nd ed.). O'Reilly Media.

Back, A. (2002). Hashcash - A denial of service countermeasure. Retrieved from http://www.hashcash.org/papers/hashcash.pdf.

Bayer, D., Haber, S., and Stornetta, W. S. (1993). Improving the efficiency and reliability of digital timestamping. In Sequences II: Methods in Communication, Security, and Computer Science (pp. 329–334). Springer.

Sasson, E. B., Chiesa, A., Garman, C., Green, M., Miers, I., Tromer, E., and Virza, M (2014). Zerocash: Decentralized anonymous payments from Bitcoin. IEEE Symposium on Security and Privacy.

Bitcoin Core. (2017). Segregated Witness (SegWit) upgrade. Retrieved from https://bitcoincore.org.

Bitcoin Foundation. (2012). About Bitcoin Foundation. Retrieved from https://bitcoinfoundation.org.

Blockchain.com. (2014). Blockchain size chart. Retrieved from https://www.blockchain.com.

Bloomberg. (2022). Bitcoin's crash and the TerraUSD collapse. Retrieved from https://www.bloomberg.com.

Bonneau, J., Miller, A., Clark, J., Narayanan, A., Kroll, J. A., and Felten, E. W. (2015). SoK: Research perspectives and challenges for Bitcoin and cryptocurrencies. 2015 IEEE Symposium on Security and Privacy (SP): 104–121. https://doi.org/10.1109/SP.2015.14.

Bukele, N. (2021). El Salvador adopts Bitcoin as legal tender. Government of El Salvador.

Buterin, V. (2014). A next-generation smart contract and decentralized application platform. Ethereum White Paper.

Buterin, V. (2020). Ethereum 2.0: The next evolution of Ethereum. Retrieved from https://ethereum.org.

Cambridge Centre for Alternative Finance. (2017). Global cryptocurrency adoption report. University of Cambridge.

Casino, F., Dasaklis, T. K., and Patsakis, C. (2019). A systematic literature review of blockchain-based applications: Current status, classification, and open issues. Telematics and Informatics, 36: 55–81. https://doi.org/10.1016/j.tele.2018.11.006.

Castro, M., and Liskov, B. (1999). Practical Byzantine fault tolerance. Proceedings of the Third Symposium on Operating Systems Design and Implementation, 173–186.

Chainalysis. (2023). Global crypto adoption index. Retrieved from https://www.chainalysis.com.

Chaum, D. (1982). Blind signatures for untraceable payments. In Advances in Cryptology: Proceedings of CRYPTO '82 (pp. 199–203). Springer.

Christidis, K., and Devetsikiotis, M. (2016). Blockchains and Smart Contracts for the Internet of Things. IEEE Access.

Christin, N. (2013). Traveling the Silk Road: A measurement analysis of a large anonymous online marketplace. Proceedings of the 22nd International Conference on World Wide Web, 213–224.

CME Group. (2017). CME Bitcoin futures launch. Retrieved from https://www.cmegroup.com.

CoinMarketCap. (2021). Bitcoin reaches $1 trillion market cap. Retrieved from https://coinmarketcap.com.

Cong, L. W., and He, Z. (2019). Blockchain disruption and smart contracts. The Review of Financial Studies, 32(5): 1754–1797. https://doi.org/10.1093/rfs/hhz007.

Crosby, M., Pattanayak, P., Verma, S., and Kalyanaraman, V (2016). Blockchain Technology: Beyond Bitcoin.

Daemen, J., and Rijmen, V. (2002). The design of Rijndael: AES-the advanced encryption standard. Springer Science & Business Media.

Dai, W. (1998). b-money proposal. Retrieved from http://www.weidai.com/bmoney.txt.

De Angelis, S., Aniello, L., Baldoni, R., Lombardi, F., Margheri, A., and Sassone, V. (2018). PBFT vs Proof-of-Authority: Applying the CAP theorem to permissioned blockchain. International Conference on Cyber Security Cryptography and Machine Learning, 48–62.

De Filippi, P. (2018). Blockchain and the law: The rule of code. Harvard University Press.

Diffie, W., and Hellman, M. (1976). New directions in cryptography. IEEE Transactions on Information Theory, 22(6): 644–654.

Dwork, C., and Naor, M. (1992). Pricing via processing or combating junk mail. Advances in Cryptology, 139–147.

FATF. (2019). Guidance for a risk-based approach to virtual assets and virtual asset service providers. Financial Action Task Force. Retrieved from https://www.fatf-gafi.org.

FATF. (2021). Guidance for a Risk-Based Approach to Virtual Assets and VASPs.

FinCEN. (2013). Application of FinCEN's regulations to virtual currencies. U.S. Department of the Treasury.

Finney, H. (2004). Reusable proof of work (RPOW) implementation. Retrieved from http://www.finney.org.

Fischer, M. J., Lynch, N., and Paterson, M. S. (1985). Impossibility of distributed consensus with one faulty process. Journal of the ACM (JACM), 32(2): 374–382.
Foley, S., Karlsen, J. R., and Putniņš, T. J. (2019). Sex, drugs, and bitcoin: How much illegal activity is financed through cryptocurrencies? The Review of Financial Studies, 32(5): 1798–1853.
Gartner. (2018). Blockchain adoption remains slow among CIOs. Retrieved from https://www.gartner.com.
Gartner. (2019). 5% of CIOs view blockchain as a game-changer. Retrieved from https://www.gartner.com.
Graglia, J. M., and Mellon, C. (2018). Blockchain and property in 2018: At the end of the beginning. The Journal of the British Blockchain Association, 1(2): 46–59.
Greenberg, A. (2013). FBI busts Silk Road and arrests Ross Ulbricht. Wired Magazine.
Haber, S., and Stornetta, W. S. (1991). How to timestamp a digital document. Journal of Cryptology, 3(2): 99–111.
Haber, S., and Stornetta, W. S. (1995). Surety's digital notarization service. Retrieved from https://www.surety.com.
Hanyecz, L. (2010). Bitcoin Pizza Day transaction record. Retrieved from https://bitcointalk.org.
Helo, P., and Hao, Y. (2019). Blockchain in operations and supply chain management: Benefits, challenges and future research opportunities. International Journal of Production Research, 57(7): 2234–2252.
Hougan, M., and Lawant, D. (2021). Cryptoassets: The guide to Bitcoin, blockchain, and cryptocurrency for investment professionals. CFA Institute Research Foundation.
Hyperledger. (2017). Hyperledger Fabric: A Distributed Operating System for Permissioned Blockchains.
Iansiti, M., and Lakhani, K. R. (2017). The truth about blockchain. Harvard Business Review, 95(1): 118–127.
Intel Corporation. (2016). Understanding Proof of Elapsed Time (PoET). Retrieved from https://software.intel.com/.
Ittay, E., and Eyal, I. (2014). Proof of Burn: A Consensus Mechanism for Bitcoin. Retrieved from https://eprint.iacr.org/2014/635.pdf.
Kahn, D. (1996). The codebreakers: The comprehensive history of secret communication from ancient times to the internet. Scribner.
King, S., and Nadal, S. (2012). PPCoin: Peer-to-Peer Crypto-Currency with Proof-of-Stake. Retrieved from https://peercoin.net/.
Krause, M. J., and Tolaymat, T. (2018). Quantification of energy and carbon costs for mining cryptocurrencies. Nature Sustainability, 1(11): 711–718. https://doi.org/10.1038/s41893-018-0152-7.
Kshetri, N. (2018). Blockchain's roles in strengthening cybersecurity and protecting privacy. Telecommunications Policy, 42(4): 335–344. https://doi.org/10.1016/j.telpol.2017.12.003.
Kuo, T. T., Kim, H. E., and Ohno-Machado, L. (2017). Blockchain distributed ledger technologies for biomedical and health care applications. Journal of the American Medical Informatics Association, 24(6): 1211–1220.
Lamport, L., Shostak, R., and Pease, M. (1982). The Byzantine generals problem. ACM Transactions on Programming Languages and Systems (TOPLAS), 4(3): 382–401.
Lamport, L. (2001). Paxos made simple. ACM SIGACT News (Distributed Computing Column) 32, 4 (Whole Number 121, December 2001), 51–58.
Mackey, T. K., and Nayyar, G. (2017). A review of existing and emerging digital technologies to combat the global counterfeit drug trade. Expert Opinion on Drug Safety, 16(5): 587–602.
Mazieres, D. (2015). The Stellar Consensus Protocol: A Federated Model for Internet-Level Consensus. Retrieved from https://www.stellar.org/.
Menezes, A. J., van Oorschot, P. C., and Vanstone, S. A. (1996). Handbook of applied cryptography. CRC press.
Merkle, R. C. (1987). A digital signature based on a conventional encryption function. Advances in Cryptology—CRYPTO '87: 369–378.
Messari. (2023). Bitcoin NFTs and spot Bitcoin ETFs. Retrieved from https://messari.io.
Mettler, M. (2016). Blockchain technology in healthcare: The revolution starts here. 2016 IEEE 18th International Conference on e-Health Networking, Applications and Services (Healthcom), 1–3.
MicroStrategy. (2020). MicroStrategy invests in Bitcoin as a treasury asset. Retrieved from https://www.microstrategy.com.
Miller, V. S. (1986). Use of elliptic curves in cryptography. Advances in Cryptology—CRYPTO'85 Proceedings, 417–426.

Nakamoto, S. (2008). Bitcoin: A peer-to-peer electronic cash system. Retrieved from https://bitcoin.org/bitcoin.pdf.

Narayanan, A., Bonneau, J., Felten, E. W., Miller, A., and Goldfeder, S. (2016). Bitcoin and Cryptocurrency Technologies: A Comprehensive Introduction. Princeton University Press.

National Institute of Standards and Technology (NIST). (2015). Secure Hash Standard (SHS): FIPS PUB 180-4. U.S. Department of Commerce.

Olnes, S., Ubacht, J., and Janssen, M. (2017). Blockchain in government: Benefits and implications of distributed ledger technology for information sharing. Government Information Quarterly, 34(3): 355–364.

Paul, G., and Maitra, S. (2007). RC4 stream cipher and its variants. CRC Press.

PayPal. (2020). PayPal enables Bitcoin transactions. Retrieved from https://www.paypal.com.

Pilkington, M. (2016). Blockchain technology: Principles and applications. Research Handbook on Digital Transformations, 225–253.

Rivest, R. L., Shamir, A., and Adleman, L. (1978). A method for obtaining digital signatures and public-key cryptosystems. Communications of the ACM, 21(2): 120–126.

Schär, F. (2021). Decentralized finance: On blockchain- and smart contract-based financial markets. Federal Reserve Bank of St. Louis Review, 103(2): 153–174.

Schneier, B. (1996). Applied cryptography: Protocols, algorithms, and source code in C. John Wiley & Sons.

SEC. (2021). Approval of Bitcoin futures ETF BITO. U.S. Securities and Exchange Commission.

Sedlmeir, J., Buhl, H. U., Fridgen, G., and Keller, R. (2020). The energy consumption of blockchain technology: Beyond myth. Business & Information Systems Engineering, 62(6): 599–608. https://doi.org/10.1007/s12599-020-00656-x.

Stallings, W. (2020). Cryptography and network security: Principles and practice. Pearson.

Stoll, C., Klaaßen, L., and Gallersdörfer, U. (2019). The carbon footprint of Bitcoin. Joule, 3(7): 1647–1661.

Swan, M. (2015). Blockchain: Blueprint for a New Economy. O'Reilly Media.

Szabo, N. (1997). Formalizing and securing relationships on public networks. First Monday, 2(9). https://doi.org/10.5210/fm.v2i9.548.

Tapscott, D., and Tapscott, A. (2016). Blockchain revolution: How the technology behind bitcoin is changing money, business, and the world. Penguin.

Wood, G. (2016). Polkadot: Vision for a heterogeneous multi-chain framework.

Wright, A., and De Filippi, P. (2015). Decentralized Blockchain Technology and the Rise of Lex Cryptographia.

Xu, X., Weber, I., and Staples, M. (2019). Hybrid Blockchain Architecture.

Yaga, D., Mell, P., Roby, N., and Scarfone, K. (2018). Blockchain technology overview. National Institute of Standards and Technology (NIST).

Yao, Y. (2013). China bans Bitcoin transactions for banks. South China Morning Post.

Yermack, D. (2015). Is Bitcoin a real currency? An economic appraisal. Handbook of Digital Currency, 31–43.

Zheng, Z., Xie, S., Dai, H. N., Chen, X., and Wang, H. (2018). Blockchain challenges and opportunities: A survey. International Journal of Web and Grid Services, 14(4): 352–375.

Zhang, R., and Xue, R. (2020). Security and privacy on blockchain. Journal of Cryptology, 33(4): 1246–1290. https://doi.org/10.1007/s00145-020-09371-9.

Zheng, Z., Xie, S., Dai, H., Chen, X., and Wang, H. (2017). An overview of blockchain technology: Architecture, consensus, and future trends. Proceedings of the 2017 IEEE International Congress on Big Data (BigData Congress), 557–564.

Zohar, A. (2015). Bitcoin: Under the hood. Communications of the ACM, 58(9): 104–113. https://doi.org/10.1145/2701411.

Zyskind, G., Nathan, O., and Pentland, A. (2015). Decentralizing privacy: Using blockchain to protect personal data. 2015 IEEE Security and Privacy Workshops, 180–184. https://doi.org/10.1109/SPW.2015.27.

CHAPTER 2

Scaling the Blockchain Horizon

Bridging Innovation and Mass Adoption

*Sivapriya Venkateswarar** and *U. Padmavathi*

2.2 Introduction

Blockchain is a revolutionary technology that redefines how we store and share information. Imagine a digital ledger that's cryptographically secure, decentralized, and shared across a network, where every piece of data is tamper-proof and transparent for everyone to see. With its unmatched features—decentralization to remove middlemen, immutable records that can't be altered, and transparent operations that build trust—blockchain is paving the way for a more secure and open digital world. It resembles a massive, publicly accessible spreadsheet that allows updating and verifying digital transactions. Beyond just powering cryptocurrencies, blockchain technology is reshaping industries like healthcare, finance, and supply chain management—offering revolutionary ways to manage data securely and transparently. However, as blockchain networks expand, so do their demands. With every new transaction added, the need for greater processing power, storage capacity, and bandwidth rises.

Despite its groundbreaking potential, blockchain technology faces serious scalability challenges that hinder its widespread adoption. However, innovative research has led to promising solutions to overcome these limitations. On-chain scaling refers to methods directly embedded within the blockchain's protocol, designed to boost its capacity to handle a growing volume of transactions and data. In contrast, off-chain scaling explores strategies that shift some of the transaction

Department of Computer Science & Engineering, Shiv Nadar University, Chennai.
Email: udayarajepadma@gmail.com
https://orcid.org/0009-0004-0263-5517, https://orcid.org/0000-0003-3835-1773
* Corresponding author: sivapriyaofficial2005@gmail.com

DOI: 10.1201/9781003540328-2

and data-handling burden away from the main blockchain. Moreover, advanced cryptographic techniques and hybrid models—combining both on-chain and off-chain methods—are being proposed to push scalability even further. When implemented effectively, these solutions could unlock the true transformative potential of blockchain. However, as scalability solutions evolve, they often collide with another critical challenge in blockchain development: the blockchain trilemma.

2.3 The Blockchain Trilemma

The blockchain trilemma, as shown in Figure 2.1, is a term that originated from one of the Ethereum co-founders; Vitalik Buterin. It asserts that a blockchain system can only achieve two out of the following three properties simultaneously: decentralization, security, and scalability. Solving this blockchain trilemma is difficult as it seeks to achieve the perfect balance. When developing blockchain applications, trade-offs are often unavoidable. Thus, when choosing an architectural design for a blockchain network, it is necessary to understand what areas affecting its performance exist and which ones require improvement.

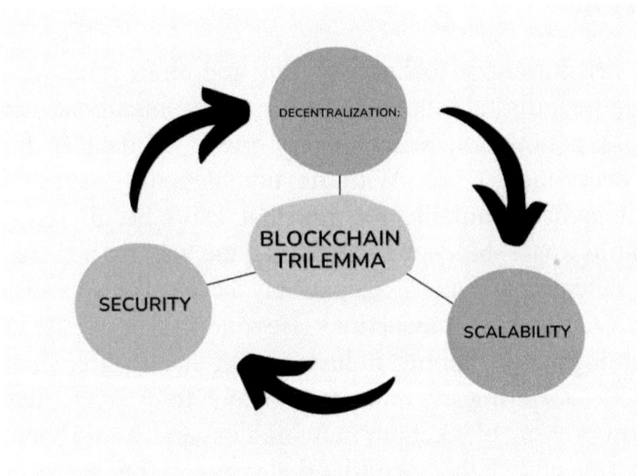

Figure 2.1. The blockchain trilemma.

2.3.1 Decentralization

Every block in a blockchain network carries transactional data which is required to validate the subsequent blocks that are added to the chain. In this case, every node (a computer or a miner) keeps a copy of all the transactions, creating a ledger that is in sync with the consensus mechanism. Decentralized networks reduce the degree of trust that peers need to have in one another and stop nodes from abusing their authority or controlling other users in a way that reduces the network's effectiveness. There is no longer a need to incorporate a third-party agency, as the system ensures that all the nodes involved in transaction processing have the same voting power.

2.3.2 Security

Blockchain security is the safety mechanism that keeps the system from malicious entities. The system employs methods like cryptographic hashing, public-private key cryptographic, and consensus mechanisms to minimize risk from improper blockchain access.

The blocks in the chain are joined by a cryptographic hash function, making the data enclosed in each block secure. SHA-256 is one of the most common hash functions used today due to its resistance to collision attacks. It is impossible to find two different inputs that produce the same hash value or reverse the hashing process. Asymmetric encryption takes place in the end-to-end systems to protect the data being stored in the network. With the help of a private key, one can decipher the message that was encrypted by its respective public key. This is called public key cryptography or asymmetric encryption. After a block is added to the chain, it is difficult to alter earlier transactions without the consent of most participants. The blockchain must be secured to guarantee the availability of the data it contains and the protection of the system and data it contains.

2.3.3 Scalability

Scalability refers to the network's ability to handle a growing number of transactions across all the nodes in the system. It is typically assessed by how long it takes for a transaction to be verified by the peer nodes. Blockchain networks require greater processing power and network bandwidth to keep up with increasing users and transactions. While boosting computational power can greatly improve scalability, it's also vital to consider the trade-offs—like the environmental impact, energy consumption, and cost.

2.4 Factors Affecting Scalability

As blockchain technology has advanced, scalability remains a key challenge. The main objective is to enhance the number of transactions a network can handle per second, enabling it to process a large volume of transactions quickly. Several key factors, as shown in Figure 2.2, influence scalability, each critical in determining its overall performance.

2.4.1 Throughput

Throughput, also known as Transactions Per Second (TPS), refers to the number of transactions a network can handle in one second. It defines a network's capability to process a given number of transactions in a given time frame. If several transactions take place in a single second, then there would be little to no waiting time for confirmation and validation of the transactions. This reduces bottlenecks during peak usage. However, higher throughput is achieved at the expense of decentralization.

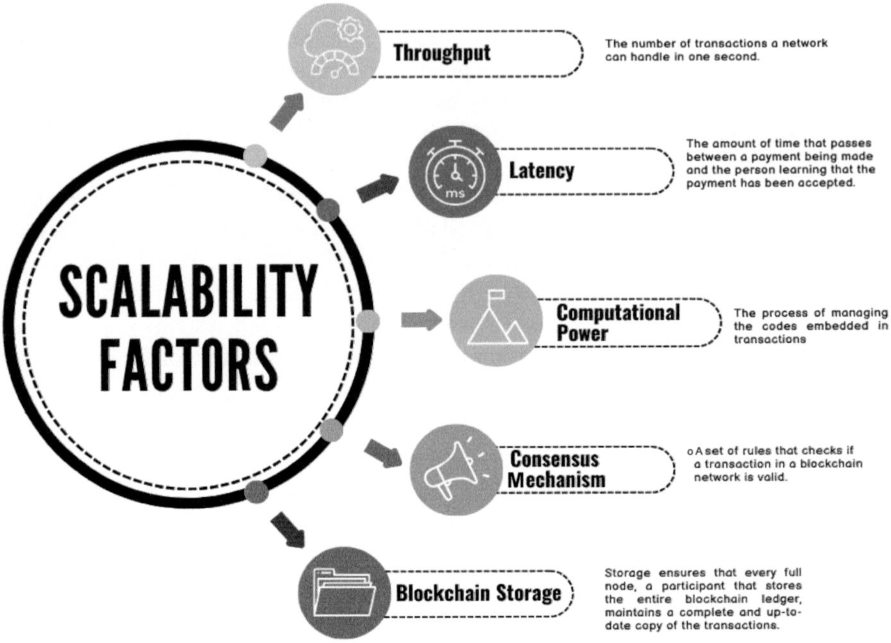

Figure 2.2. Factors affecting Scalability.

Nodes with high computational resources would be required to increase throughput to support more numbers of transactions or higher frequency of block creation, this would lead to centralization or power being provided only to a few members of the network.

2.4.2 Latency

Latency can be described as the amount of time between a payment being made and the person learning that the payment has been accepted. This confirmation indicates that the transaction has been accepted and is in progress, but it still needs additional blocks to be added to the blockchain before it is fully finalized. If the latency increases, the amount of time taken for a transaction to get verified and placed in the block will increase. Hence, there is a possibility that blocks get accumulated as they wait to be recorded, consequently creating a backlog that restricts the network's ability to handle more transactions in a given timeframe. This will stall the chain formation process. In conclusion, higher latency directly impacts throughput.

2.4.3 Computational Power

Computation can be described as the process of managing the codes embedded in transactions. A key problem that has been closely associated with the failure of scalability is computational power. It affects how efficiently the blocks are created, how fast transaction implementation or validation takes place, and the consensus-building process. Overall computational power will enhance the capability of nodes to handle simultaneous transactions per second and can also minimize the amount of time it takes to solve blocks and forward them to the rest of the nodes in the network.

2.4.4 Consensus Mechanism

A consensus mechanism is a set of rules that checks if a transaction in a blockchain network is valid. It requires agreement from most of the participants (nodes) on the state of the blockchain, allowing all nodes to stay synchronized and secure. Deciding on a consensus mechanism should be carefully done as it has a direct impact on the scalability levels of a blockchain. The most widely used types are Proof of Work (PoW) and Proof of Stake (PoS).

Proof of Work (PoW) operates on a straightforward objective: A miner, a node that participates in validating transactions and adding them to the blockchain, is rewarded with cryptocurrency when they successfully validate a block. This process usually requires miners to solve complex mathematical puzzles, proving they've invested computational resources to secure the network. A set of operations generates a hash value for the block. This value generated should be less than the predetermined value to ensure that the quality, as well as the functionality of the delivered product, is enhanced. The energy-intensive nature of the process, combined with the time required to validate blocks, reduces the overall throughput of the network. This makes PoW less efficient at handling high volumes of transactions.

Proof of Stake employs an unpredictable validation process rather than an inter-miner competition. When a node wants to become a validator, he/she has to stake out a particular number of coins. It efficiently achieves higher transaction throughput than PoW. However, there is a trade-off between security and scalability as this mechanism relies on the distribution and the size of staked tokens. Although PoW provides high security at the cost of scalability, PoS offers higher throughput and lower latency. Hence, both mechanisms hold their trade-offs in terms of decentralization and security.

2.4.5 Blockchain Storage

Storage ensures that every full node, a participant that stores the entire blockchain ledger, maintains a complete and up-to-date copy of the transactions. Storage comes in two primary forms: raw transaction data, and the database. Raw transaction data refers to the unprocessed transaction information necessary to build a block. The database describes the structure in which the blockchain network stores all its blocks and related information. As the blockchain's database grows, the computational load to process and verify new blocks increases, making the system more resource-intensive. When complete nodes cannot synchronize with the latest ledger, state bloat takes place. The factors causing state bloat are the ledger's age, further block insertions, maximum block size, and the data size for verification and state transitions.

2.5 Types of Solutions to Improve Scalability

Blockchain contains a unique architecture of distinct layers, each playing a vital role in its ecosystem. These interconnected layers work together to provide the characteristics of blockchain technology. Without this well-balanced structure, the promise of seamless and trustworthy transactions would be out of reach. Each solution designed for a specific layer in the blockchain architecture plays a pivotal role in overcoming unique challenges, such as enhancing scalability, improving data propagation, or enabling seamless cross-chain communication. As illustrated in Figure 2.3 and Figure 2.4, these solutions are categorized across three distinct layers—Layer 0, Layer 1, and Layer 2—each contributing innovative strategies to ensure the overall efficiency and robustness of blockchain systems.

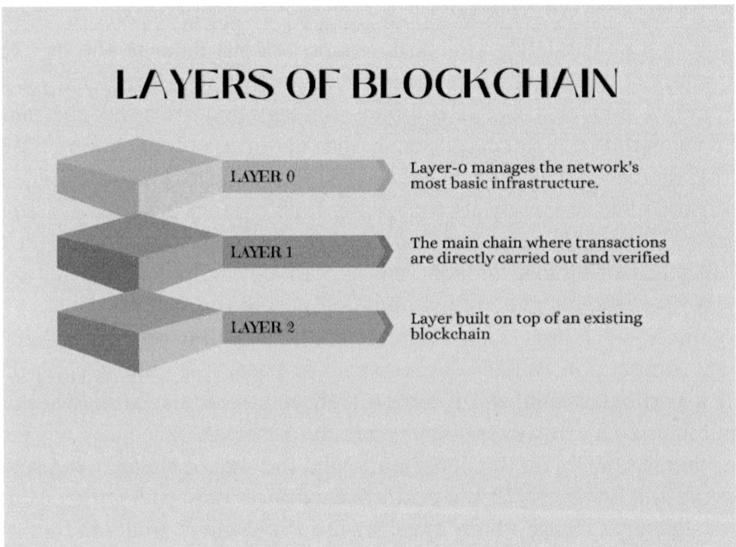

Figure 2.3. Layers of blockchain.

2.5.1 Layer 0

At the base of the blockchain stack, Layer-0 manages the network's most basic infrastructure. It links higher blockchain strata with the real world. Developers can craft personalized Layer 1 blockchains by leveraging basic protocols of Layer 0 like node connectivity, data transmission, network security, etc. The design and definition of consensus mechanisms are done at layer 0, but its implementation involves numerous layers of blockchain architecture. The unique selling proposition for this layer is its ability to support cross-chain connectivity, as it permits communication between several blockchain networks. With its essential components—internet, hardware, node infrastructure, and communication and interoperability protocols—Layer 0 not only ensures the seamless operation of Layer 1 but also paves the way for advanced innovations in data propagation and scalability, setting the stage for a truly interconnected blockchain ecosystem.

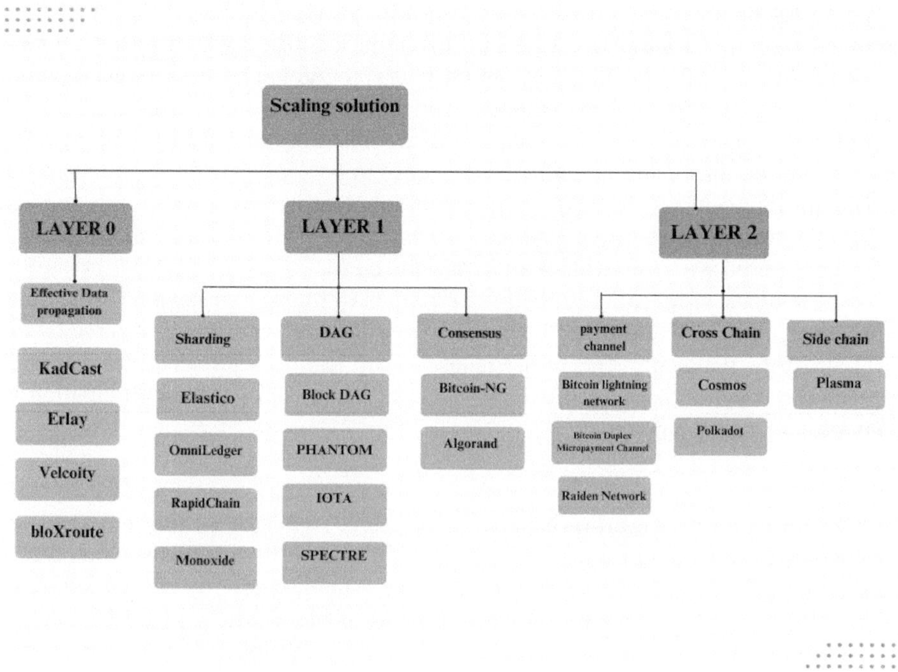

Figure 2.4. Solutions for scaling per distinct layer.

a. Effective Data Propagation

It is the heart of blockchain's integrity and performance. Data contained in blocks or unbundled transactions in a network can efficiently propagate using P2P protocols. However, as transaction volumes and sizes grow across blockchain platforms, the challenge of scalability becomes intrinsically tied to optimizing data propagation. To address this, Layer 0 introduces innovative solutions designed to enhance data propagation and bolster network scalability, including the following approaches:

Kadcast

In blockchain, transactions take place with peer-to-peer connections among all nodes. Blocks are broadcast across their respective network supporting local verification. Modern systems often rely on flooding as a fundamental broadcasting technique. In this approach, each connected node broadcasts 'received' messages to its peers, continuing the process until the message has reached every node within the network. Widely used in unstructured overlays, flooding ensures comprehensive message delivery but also poses challenges in terms of efficiency and scalability as networks grow. This duplication in message forwarding generates a huge amount of network traffic and uses processing power. Based on the hierarchical Kademlia architecture, Kadcast (Rohrer and Tschorsch 2019) offers a more efficient broadcast overlay trying to preserve principles of blockchain decentralization while improving broadcast consistency.

Kadcast deploys the structured peer-to-peer protocol of Kademlia; nodes are arranged in a binary routing tree according to unique identifiers which are large binary numbers usually 160 bits long, and similar to cryptographic hashes. In unstructured networks, nodes are connected randomly, while in Kademlia they are structured using a DHT (Distributed Hash Table). Nodes forward messages to peers that are closer to the destination, thus avoiding redundancy, hence improving data propagation speed. In Bitcoin-like settings, Kadcast increases block distribution speed by an average of thirty percent. The improvement was much greater with Ethereum-like scenarios when configured with lower block intervals and sizes.

Faster block propagation directly contributes to higher transaction throughput. Furthermore, Kadcast addresses the blockchain trilemma: security is bolstered by the DHT structure, which prevents message loss or duplication, while decentralization is preserved through a distributed overlay network that ensures equal participation of all nodes during propagation.

Erlay

By boosting connectivity, Erlay (Naumenko et al.2019) reduces flooding and improves security and the bandwidth used for transaction relays. Its mechanism involves a node sending 'received' messages back to a very small, randomly chosen subset of peers, also called Low-Fanout Flooding, instead of broadcasting every transaction to each node. Thus, there is less need for message distribution, reducing overall network traffic. Nodes send each other brief transaction IDs periodically to highlight the ones they haven't received and just request those. That way, all nodes eventually get every transaction. Such a method greatly reduces duplicate messages across the network and saves bandwidth. Instead of traditional flooding, Erlay employs a smart mechanism called Low-Fanout Flooding, where a node sends 'received' messages to only a small, randomly chosen subset of peers. This targeted approach minimizes message distribution, significantly cutting down on network traffic.

Erlay is a solution to the scalability challenge in blockchain trilemma while maintaining the other two properties. It will, therefore, be a strong solution for improving performance on blockchain networks without being at the expense of decentralization. On its part, Erlay ensures security as individual nodes get all transactions and verify them in an existing protocol-compliant manner.

Velocity

Velocity (Chawla et al. 2019) revolutionizes block propagation by blending rateless erasure coding with traditional methods, addressing key inefficiencies and limitations of conventional systems. In this innovative approach, a block is broken down using fountain codes into numerous small pieces called symbols. Nodes can receive any subset of these symbols and, once enough are collected, reconstruct the original block. As peers share the symbols with others, a ripple effect occurs, ensuring that eventually, all nodes gather enough symbols to fully rebuild the block. This dynamic process enhances efficiency, enabling faster and more reliable data propagation across the network. Less data is sent over networks as fewer symbols are transmitted rather than a complete block. Traditional Flooding solution faces rapid increases in latency and bandwidth requirements. Velocity's encoding approach scales well and allows for faster transaction throughput because it supports key block lengths without noticeably lengthening propagation times. This proposal thus fixes one of the main limitations of the scalability of blockchain networks. Despite higher orphan rates under Velocity, the protocol supports increased block sizes without compromising security and consensus mechanisms

Velocity does a good job regarding blockchain trilemma in security, ensuring that all nodes receive the same blocks and are at a consensus. Since nodes with different capacities can participate and behave equally, single nodes do not demand a lot of resources in terms of processing and bandwidth, it can be claimed that this strategy does not result in centralization of any kind.

bloXroute

bloXroute (Klarman et al. 2018) achieves scalability by improving the throughput of blockchain networks by more than three orders of magnitude. bloXroute introduces a BDN (Blockchain Distribution Network), instead of a peer-to-peer network, to provide the needed transactional throughput without bypassing the decentralized nature of blockchain networks. The transport-layer network adds a necessary boost to the speed and scalability of blockchains without changing their underlying protocols. A bloXroute uses system-wide caching, the network can accommodate larger blocks with faster propagation. Cut-through routing enhances the efficiency of BDN servers by allowing them to forward the first bytes of an incoming block to the next node as soon as they are received. This eliminates the need to wait for the entire block to arrive, enabling faster transmission and reducing latency. bloXroute further provides an efficient broadcast primitive to blockchain nodes via a network of gateways. Each node in a blockchain network runs a gateway process that serves as an intermediary between the blockchain and the bloXroute BDN. This setup makes the nodes operate in a way that suggests they belong to the same Local Area Network, even if geographically dispersed.

Concerning the blockchain trilemma, bloXroute ensures decentralization through a small set of servers, none of which the nodes on the network need to trust. Likewise, it ensures security is maintained because it propagates blocks after they have been encrypted, which hides the number and total size of transactions for added privacy and security. The key to encryption is only revealed after the block has been propagated to ensure that even bloXroute is unable to impact the propagation process based on the content of the block is shown in the Table 2.1.

2.5.2 Layer 1

Layer-1 Blockchain refers to the base layer of the architecture. It's the main chain where transactions are directly carried out and verified. It provides the required framework for smart contracts and decentralized apps. This layer enforces the consensus rules established at Layer 0 by meticulously validating transactions. It ensures integrity by checking digital signatures, verifying account balances, and preventing double-spending, safeguarding the reliability and trustworthiness of the blockchain network. An immutable record cannot be altered if it has been added to the blockchain ledger via consensus-building procedures. This has been one of the

Table 2.1. Summary of Proposals for Data propagation.

S. NO	Proposed Approaches	Methods Used
1.	KadCast	Kadaemila
2.	Erlay	Low-Fanout Flooding
3.	Velocity	Symbols
4.	bloXroute	Blockchain distribution network

key features of the blockchain system that has led to its adoption as a secure, reliable, and respectable platform that deserves trust.

Layer-1 solutions involve changes in the code base of a network. On-chain scaling is a structural or integral change in the chain. Thus, it is directly implemented on the blockchain protocol to achieve higher throughput, lower latency, without compromising security and decentralization. On-chain scaling has the following properties:

1. Sharding
2. DAG
3. Consensus

1. Sharding

Sharding is a technique used to improve scalability by splitting blockchain networks into smaller units called “shards”. Each shard handles its transactions and smart contracts within a discrete slice of the transactional data. This division of labour may cause faster processing and scalability as every single shard independently executes their transactions with no reliance on each other. In theory, this strategy can scale more by processing transactions simultaneously and adding shards if needed. However, this independence introduces a trade-off. Smaller shards are inherently more vulnerable to threats, such as the 51% attack, where an attacker gains control of a shard due to reduced hash power requirements. The decreased hash power needed to manage individual segments is the reason behind this. This compromise underscores sharding’s challenge in maintaining security within the blockchain trilemma. To address these challenges and maximize its potential, several innovative sharding proposals have been introduced:

ELASTICO

ELASTICO (Luu et al. 2016) is a new protocol that attempts to improve the scalability and security of blockchains, particularly the permissionless ones. This is a sharding method of dividing the mining network into smaller groups known as committees where each committee is responsible for a set of transactions. As a result, transaction rates on the network grow linearly with the amount of processing power available. Firstly, ELASTICO begins with an identity setup phase where each node generates a public-private key pair and registers its identity. Then each node with this identity is assigned to a committee. This randomness makes it exceptionally difficult for attackers to concentrate their malicious nodes within a single committee, safeguarding the network from coordinated attacks. The committees are then arranged in an overlay network. This architecture allows these committees to communicate and coordinate their work without being directly connected to the underlying physical network. Each committee reaches a consensus on its transactions and results from all committees are combined to form the final blockchain state. As such, ELASTICO provides robust protection against Byzantine adversaries, sustaining the security and operation of blockchain even in the presence of numerous bad actors.

ELASTICO's architecture provides robust defenses against Byzantine adversaries, ensuring the blockchain remains operational and secure even in the presence of a significant number of malicious actors. The randomness in node assignment plays a crucial role here, making it nearly impossible for attackers to predict or concentrate their malicious nodes within a single committee. This unpredictability safeguards decentralization, delivering enhanced scalability without compromising the core features of blockchain security.

OmniLedger

OmniLedger (Kokoris-Kogias et al. 2018) is proposed to be a scalable distributed ledger that attains high levels of scalability and throughput shown by payment processors such as Visa, without sacrificing security and decentralization. The design of the system uses an architecture with sharding, as the ledger is partitioned into small, manageable pieces (known as shards), each processed by different subsets of validators. Experimental evaluations show that OmniLedger scales linearly with the number of validators, coming up with high throughput and confirming ordinary transactions within less than two seconds. The Atomix protocol allows efficient sharding and cross-shard transactions. Atomix ensures atomicity—meaning that a transaction is either fully processed across all relevant shards or not processed at all. This guarantees the consistency of the network's state, eliminating partial or conflicting updates and maintaining trust in a fragmented blockchain ecosystem. Any proposed transaction is sent to all the shards involved, and each shard independently verifies the transaction. If a transaction is valid, then the pre-commit message will be signed by each shard and sent to all other participating shards in that particular transaction. The transaction commits after a shard has received enough pre-commit votes from other shards. If one shard aborts, the transaction is rolled back in all shards. By all means, OmniLedger is a major step in the design of scalable and secure distributed ledgers and hence substantially renders a feasible path to mainstream adoption of blockchain technology.

RapidChain

RapidChain (Zamani et al. 2018) provides solutions for issues across a wide spectrum of settings that involve high communication overhead and weak security guarantees. This suggested protocol accomplishes full sharding of communication, computing, and storage overhead without requiring any trusted setup and is robust to Byzantine faults from up to one-third of its members. The key to the design of RapidChain lies in this combination of the latest cutting-edge protocols and mechanisms in the form of the Intra-Committee Consensus Algorithm, the Gossiping Protocol, the Cross-Shard Transaction Verification, and the Reconfiguration Mechanism. Some key features of

RapidChain are its Optimal Intra-Committee Consensus algorithm, Novel Gossiping Protocol for Large Blocks, and its Secure Re-Configuration Mechanism. The Intra-Committee Consensus algorithm ensures that there is efficient consensus within each shard. The gossip protocol ensures the rapid and reliable propagation of large-size blocks within the network. Cross-shard transactions are verified when a multishard transaction is properly executed and recorded in all the shards associated with it. The reconfiguration technique ensures that the system stays secure and resilient by rearranging the validators among several shards. In a network of 4K nodes, empirical evaluation results show that RapidChain goes to over 7,300 transactions per second with confirmation latency, which is estimated to be around 8.7 s.

Monoxide

Asynchronous Consensus Zones (Wang and Wang 2019) enhance blockchain scalability by running many single-chain consensus systems that are independent but run parallel with one another. Every zone contains independent communication, computation, and storage, hence reducing the burden on the nodes. Eventual atomicity can ensure correctness and efficiency, unlike traditional two-phase commit protocols for cross-zone handling. In the case of eventual Atomicity, two zones process their part of the transaction independently. These zones eventually communicate to ensure that the transaction is processed across each other correctly. Chu-ko-nu mining preserves security across zones by enabling the creation of several blocks in various zones for the resolution of a single proof-of-work puzzle. The approach has significant improvements both in throughput and capacity and solves the limitations of traditional blockchain systems is shown in the Table 2.2.

2. Directed Acyclic Graph

DAG-based systems provide parallel processing, as opposed to traditional blockchains, which sequentially process transactions. This approach enables entire batches of transactions to be confirmed and added to the ledger simultaneously, streamlining the process like never before. By leveraging a DAG (Directed Acyclic Graph) structure, the system inherently supports a higher transaction rate, eliminating the need for traditional blocks. The network can accommodate a large number of transactions at once. This continuous transaction flow eliminates the bottlenecks of block creation and propagation. Unlike traditional block generation, every new transaction in a DAG has to refer to and validate one or more previous transactions; hence, multiple transactions can be simultaneously processed and confirmed. The structure grows as

Table 2.2. Summary of Proposals for Sharding.

S. NO	Proposed Approaches	Methods Used
1.	ELASTICO	Formation of committee (shards)
2.	Omniledger	Atomix protocol
3.	RapidChain	Intro-committee Consensus Algorithm
4.	Monoxide	Asynchronous Consensus Zone

a web with transactions interlinked. Following are some approaches introduced to enhance the scalability along with DAG:

Block DAG

Block DAG (Block DAG 2024) is an alternative to the traditional blockchain structure used in Bitcoin and Ethereum. Each block can reference multiple predecessors by allowing the creation of a more complex, web-like structure where blocks can incorporate information from previous blocks, not just the last one in the chain. Even if multiple miners create blocks simultaneously, these blocks can still be integrated into the DAG without being discarded. Initially, each block in the DAG includes hashes to multiple previous blocks. Transactions flow through the system, with new blocks validating and including data from numerous preceding transactions. By using the original DAG structure, the protocol selects only transactions from all referenced blocks that do not intersect with each other. Consistency and maximality principles help to create stable and complete transaction sets without any conflict. Therefore, the protocol tuning system is perking up on block formation and distribution that may help to better the network performance without conceding security or decentralization.

PHANTOM

PHANTOM (Sompolinsky and Zohar 2018) introduces a groundbreaking approach to blockchain by extending the traditional structure into a block Directed Acyclic Graph (DAG), creating an intrinsically permissionless ledger. This innovative proof-of-work technology leverages a tunable parameter, k, to optimize throughput, offering unparalleled flexibility. Unlike conventional protocols, PHANTOM resolves the long-standing security versus scalability tradeoff by controlling the tolerance for simultaneously produced blocks. The result is a system that scales smoothly while preserving the strong security underpinnings necessary for decentralized networks.

IOTA

IOTA's (Iota Foundation. 2019) core design is distributed ledger technology for the Internet of Things. Contrary to traditional implementations of blockchains, IOTA uses another form of data structure known as the Tangle, a variant of Directed Acyclic Graph. In this case, every new transaction in the Tangle will refer to the previous two, hence making a web-like structure instead of a linear chain as in conventional blockchains. Every transaction is added to the network in real-time without requiring block formations. By avoiding the delays usually involved in block generation and propagation, this method allows for quicker, more effective transaction processing as well as a more seamless network experience. IOTA eradicates the need for miners and their energy consumption. Each transaction must validate two predecessors to ensure that the network retains a consistent and secure ledger. IOTA offers a robust infrastructure, that is scalable for IoT and other high-throughput applications of the future due to its ability to enable parallel and seamless transaction processing with decentralized validation. Therefore, it does not sacrifice the blockchain trilemma.

SPECTRE

SPECTRE (Sompolinsky et al. 2016) stands for Serialization of PoW Events: Confirming Transactions via Recursive Elections. It is a consensus protocol based on proof-of-work events, which sets a serialization to guarantee security and scalability for blockchain networks. SPECTRE has a directed acyclic graph of blocks, so the creation of blocks happens simultaneously, improving scalability. SPECTRE remains secure if an attacker controls as much as 50% of the computational power, without any security degradation as throughput increases. Transaction confirmation is achieved through vote chaining across multiple blocks in the DAG. Such voting ensures a fast and secure validation process. This mechanism ensures a swift yet secure validation process, prioritizing honest transactions for immediate confirmation while delaying conflicting ones for further assessment. Based on a block DAG structure that distributes validation and consensus procedures across the network, SPECTRE will promote scalability improvements and a decentralized voting mechanism that uses recursive elections to arrange blocks and transactions. Naturally, effective decentralization in this setting is predicated on keeping a tight rein on propagation over the network, computational overhead, and security assumptions as shown in the Table 2.3.

3. Consensus

Consensus mechanisms ensure that every node in the network shares an identical, trustworthy view of the ledger. Effective consensus is one of the prime factors behind the integrity, security, and high performance of blockchains. Consensus mechanisms are essential enablers of on-chain scaling as they directly impact transactional throughput, latency, security, and energy efficiency. Hence, innovations in consensus mechanisms are the key to developing blockchain networks that will have scalability features to bounce back with wide adoption and a wide range of applications.

Bitcoin-NG

Bitcoin-NG (Eyal et al. 2015) introduces a groundbreaking approach to blockchain architecture, separating the process of electing entities that extend the blockchain from the actual creation and confirmation of transaction blocks. This innovative design achieves higher transaction throughput and lower latency without compromising security, preventing any single entity from dominating the network. Bitcoin-NG achieves significant performance improvement over the traditional protocol by combining key blocks and microblocks. First, Bitcoin-NG divides time

Table 2.3. Summary of Proposals for Directed Acyclic Graphs.

S. NO	Proposed Approaches	Methods Used
1.	Block DAG	Directed Acyclic graph
2.	PHANTOM	Atomix protocol
3.	IOTA	Data structure called Tangle
4.	SPECTRE	Proof of Work events

into epochs where each is governed by a single leader elected through the creation of a so-called key block using a mechanism very similar to that in Bitcoin's Proof-of-Work. From here, the leader generates microblocks serializing transactions during their epoch. This separation will enable the continuous processing of transactions without frequent leader elections. The key block contains an element of reference to the previous block, timestamp, coinbase transaction, target value, and a nonce field. After generating the microblock during their epochs, these blocks allow for the continuous processing of transactions, significantly improving throughput. It closes with the election of a new leader, which is performed by creating the next key block. The new key block refers to the previous delay and a chain of key blocks is created. Extensive experiments validate the protocol's properties of robustness and scalability, showing that it can sustain even higher volumes of transactions, as needed for increased adoption of cryptocurrencies. While enhancing scalability, Bitcoin-NG strives to maintain decentralization and security but does introduce temporary centralization during each leader's epoch. It increases the protocol's overall complexity due to this design; however, these are considered manageable trade-offs that make Bitcoin-NG a promising approach to the blockchain trilemma.

Algorand

Algorand (Gilad et al. 2017) guarantees the finality of low-latency transactions with an availability assumption that all users have a consistent view of the chain even under network partitions. Algorand's scalability is driven by a unique committee-based approach to consensus, where members are selected in a way that prevents attackers from exploiting the Verifiable Random Function (VRF) process. Algorand experimental results show that it confirms transactions in under a minute and scales effectively to a large number of users. Unlike conventional systems, Algorand weights users by their account balances, granting more influence in the consensus process to those with higher stakes. This guards against malicious agents preparing many 'weak' accounts to launch a flooding attack. Algorand achieves committee selection through the use of a non-interactive and private VRF. Since selection may sound unrealistic or a little arbitrary, a user can locally check, by running a VRF using their private key, if they've been selected to belong to a committee for a certain round. If selected, they should proceed to provide a consensus for that round. By using a small committee, Algorand can make fast decisions with low computational overhead. To provide further assurance of integrity within the consensus process, Algorand keeps recycling its committee members after participation.

Algorand is a well-balanced approach to the blockchain trilemma, making imperative improvements in scalability while having strong security and some decentralization. It reduces sacrifices efficiently but does not get rid of them, like any other blockchain solution. In every consensus round, only a small committee of randomly chosen users is included at a time. While these committees change rapidly, at that moment, they have had a significant influence on the block validation process is shown in the Table 2.4.

Table 2.4. Summary of Proposals for Consensus.

S. NO	Proposed Approaches	Methods Used
1.	Bitcoin-NG	Uses Microblocks, keyblocks, and PoW
2.	Algorand	Verifiable Random Function (VRF)

2.5.3 Layer 2

Layer 2 solutions are transformative frameworks or protocols built atop the foundational Layer 1 blockchain to enhance scalability and efficiency. By offloading transactions from the main blockchain, Layer 2 systems alleviate congestion while retaining the security and decentralization of the underlying Layer 1. These solutions are meticulously designed to integrate seamlessly with the base chain, ensuring that the core properties of security and decentralization are preserved. The hallmark of Layer 2 lies in its ability to provide cryptographic and verifiable "proofs," ensuring the integrity of state changes before they are settled on the main chain. This approach enhances scalability and fortifies trust, making Layer 2 an indispensable layer in the evolution of blockchain technology.

Layer 2 solutions are subsets of non-on-chain scaling techniques specifically made to expand the capabilities of the primary blockchain by including an additional decentralized layer that handles transactions off-chain. These solutions handle transactions off the chain before periodically settling their results on the main chain. This lessens the burden on the main chain and enhances general network performance. Second-layer solutions, like payment channels, cross-chains, sidechains, and off-chain computations, take part in non-on-chain scaling.

a. Payment Channel

Payment channels allow participants to do many transactions among themselves, with only the first and last states being recorded on-chain. This design drastically reduces the burden on the blockchain, hence making it more scalable and cheaper in transactions. Two participants can create a multi-signature address on the blockchain. They both send some amount of cryptocurrency to this address. The first transaction to this address gets recorded on the main blockchain, opening the payment channel. Numerous transactions can be done off-chain by participants. In simple terms, the transactions are updates of the balance of the funds in the multi-signature address. These updates get exchanged between participants but are never broadcast to the blockchain. When participants intend to close the payment channel, they broadcast the last signed balance sheet to the blockchain. This closing transaction gets embedded in the main blockchain and marks the end of the payment channel. In this way, payment channels are an excellent Layer 2 scaling solution, strengthening the scalability, speed, and cost efficiency of blockchain networks.

Bitcoin Lighting Network

The Bitcoin Lightning Network (Poon and Dryja 2016). is all about scaling Bitcoin transactions beyond the perceived limitations of the blockchain. Off-chain transaction solutions are proposed using micropayment channels. This can significantly increase throughput without giving up on security and decentralization for the Bitcoin network. A new signature hash type addresses transaction malleability, enabling the Blockchain to enforce transactions between untrusted parties if needed. Two parties generate a 2-of-2 multi-signature address where both must sign off on any spending transactions. They create an initial funding transaction but do not broadcast it immediately. A newer transaction can be generated by both parties to update the balance in the channel. At channel closing, the parties simply broadcast the most recent transaction, which defines the final balance. Any dispute can be solved by invalidating older transactions, as ensured through a penalty mechanism so that only the latest one gets confirmed. The Lightning Network is capable of routing payments through several different channels, which enables payments between parties who don't have a direct channel open. It achieves this through hash-locked and time-locked contracts to secure the process of routing from fraud events.

One of the most groundbreaking solutions to the scalability challenge in Layer 2 is the Lightning Network. Enabling off-chain transactions dramatically boosts transaction velocity while alleviating the load on the main blockchain. Although the network introduces a slight centralization risk with the emergence of hubs, its robust security remains intact, as it directly inherits the proven security model of the Bitcoin blockchain. The Lightning Network stands as a testament to innovation, balancing speed and security to propel blockchain scalability to new heights.

Bitcoin Duplex Micropayment Channels

Bitcoin Duplex Micropayment Channels (McCorry et al. 2016) utilize off-blockchain transactions to create long-lived user payment channels. First, two users make a shared account with a multi-sig output, requiring both signatures for a transaction. They also return a refund transaction to guarantee money back in case the proper closure of the channel is not affected. A sender can make incremental micropayments by creating and signing update transactions, which, rather than being directly broadcast to the network, are held by the receiver only. The protocol institutes mechanisms for preventing fraudulent behavior, in which old transactions get invalidated in case new ones are created, and it uses hashed timelock contracts to ensure that payments will be processed only if the intended recipient receives his funds. On this basis, duplex micropayment channels could make Bitcoin infinitely scalable and suitable for real-time, high-frequency transactions such as micropayments with near-negligible fees and processing times. This innovation opens the gateway to a network capable of handling a vast volume of transactions within the Bitcoin ecosystem effectively.

Raiden Network

The Raiden Network (Raiden Network 2019) emerges as Ethereum's answer to scaling challenges, offering lightning-fast transaction settlements with minimal fees. It runs off the main Ethereum blockchain similar to what the Lightning Network does for Bitcoin. Raiden empowers the off-chain by transferring ERC20 tokens between parties. These transfers do not need to be instantly confirmed on the Ethereum blockchain, thereby reducing congestion and fees. Much like duplex micropayment channels, Raiden deploys bidirectional payment channels. Two users

Table 2.5. Summary of Proposals for Payment Channels.

S. NO	Proposed Approaches	Methods Used
1.	Bitcoin Lightning Network	Multi-signature
2.	Bitcoin Duplex Micropayment Channel	Micropayment
3.	Raiden Network	ERC20 tokens

may open a channel, deposit some money in it, and conduct a series of off-chain transactions. Only the opening and closure need to be committed to the blockchain. The Raiden Network creates a dynamic web of interconnected payment channels, enabling transactions between participants without a direct link. While still under active development, Raiden continues to evolve with regular upgrades. A main-net implementation already exists, but its full integration into the broader Ethereum ecosystem is an ongoing journey, promising to unlock new levels of scalability and efficiency for decentralized applications. Raiden, if taken as a whole, offers a doff-balanced solution to the trilemma. It does lean toward scalability and security, with manageable compromises in decentralization and complexity is shown in the Table 2.5.

b. Cross-Chains

Cross-chain interoperability enables layer-2 protocols to facilitate transactions and interactions between different blockchain networks. Interoperability freely moves assets and data across different chains, improving liquidity and ease of use. This would be one of the intrinsic elements that guarantee more connectivity and efficiency in the blockchain ecosystem at the cost of security threats and complexity safeguarding. Unlike traditional transactions that rely on centralized exchanges or intermediaries—creating risks tied to these middlemen—interoperability reduces the need for such intermediaries, lowering the risks associated with counterparty failures.

Cosmos

Cosmos (Cosmos Network 2019) is a decentralized network of independent, scalable systems. The main goal here is building the "Internet of Blockchains" that will allow the different chains to communicate and interact with each other in a decentralized manner. The Cosmos project has set high goals for a decentralized, interoperable, and scalable blockchain ecosystem that can function effectively. Paired with the IBC protocol, its modular architecture enables the implementation of bespoke blockchains that can communicate with one another to prove a robust base for many applications and use cases. Being just a network that focuses on scalability, interoperability, and customizability, Cosmos puts quite a lot on its plate toward the further development of the blockchain industry.

Polkadot

Polkadot (Wood 2016) is the next generation of blockchain protocol, aimed at empowering a heterogeneous multi-chain framework. It is designed to allow different

Table 2.6. Summary of Proposals for Cross-Chain.

S. NO	Proposed Approaches	Methods Used
1.	Cosmos	IBC protocol
2.	Polkadot	Parallel processing

blockchains to transfer messages and value in a trust-free fashion, sharing their unique features while pooling their security. Through cross-chain communication and parallel processing, Polkadot considers the realization of a more unified and efficient blockchain ecosystem—thereby laying out the foundation for a quite varied array of applications and use cases in a decentralized world is shown in the Table 2.6.

c. Sidechain

A sidechain is another blockchain that runs parallel to a main or parent blockchain. Sidechains have only two major functions. First, it allows the secure transfer of assets and data between the sidechain and the main blockchain, ensuring both security and decentralization are maintained. Second, it addresses some of the main blockchain's limitations, such as improving scalability, increasing transaction speed, or enabling more complex functionalities that the parent blockchain may struggle to support.

Plasma

Plasma (Poon 2017) is a framework designed to run smart contracts. Plasma enables the secure transfer of assets and data between itself and the parent blockchain, ensuring security and decentralization. However, it scales a tremendous amount of state updates per second to give way for decentralized financial applications. Plasma empowers the self-facing behavior of smart contracts via economic incentives and network transaction fees. It reframes blockchain computation into MapReduce functions and makes use of Proof-of-Stake token bonding. Plasma uses fraud proofs to enforce state transitions on some parent blockchains, such as Ethereum. Plasma is designed for multi-party, off-chain channels holding state and state transitions enforced by the generation of fraud proofs. In effect, nodes of the Plasma chain should not need to constantly interact with the root blockchain except for submitting periodic commitments. In the event of block withholding or Byzantine behavior, participants can conduct a mass exit to the root chain, which processes the withdrawals after some delay to allow for disputes. Plasma is a tremendous improvement in smart contract scalability through high throughput, autonomous operation, and security while reducing on-chain interactions is shown in the Table 2.7.

Table 2.7. Summary of Proposals for Sidechain.

S. NO	Proposed Approaches	Methods Used
1.	Plasma	MapReduce functions and PoS

2.6 Conclusion

The scalability of blockchain technology is full of immense opportunities and challenges. As advancements in scalability solutions such as sharding, off-chain scaling, and innovative consensus mechanisms continue to evolve, they hold the key to preparing blockchain systems for mass adoption. These technologies are pivotal in improving transaction throughput, reducing latency, and lowering transaction costs, making blockchain more efficient and accessible across various sectors, from financial services to supply chain management. This, however, comes with several issues it has to address, such as data propagation delays, network bandwidth limitations, and the need for infrastructure that is at once robust and resilient. Moreover, developers should ensure that various solutions to scaling are compatible and able to interoperate with the current protocols of blockchains. The quest for scalable blockchain solutions balances wide opportunities against major pitfalls, with ongoing research and development on the verge of unlocking all the potential of the technology. While the fine line held between scalability, decentralization, and security trade-offs brings into being a future in which at-scale decentralized applications can be reckoned to fulfill their transformative promise, it is nonetheless very much up in the air.

References

BlockDAG. (2024). blockDAG. https://blockdag.org/.

Chawla, N., Behrens, H., Tapp, D., Boscovic, D., and Candan, K. S. (2019). Velocity: Scalability improvements in block propagation through rateless erasure coding. IEEE Blockchain Conference (BLOC), 447–454. https://doi.org/10.1109/BLOC.2019.8751427.

Cosmos Network. (2019). Cosmos. https://cosmos.network/.

Eyal, I., Gencer, A. E., Sirer, E. G., and Van Renesse, R. (2015). Bitcoin-NG: A scalable blockchain protocol. 12th USENIX Symposium on Networked Systems Design and Implementation (NSDI 2016). https://www.usenix.org/conference/nsdi16/technical-sessions/presentation/eyal.

Gilad, Y., Hemo, R., Micali, S., Vlachos, G., and Zeldovich, N. (2017). Algorand: Scaling Byzantine agreements for cryptocurrencies. Proceedings of the 26th Symposium on Operating Systems Principles (SOSP '17), 51–68. https://doi.org/10.1145/3132747.3132757.

Iota Foundation. (2019). IOTA. https://www.iota.org/.

Klarman, U., Basu, S. S., Kuzmanovic, A., and Sirer, E. G. (2018). bloXroute: A scalable trustless blockchain distribution network. Whitepaper. https://api.semanticscholar.org/CorpusID:20050445.

Kokoris-Kogias, E., Jovanovic, P., Gasser, L., Gailly, N., Syta, E., and Ford, B. (2018). OmniLedger: A secure, scale-out, decentralized ledger via sharding. 2018 IEEE Symposium on Security and Privacy (SP), 583–598. https://doi.org/10.1109/SP.2018.000-5.

Luu, L., Narayanan, V., Zheng, C., Baweja, K., Gilbert, S., and Saxena, P. (2016). A secure sharding protocol for open blockchains. Proceedings of the ACM SIGSAC Conference on Computer and Communications Security (CCS), 17–30. https://doi.org/10.1145/2976749.2978389.

McCorry, P., Möser, M., Shahandashti, S. F., and Hao, F. (2016). Towards Bitcoin payment networks. Lecture Notes in Computer Science, 9722: 57–76. https://doi.org/10.1007/978-3-319-40253-6_4.

Naumenko, G., Maxwell, G., Wuille, P., Fedorova, A., and Beschastnikh, I. (2019). Erlay: Efficient transaction relay for Bitcoin. Proceedings of the 2019 ACM SIGSAC Conference on Computer and Communications Security (CCS '19), 817–831. https://doi.org/10.1145/3319535.3354237.

Poon, J. (2017). Plasma: Scalable autonomous smart contracts. Whitepaper. https://api.semanticscholar.org/CorpusID:13266881.

Poon, J., and Dryja, T. (2016). The Bitcoin Lightning Network: Scalable off-chain instant payments. https://lightning.network/lightning-network-paper.pdf.

Raiden Network. (2019). Raiden Network. https://raiden.network/.
Rohrer, E., and Tschorsch, F. (2019). Kadcast: A structured approach to broadcast in blockchain networks. Proceedings of the 1st ACM Conference on Advances in Financial Technologies (AFT '19), 199–213. https://doi.org/10.1145/3318041.3355469.
Sompolinsky, Y., and Zohar, A. (2018). PHANTOM: A Scalable BlockDAG Protocol. *IACR Cryptol.* ePrint Arch., 2018, 104. https://api.semanticscholar.org/CorpusID:3538000.
Sompolinsky, Y., Lewenberg, Y., and Zohar, A. (2016). SPECTRE: A fast and scalable cryptocurrency protocol. IACR Cryptology ePrint Archive, 2016(1159). https://api.semanticscholar.org/CorpusID:20050445.
Wang, J., and Wang, H. (2019). Monoxide: Scale-out blockchains with asynchronous consensus zones. 15th USENIX Symposium on Networked Systems Design and Implementation (NSDI 2019). https://www.usenix.org/conference/nsdi19/presentation/wang.
Wood, G. (2016). Polkadot: Vision for a heterogeneous multi-chain framework. Whitepaper. https://api.semanticscholar.org/CorpusID:195177332.
Zamani, M., Movahedi, M., and Raykova, M. (2018). RapidChain: Scaling blockchain via full sharding. Proceedings of the ACM SIGSAC Conference on Computer and Communications Security (CCS), 931–948. https://doi.org/10.1145/3243734.3243853.

CHAPTER 3

Privacy-Focused Blockchains

Manmohan Pundir, Abhimanyu Kumar* and *Vinay Prasad Tamta*

3.1 Introduction

Blockchain technology has revolutionized various domains with its decentralized and distributed nature, functioning as a digital ledger that records transactions across multiple computers. This ensures that records are immutable and tamper-proof through a consensus mechanism, requiring network participants' agreement to validate any changes. Blockchain underpins cryptocurrencies like Bitcoin and Ethereum, offering unparalleled security and transparency. Its applications extend beyond finance to industries such as supply chain management, healthcare, and voting systems, enhancing data integrity and operational efficiency.

The internet, in its early days, faced challenges in adoption due to concerns about obscurity and reliability. Over time, it evolved into a versatile solution addressing data security concerns across various sectors. In 2008, Satoshi Nakamoto introduced Bitcoin (Nakamoto 2008), which gained popularity for its accessible and secure decentralized system. This success led to the development of other cryptocurrencies like Ethereum and Litecoin and emphasized the need for transparent transaction records, which led to the emergence of blockchain technology. Blockchain employs strong cryptography, hashing, and timestamps to create a secure, distributed ledger system, synchronizing transactions across a global peer-to-peer network without intermediaries like banks. Beyond virtual currencies, blockchain technology holds promise for transforming record-keeping in areas such as supply chain management, making it one of the most significant innovations since artificial intelligence.

Despite the advantages of transparency and immutability, privacy remains a significant concern within blockchain systems. The open and transparent nature of most blockchains means that transaction details and participant identities can be

School of Computing, DIT University, Dehradun, India.
Emails: abhi.kumar@nituk.ac.in, ORCID ID: https://orcid.org/0000-0002-8933-9996;
vinayprasadtamta@gmail.com, ORCID ID: https://orcid.org/0009-0006-5707-3966
* Corresponding author: manmohan.pundir@dituniversity.edu.in, ORCID ID: https://orcid.org/0009-0005-6989-7981

DOI: 10.1201/9781003540328-3

exposed, potentially compromising sensitive information. This is particularly critical for applications involving private financial transactions, personal data, or confidential business dealings. This chapter explores how Elliptic Curve Cryptography (ECC) enhances privacy in blockchain systems. ECC offers a robust framework for securing digital communications and transactions, providing both efficiency and strong security guarantees. The chapter delves into the mathematical foundations of ECC, including key generation and management processes, and examines its application in cryptographic protocols.

Furthermore, the chapter investigates privacy-enhancing techniques in blockchain systems, including Confidential Transactions, Zero-Knowledge Proofs, Ring Signatures, and Stealth Addresses. These techniques address privacy concerns by obscuring transaction details and protecting user identities. Case studies of privacy-focused blockchains, such as Zcash and Monero, are presented to illustrate the application of these techniques in real-world scenarios.

Finally, the chapter addresses the current challenges faced by privacy-focused blockchain technologies, such as scalability, regulatory concerns, and usability issues. It also explores future research and development directions, highlighting potential advancements in cryptographic techniques and the integration of privacy features into mainstream blockchain systems. This exploration provides a comprehensive understanding of how ECC and privacy-enhancing techniques contribute to the evolution of blockchain technology and its applications.

3.1.1 Overview of Blockchain Technology

Blockchain technology is a decentralized system that uses a distributed ledger to track and record transactions. This ledger is maintained across multiple computers, making it extremely challenging to alter any previous records without modifying all subsequent blocks and securing consensus from the entire network. Blockchain underpins cryptocurrencies like Bitcoin and Ethereum and is gaining adoption across various industries due to its strong security features and transparency.

3.1.2 Historical Overview of Blockchain in the Aspect of Privacy

- 2008: Introduction of Bitcoin

  Bitcoin, introduced by an anonymous person or group known as Satoshi Nakamoto, was the first implementation of blockchain technology. While Bitcoin provides pseudonymity, where users' identities are hidden behind cryptographic addresses, it does not offer complete privacy. All transactions are recorded on a public ledger, allowing for the possibility of tracing transactions back to individuals through various methods.

- 2014: Emergence of Privacy Coins

  With the realization that Bitcoin's pseudonymity was insufficient for privacy conscious users, the concept of privacy coins emerged. Monero, launched in April 2014, was one of the first cryptocurrencies designed with privacy in mind. Monero uses ring signatures, stealth addresses, and confidential transactions to obscure the details of transactions and enhance user privacy.

- 2017: Ethereum and Privacy Enhancements

  Ethereum, the second-largest blockchain platform, began exploring privacy enhancements. Projects like zk-STARKs (Zero-Knowledge Scalable Transparent Arguments of Knowledge) were developed to provide scalability and privacy. These techniques allow for complex computations to be performed off-chain while maintaining privacy and security.

- 2018: Introduction of Mimblewimble Protocol

  The Mimblewimble protocol, introduced by an anonymous developer under the pseudonym Tom Elvis Jedusor, brought a new approach to blockchain privacy and scalability. Cryptocurrencies like Grin and Beam implemented Mimblewimble, which combines Confidential Transactions with a novel way of structuring blockchain data to enhance privacy and reduce blockchain size.

- Ongoing Developments

  The field of blockchain privacy is continuously evolving. Research and development efforts are ongoing in various areas, including homomorphic encryption, multi-party computation, and other advanced cryptographic techniques. The goal is to enhance the privacy and security of blockchain transactions while maintaining the transparency and integrity that are core to blockchain technology.

3.1.3 Purpose and Scope of the Chapter

This chapter explores the role of Elliptic Curve Cryptography (ECC) in enhancing privacy within blockchain systems focusing on the key establishment techniques. It covers the mathematical foundations of ECC, its application in cryptographic protocols, and various privacy-enhancing techniques used in modern blockchain implementations. The chapter includes case studies of privacy-focused blockchains and discusses the challenges and future directions in this field.

3.2 Elliptic Curve Cryptography

ECC uses the mathematical properties of elliptic curves to enable secure communication, digital signatures, and key exchange (Khodaiemehr et al. 2023). This section presents an overview of elliptic curve groups and their geometric representations.

3.2.1 Geometric Representation

The elliptic curve is symmetric about the x-axis, meaning that each point (x,y) has a corresponding point $(x,-y)$. It includes a point at infinity (∞), which serves as a crucial aspect of its geometry. The addition of two points on the curve involves drawing a line through them, determining the intersection point with the curve, and then reflecting that intersection point about the x-axis. For the case of doubling a point, the tangent line at that point is used instead of a secant line. The shape of the curve itself is determined by the coefficients a and b in the defining equation $y^2 = x^3 + ax + b$.

3.2.2 Group Structure

The points on the elliptic curve form an abelian group under the operation of point addition. The sum of two points P and Q results in a third point R that also lies on the curve. The identity element for this group is the point at infinity (∞). If two points $P = (x_1,y_1)$ and $Q = (x_2,y_2)$ satisfy $x_1 = x_2$ and $y_1 = -y_2$, then their sum $P + Q = \infty$. The formulas for point addition depend on whether P and Q are distinct or identical. For $P \neq Q$, the slope λ is calculated as $\lambda = \frac{y_2 - y_1}{x_2 - x_1}$, while for $P = Q$, it is given by $\lambda = \frac{3x_1^2 + a}{2y_1}$. The resulting point coordinates are $x_3 = \lambda^2 - x_1 - x_2$ and $y_3 = \lambda\,(x_1 - x_3) - y_1$.

3.2.3 Elliptic Curve Groups and Operations

In Elliptic Curve Cryptography (ECC), the points on an elliptic curve form a mathematical group, with two primary operations: point addition and point doubling (Aydın and Aydın 2006). These operations are integral to ECC algorithms, underpinning key exchange, digital signatures, and encryption processes. Figures 3.1 and 3.2 illustrate the mechanics of these operations.

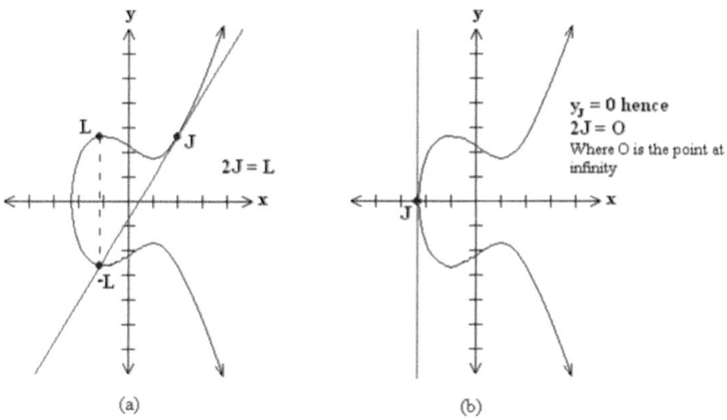

Figure 3.1. Point Addition.

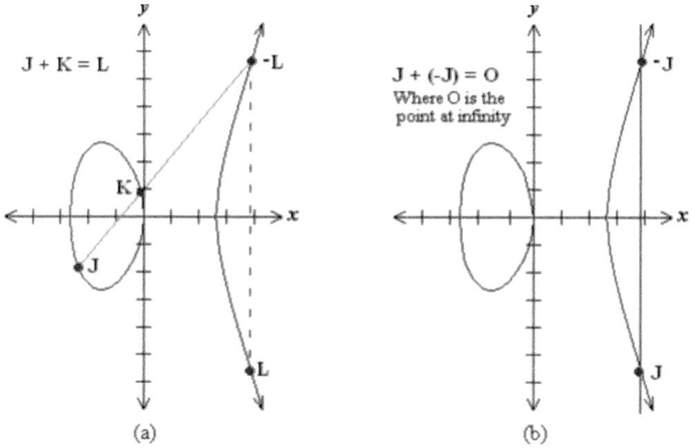

Figure 3.2. Point Doubling.

- **Point Addition:** Point addition on an elliptic curve combines two distinct points P and Q to produce a third point R that lies on the curve. The process involves drawing a straight line through P and Q, determining the intersection of this line with the curve, and then reflecting the intersection point across the x-axis to obtain R. This operation satisfies the commutative property, meaning $P + Q = Q + P$, as well as the associative property, ensuring consistency in group operations.
- **Point Doubling:** Point doubling is a special case of point addition where a point P is added to itself to produce another point $Q = 2P$. The tangent line at P is used instead of a secant line to find the intersection point on the curve. This intersection is then reflected across the x-axis to determine Q. Point doubling plays a crucial role in elliptic curve cryptography, particularly in scalar multiplication operations.

3.2.4 ECC's Resistance Against Various Attacks

The security of Elliptic Curve Cryptography (ECC) depends on the careful selection of curve parameters, including the curve equation, base point, and prime field size. Organizations such as NIST provide guidelines for choosing secure elliptic curves to defend against known cryptographic attacks. ECC's security is mainly determined by the size of the underlying finite field and the bit-length of the private key. Larger key sizes offer improved protection against brute-force and index calculus attacks.

To mitigate side-channel attacks, techniques like randomized scalar multiplication are used (Roche et al. 2019) introduced algorithms to retrieve a secret scalar from noisy blinded scalars, enhancing resistance to horizontal side-channel attacks. These algorithms are particularly effective under extensive blinding factors and a bit error rate above 10%. Implementing ECC algorithms in a constant-time manner helps prevent timing attacks by ensuring that execution time does not depend on the secret data. Several ECC-based schemes demonstrate resistance to various attacks.

- **ECC-based Blind Digital Signature:** Introduced by (Chaum 1983), ECC-based blind signatures secure digital payments and electronic voting systems. This method ensures that the signer remains unaware of the message content, providing unforgeability, non-reusability, and integrity essential for electronic cash systems and secure voting.
- **ECC-based Digital Signature:** Digital signatures derived from ECC are intrinsically linked to the signer's private key. Verifiability is crucial for resolving disputes in contractual agreements. ECC-based digital signatures are grounded in the intractability of the Elliptic Curve Discrete Logarithm Problem (ECDLP). Signature schemes such as Elgamal, Schnorr, DSA, and Nyberg fall under this category.
- **ECC-based Encryption:** ECC is known for its computational efficiency and robust security with smaller key sizes that enhance performance. It uses algebraic structures to generate and secure key pairs, crucial for resisting Man-in the-Middle Attacks (MiMA). ECC encryption methods, including re-encryption and proxy encryption schemes, support scalable security in cloud computing environments.

- **ECC-based Threshold Signature:** This scheme utilizes ECC and Shamir's threshold (Rivest et al. 1978) to create a decentralized signature mechanism without a Trusted Third Party (TTP). It allows a group of participants to collaboratively generate a signature, with security based on the difficulty of solving the ECDLP. The scheme uses the Chinese Remainder Theorem (CRT) to establish threshold capabilities, pointing towards new cryptographic integrations of CRT-based secret sharing.
- **Resistance Against Side-Channel Attacks-Randomized Scalar Multiplication:** This technique mitigates side-channel attacks by introducing randomness into the scalar multiplication process. This randomness makes it difficult for attackers to obtain useful information from power consumption or electromagnetic emissions. Algorithms that retrieve a secret scalar from noisy blinded scalars, introduced by Roche, provide robust protection under certain conditions.
- **Resistance Against Timing Attacks-Constant-Time Algorithms:** Implementing ECC in a constant-time fashion ensures that execution time does not depend on secret data. This prevents attackers from inferring private keys based on variations in execution time. Jancar (Jancar et al. 2021) highlighted the importance of constant-time implementations to safeguard against timing attacks.
- **Resistance Against Brute-Force Attacks-Large Key Sizes:** ECC's security is enhanced by using large key sizes, making brute-force attacks computationally infeasible. A 256-bit key in ECC offers security comparable to a 3072-bit key in RSA, providing substantial protection due to the computational complexity involved.
- **Resistance Against Index Calculus Attacks-Secure Curve Parameters:** Selecting secure curve parameters helps resist index calculus attacks, which are designed to solve discrete logarithm problems more efficiently than brute-force methods. Parameters recommended by standards organizations like NIST are specifically chosen to prevent such attacks, ensuring the ECC curves remain secure.
- **Resistance Against Man-in-the-Middle Attacks (MiMA)-Strong Encryption:** ECC encryption methods, including re-encryption and proxy encryption schemes, provide strong protection against MiMA by ensuring that intercepted communications cannot be deciphered or altered without detection. ECC's algebraic structure enables secure key exchange protocols that resist MiMA by securely establishing shared keys between parties.
- **Resistance Against Quantum Attacks-Post-Quantum Cryptography:** While ECC is currently vulnerable to quantum attacks, efforts are underway to develop quantum-resistant algorithms. These include lattice-based, hash-based, and other post-quantum cryptographic methods that aim to provide quantum safe alternatives to ECC, ensuring long-term security against quantum computers.

3.3 Integration of ECC in Blockchain Technology

Elliptic Curve Cryptography (ECC) is integrated into various emerging technologies such as blockchain, Internet of Things (IoT), secure messaging and communication, public and private key management, cloud computing, etc., to provide secure and efficient cryptographic solutions. Blockchain technology combined with ECC offers several advantages, including.

3.3.1 Digital Signatures in Bitcoin

Bitcoin uses Elliptic Curve Cryptography (ECC) with cryptographic parameters that include a prime modulo of an extraordinarily large number and specific elliptic curve coefficients ($a = 0$, $b = 7$). The base point P, expressed in hexadecimal, and the order of the curve (secp256k1 standard) are integral to the system. In Bitcoin, a private key is a random number selected from a defined range. The public key is obtained through scalar multiplication of the private key with the base point P:

public key = private key × P

This process, involving very large hexadecimal numbers, generates a new point (x,y) on the elliptic curve, forming the public key. While deriving the public key from the private key and base point is straightforward, calculating the private key from the public key is computationally challenging, ensuring system security (Pal et al. 2021).

3.3.2 Public and Private Key Management

As depicted in Figure 3.3, blockchain users generate ECC key pairs to secure their cryptocurrency holdings and transactions. A Bitcoin wallet functions like a bank

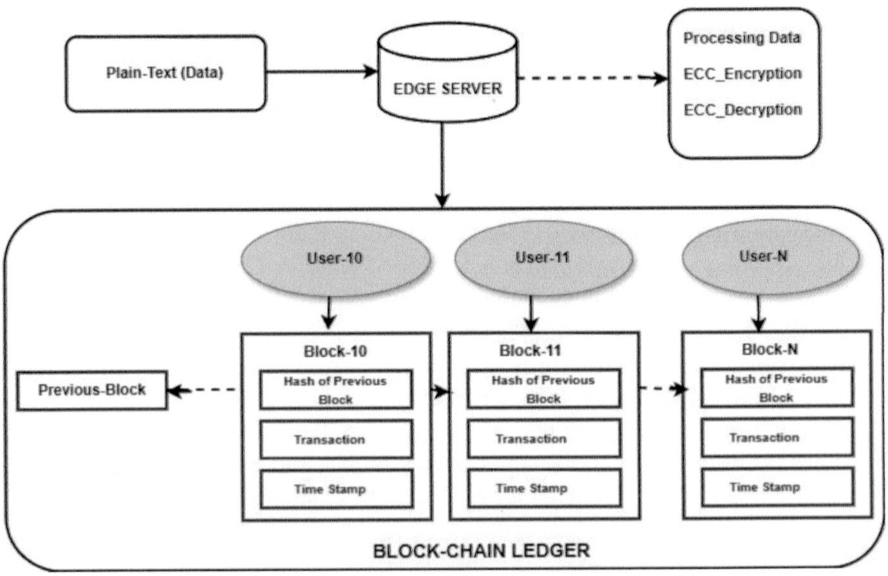

Figure 3.3. Integration of ECC in Blockchain Technology.

account for storing Bitcoin. Access and usage of the Bitcoin in the wallet require the private key. Security relies on safeguarding this private key; if compromised, the Bitcoin can be stolen. Efficient key management methods for Bitcoin wallets include local key storage, password-protected wallets, offline key storage, and password-driven keys.

3.3.3 Smart Contracts

ECC secures smart contracts on blockchain platforms, ensuring only authorized parties can execute and interact with them. Smart contracts simplify processes, boost confidence, and enhance security, evolving into distributed ledgers that reduce the need for centralization. A prototype integrating smart contracts with blockchain achieved key security goals, particularly in real estate transaction management. The adoption of elliptic-curve cryptography and Secure Socket Layer (SSL) enhances security (Choudhary et al. 2023). Experiments show that ECC, despite its complexity, offers smaller, faster keys and robust security compared to RSA.

3.4 Privacy in Blockchain

3.4.1 Importance of Privacy in Blockchain Networks

Privacy is essential in blockchain networks to protect users' identities, transaction details, and sensitive data. It helps prevent unauthorized access, surveillance, and potential misuse of information. Key aspects of blockchain that contribute to privacy include consensus mechanisms, cryptography, immutable ledgers, and smart contracts. Figure 3.4 shows the Security and Immutability in Blockchain Networks.

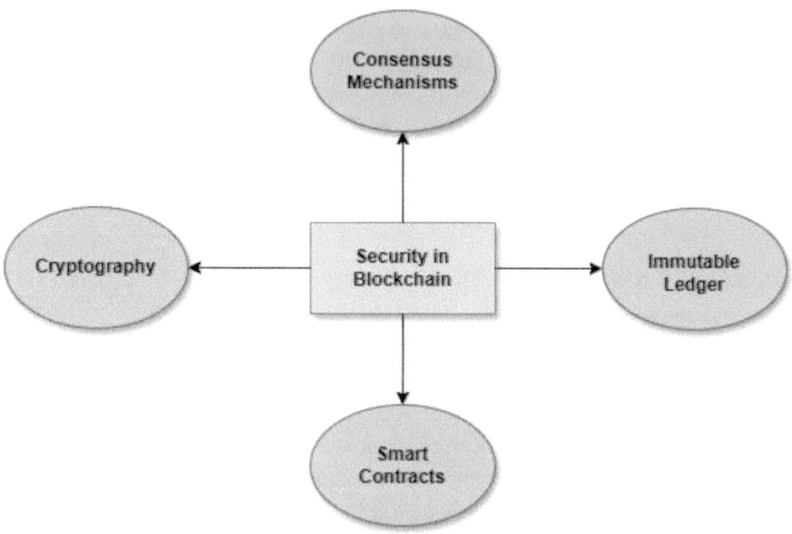

Figure 3.4. Security and Immutability in Blockchain Networks.

3.4.2 Consensus Mechanisms and Privacy

Consensus methods play a crucial role in upholding the integrity and security of blockchain networks. They ensure consensus across all nodes regarding the current state of the ledger. Different consensus mechanisms offer varying levels of privacy (Mohammed et al. 2023):

- **Proof of Work (PoW):** PoW is known for its strong security guarantees, primarily due to the computational difficulty involved in solving cryptographic puzzles. However, traditional PoW systems do not inherently include privacy features, as transactions are typically broadcasted in a transparent manner. To address this, PoW can be augmented with advanced cryptographic techniques, such as Zero-Knowledge Proofs (ZKPs) or ring signatures, which allow transactions to be verified without revealing sensitive information. This integration can significantly enhance privacy while maintaining the robust security of PoW.
- **Proof of Stake (PoS):** Proof of Stake (PoS) provides a more energy-efficient option compared to Proof of Work (PoW) by enabling validators to generate new blocks based on the number of coins they possess. Regarding privacy, PoS systems can be specifically built to reduce the necessity of publicly revealing staking amounts and validator identities. For instance, privacy-enhanced PoS models can use techniques like confidential staking or stealth addresses, ensuring that only the necessary parties have access to the details of staking amounts, thereby reducing the exposure of participants' financial activities.
- **Delegated Proof of Stake (DPoS) and Byzantine Fault Tolerance (BFT):** DPoS and BFT mechanisms involve a smaller set of trusted validators or delegates to maintain the blockchain network. While these systems are efficient, they can still benefit from privacy-preserving techniques. By incorporating cryptographic methods such as threshold encryption or secure multiparty computation (SMPC), DPoS and BFT can protect the identities of validators and obscure transaction details from the broader network. This ensures that even in a more centralized validation process, the privacy of both validators and participants remains safeguarded.

3.4.3 Immutable Ledger and Privacy

The unchangeable nature of blockchain ledgers guarantees that once data is recorded, it remains permanent and cannot be modified or erased. While this feature enhances transparency and security, it also creates challenges for maintaining privacy (Rao et al. 2022).

- **Transaction Privacy:** Immutable ledgers record all transactions, making it essential to use cryptographic techniques, such as zero-knowledge proofs, to ensure that sensitive details remain confidential.
- **Data Encryption:** Encrypting data before adding it to the blockchain ensures that even if the ledger is immutable, the sensitive information remains private and secure. Techniques like homomorphic encryption allow for data to be encrypted yet still processed.

- **Anonymity and Pseudonymity:** Using pseudonyms instead of real identities helps maintain user privacy while still allowing the ledger to remain transparent and verifiable. Techniques like stealth addresses and ring signatures can provide additional layers of anonymity.
- **Selective Disclosure:** Users can selectively disclose information to authorized parties without revealing the full content of their transactions. This is crucial for complying with regulatory requirements while maintaining privacy.
- **Data Minimization:** Storing only essential data on the blockchain and keeping other sensitive information off-chain can help enhance privacy. Off-chain data can be protected using secure data storage methods and accessed through secure channels.

3.4.4 Smart Contracts and Privacy

Smart contracts are autonomous agreements in which the conditions are integrated directly into the code. Although they offer numerous benefits, they also raise concerns around privacy (Wu et al. 2023).

- **Private Smart Contracts:** These contracts leverage cryptographic techniques, such as zk-SNARKs or secure multi-party computation (sMPC), to execute transactions and enforce agreements without revealing the underlying data to the public.
- **Confidential Transactions:** Smart contracts can incorporate confidential transaction protocols to ensure that transaction details, such as amounts and parties involved, remain private. Techniques like confidential assets and bulletproofs can enhance transaction privacy.
- **Data Privacy in Decentralized Applications (dApps):** dApps built on blockchain can use smart contracts to handle sensitive user data securely, ensuring privacy and compliance with regulations. They can implement privacy preserving protocols to manage data access and sharing.
- **Role-Based Access Control (RBAC):** Smart contracts can enforce role-based access control, ensuring that only authorized parties can access specific data or perform certain actions. This helps in maintaining privacy while enabling complex workflows.
- **Auditability and Compliance:** Privacy-preserving smart contracts can be designed to ensure auditability and compliance with regulatory requirements without compromising on user privacy. They can provide selective disclosure mechanisms for auditors.
- **On-Chain and Off-Chain Privacy Solutions:** Combining on-chain privacy techniques with off-chain solutions can enhance the overall privacy of smart contract operations. Off-chain computation can handle sensitive data processing, while on-chain smart contracts enforce the rules and logic.

3.5 Key Establishment for Blockchain

3.5.1 Key Management

The security of any cryptographic system largely depends on how well its cryptographic keys are managed. In Blockchain networks, Public Key Infrastructure (PKI) is commonly used to verify the identities of devices and users. However, managing these keys securely and efficiently is challenging. If an attacker gains access to the keys—whether through brute force, side-channel attacks, physical access, or exploiting weak encryption—the security of the entire system could be at risk. Therefore, strong key management practices are crucial to safeguarding the integrity and privacy of the Blockchain network (Pal et al. 2021).

3.5.2 Bitcoin Wallet Key Management

Bitcoin wallets, like traditional bank accounts, store digital currency and rely on private keys to authorize transactions. There are various methods for managing keys in Bitcoin wallets:

- **Local Key Storage:** This method stores private keys directly on the user's device, usually in a file system or database associated with the Bitcoin client. While this provides quick access for transactions, it exposes the keys to risks like hacking, malware, and unauthorized physical access.
- **Password-Protected Wallets:** In this approach, private keys are protected by a user-generated password. The Bitcoin software can only access the keys when the correct password is entered. This adds a layer of security but can be vulnerable to keylogging or brute-force attacks. Additionally, if the password is forgotten, access to the Bitcoin balance may be lost permanently.
- **Offline Key Storage:** To avoid online risks, some users store their private keys offline on devices like USB drives or in the form of paper wallets (keys printed as barcodes). This method reduces the risk of online attacks but makes the keys less accessible for transactions.
- **Password-Generated Keys:** Here, the key pair is created using a user provided password. However, this approach can be compromised by rainbow table attacks, where attackers use precomputed tables of common passwords to find the corresponding private key, especially if the password is weak.
- **Hosted Wallets:** In this approach, a third-party service provider manages the user's account details and private keys on their servers. Users access their Bitcoin wallet through web authentication. While convenient, this method depends on the security measures of the service provider, which can be a risk.

3.5.3 Blockchain-Based PKI Approaches

Various methods have been proposed to integrate PKI with Blockchain technology, aiming to enhance security and reduce reliance on third parties:

- **Multi-Layered Approach:** In this approach, the Blockchain network is structured in layers, with inner layer IoT nodes having more privileges than outer layer nodes. A Centralized Certificate Authority (CCA) manages the public keys of the inner layer nodes, which then manage the public keys of the outer layer nodes. This hierarchical structure helps organize and secure the network.
- **Instant Karma PKI:** This approach involves recording the actions of the Certificate Authority (CA) on the Blockchain. The network's nodes monitor and document the CA's behavior. If the CA acts improperly, the network's consensus can identify and address the issue, ensuring the authentication process remains trustworthy.
- **Guardtime Approach:** In this method, a Physical Unclonable Function (PUF) is used to identify IoT devices. A PUF generates a unique key pair based on the physical properties of a device. This decentralized method of key generation reduces dependency on the CA by relying on the device's intrinsic characteristics.

3.6 Elliptic Curve-Based Key Establishments Scheme

ECC is a versatile cryptographic scheme that finds applications in various other cryptographic schemes and systems, including Attribute-Based Encryption (ABE), Identity-Based Encryption (IBE), Certificateless Public Key Infrastructure (CL-PKI), and Public Key Infrastructure (PKI).

Elliptic Curve finds applications in various aspects of secure communication. In PKI, ECC is employed for establishing and managing shared secret keys in group communication (Kim et al. 2004), but it raises concerns regarding scalability due to the increasing reliance on Certificate Authorities. In IBE, ECC allows users to create shared secret keys based on their unique identities, offering computational efficiency and security benefits, though the issue of Key Escrow remains a challenge. ECC with hierarchical or tree-like structures to enhance scalability and key management in cryptographic systems. It is often used in scenarios where multiple entities need to establish secure communication channels while efficiently managing cryptographic keys. ECC is also utilized in ABE and CL-PKI, contributing to the security and flexibility of these cryptographic systems. Table 3.1 summarizes various key establishment schemes.

3.6.1 Public Key Infrastructure (PKI)

In Figure 3.5, the key establishment scheme for public key infrastructure is shown. The user and verifier begin by initiating the establishment of a secure communication channel. The user generates a public-private key pair (K_{pub},K_{priv}), with the public key K_{pub} being shared while the private key K_{priv} remains confidential.

To validate the user's identity and ensure the integrity of communication, the user requests a digital certificate containing their public key from a certification authority (CA). This request goes through a registration authority (RA) for validation, ensuring

Table 3.1. Key Establishment Scheme.

Scheme:	Public Key Infrastructure (PKI)
Description:	• Establishes and manages shared secret keys for secure communication. • Encrypts using the recipient's public key (from the digital certificate); decrypts with the private key. • Commonly used for secure communications, digital signatures, and authentication. • Applied in SSL/TLS for web security, secure email, and file transfers. • Depends on Certificate Authorities; scalability concerns.
Scheme:	ID-Based Encryption (IBE)
Description:	• Uses identity information like email addresses to generate public keys. • Encryption based on the recipient's identity; private keys are issued by a Trusted Third Party (TTP). • Suitable for higher security levels with reasonable performance. • Ideal for environments where centralized PKI is impractical, such as in IoT devices. • Simplifies key management, scalable and flexible.
Scheme:	Attribute-Based Encryption (ABE)
Description:	• Uses attributes associated with users' identities to generate keys; encrypts data based on these attributes. • Decrypts only if user attributes match the defined access control policies. • Ideal for devices needing quick key exchange; suitable for fine-grained access control. • Used in cloud storage, data sharing platforms, and secure data outsourcing.
Scheme:	Certificateless Public Key Infrastructure (CL-PKI)
Description:	• Hybrid approach combining PKI and IBE; uses CA for user identity verification. • Generates public keys from user identities; encryption and decryption based on these keys. • Aims to overcome limitations of PKI and IBE by integrating their benefits. • Reduces dependency on trusted third parties and eliminates certificate management issues.

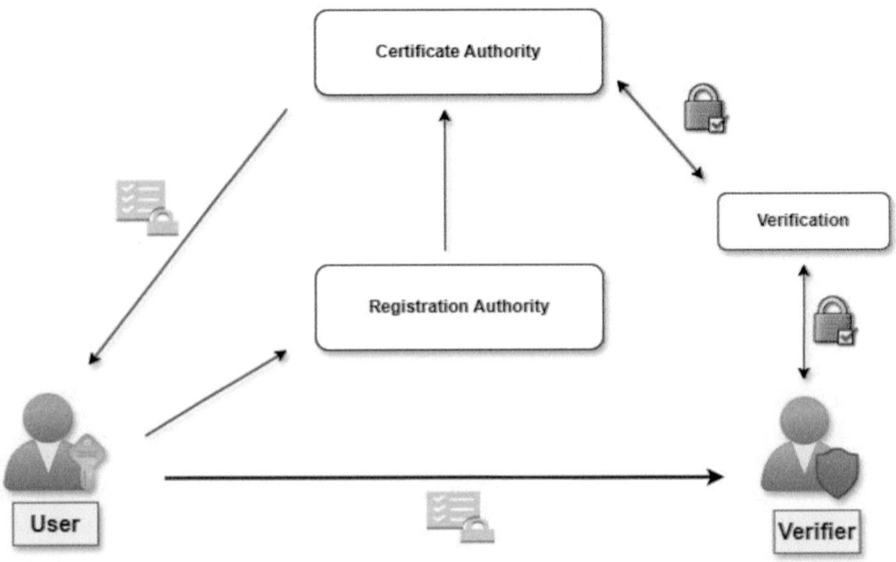

Figure 3.5. Public Key Infrastructure.

Table 3.2. Common PKI Use Cases.

Use Case	**Description**
SSL/TLS Certificates for Securing Web Browsing	Ensures the use of encryption protocols to secure and safeguard the communication between a user's browser and a web server, thereby preventing unauthorized access, interception, and alteration of data.
Digital Signatures on Software	Verifies the authenticity and integrity of software applications, ensuring that the software has not been altered or corrupted since it was signed by the publisher.
Restricted Access to Enterprise Intranets and VPNs	Provides secure access to internal networks and resources by authenticating users and devices, ensuring that only authorized personnel can access sensitive information.
Password-free WiFi Access Based on Device Ownership	Enables secure and seamless WiFi connectivity by using digital certificates stored on devices to authenticate users, eliminating the need for passwords.
Email and Data Encryption	Protects the confidentiality and integrity of email communications and sensitive data by encrypting the content, ensuring that only intended recipients can access and read the information.

its authenticity before being accepted. The CA then issues the certificate (Kumar and Ray 2022), signing it to authenticate its validity as:

$$\text{Certificate} = \{K_{pub}, \text{User Info}, \text{CA Signature}\}$$

This digital certificate, including the user's public key information, is securely transmitted to the receiver. Upon reception, the receiver extracts the sender's public key K_{pub} from the certificate. The Verification Authority (VA) ensures the certificate's authenticity and validity, establishing trust in the user's public key. Subsequently, the user signs data/messages M with their private key K_{priv}, producing a digital signature σ as $\sigma = \text{Sign}_{Kpriv}(M)$. For transmission, the verifier uses the user's public key K_{pub} to verify the signature σ, ensuring successful verification and validating the received information. The verification process represented as $\text{Verify}_{Kpub}(M, \sigma)$. Common PKI use cases are shown in the Table 3.2.

3.6.2 Identity-Based Encryption (IBE)

IBE utilizing Elliptic Curve is illustrated in Figure 3.6. The block diagram highlights the key components and processes involved in IBE. In this system, the sender uses the receiver's public identity (ID) to encrypt the message.

- **Sender-Secret-ID:** The sender's unique identity used in the encryption process.
- **Receiver Secret Key (ID):** The private key generated for the receiver based on their identity.
- **Public Parameters:** The publicly available parameters required for encryption and decryption, set by the key generation authority.

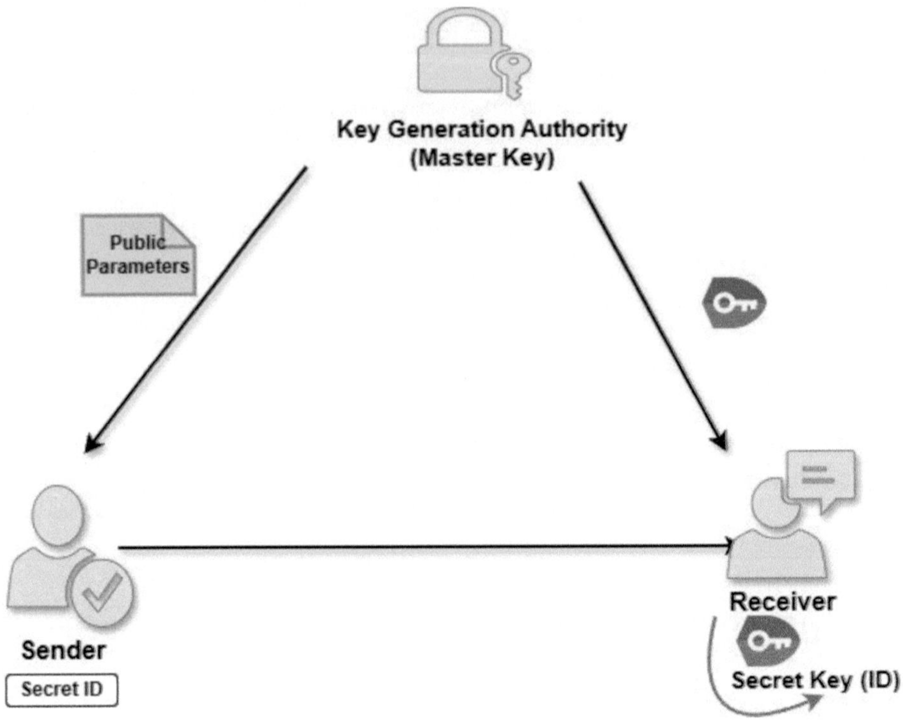

Figure 3.6. Identity-Based Encryption (IBE).

- **Key Generation Authority (Master Key):** The central authority responsible for generating and distributing private keys. It uses the master key to derive the receiver's secret key based on their ID.
- **Process:** The process begins with the KGA generating a master key s and public parameters, including a generator P of the elliptic curve group. For key extraction, given a user's identity ID, the KGA computes the user's private key d_{ID} as $d_{ID} = H_1(\mathrm{ID}) \cdot s$, where H_1 is a hash function mapping the identity to a point on the elliptic curve (Mezrag et al. 2022). To encrypt a message M using the receiver's identity ID, the sender computes the public key $Q_{ID} = H_1(\mathrm{ID})$ chooses a random r, and generates the ciphertext (C_1, C_2) where $C_1 = rP$and $C_2 = M \oplus H_2(rQ_{ID})$ with H_2 being a hash function. The receiver decrypts the ciphertext (C_1, C_2) using their private key d_{ID} by computing

$$M = C_2 \oplus H_2(d_{ID} \cdot C_1)$$

This method simplifies key management and enhances security by utilizing ECC's cryptographic properties. Further common IBE use cases are shown in Table 3.3.

Table 3.3. Common IBE Use Cases.

Use Case	Description
Secure Email Communication	Ensures that email content is encrypted using the recipient's identity, making it easy to manage keys and protect against unauthorized access.
Secure Document Sharing	Allows secure sharing of documents by encrypting them with the recipient's identity, ensuring only intended recipients can decrypt and access the content.
Authentication in Online Services	Simplifies user authentication for online services by using identity-based encryption, eliminating the need for complex key management.
Access Control in Enterprises	Manages access control by encrypting sensitive data with the identities of authorized employees, ensuring only those with the correct identity can decrypt the information.
Secure IoT Communications	Provides secure communication channels for IoT devices by using identity-based encryption to ensure that only authenticated devices can exchange data.
Digital Rights Management (DRM)	Protects digital content by encrypting it with the consumer's identity, ensuring that only legitimate users can access and use the content.

3.6.3 Attribute-Based Encryption (ABE)

ABE for key establishment is the process that commences with an authority monitoring the system, responsible for managing the overall framework. Users within the system interact with this authority to generate their individual keys.

Initially, a master key is generated by the authority, while users keys are distributed based on predefined attributes, unlike in IBE where a unique ID is generated (Guo et al. 2021). Access policies, defining the rules for data access, are established by the authority. Users' keys are distributed based on these policies, ensuring that access is granted according to specified attributes.

ABE working process shown in the Figure 3.7, where when a user requests access to encrypted data, they submit a secret key request to the authority. The authority utilizes this request to extract the necessary key relevant to the user's attributes and

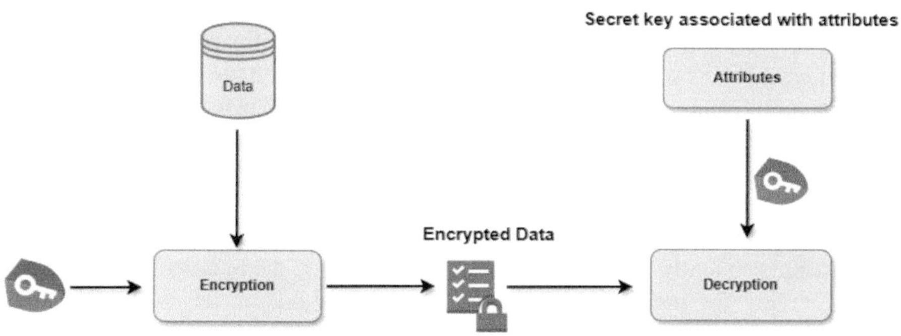

Figure 3.7. Attribute-Based Encryption (ABE).

Table 3.4. Common ABE Use Cases.

Use Case	Description
Fine-Grained Access Control in Cloud Storage	Enables secure access to data stored in the cloud, ensuring that only users with the appropriate attributes can decrypt and retrieve the information.
Secure Healthcare Data Management	Ensures that sensitive healthcare data is encrypted and only accessible to medical personnel with the appropriate attributes, protecting patient privacy and data security.
Access Control in IoT Networks	Manages access to IoT device data based on user and device attributes, ensuring that only authorized entities can interact with specific IoT devices and their data.
Secure Communication in Ad Hoc Networks	Facilitates secure communication between nodes in ad hoc networks by using attribute-based encryption to ensure that only nodes with matching attributes can decrypt messages.
Fine-Grained Access Control in E-Government Systems	Ensures that sensitive government data is encrypted and accessible only to government employees with the necessary attributes, enhancing data security and privacy.
Secure Sharing of Research Data	Facilitates the secure sharing of encrypted research data among collaborators, allowing only those with the requisite attributes to decrypt and access the information.

access policies. Once obtained, this key allows the user to decrypt the encrypted data relevant to their specified attributes. This encryption and decryption method, which is attribute-based, provides precise control over data access. It ensures that only authorized users with corresponding attributes may access specific information, hence preserving data confidentiality and security. Table 3.4 presents common ABE use cases in attribute-based encryption schemes.

3.6.4 Certificateless Public Key Infrastructure (CL-PKI)

In CL-PKI key establishment process, the Certificate Authority (CA) plays a central role. To initiate the process, the CA generates key material crucial for cryptographic operations (Sey et al. 2022). However, instead of directly issuing complete private keys, the CA provides users with partial private key components. Simultaneously, users generate their own key material, such as identifiers and nonces.

To compute their private keys, users combine the partial private key components obtained from the CA with their key material. This fusion results in the generation of the complete private keys required for encryption and decryption.

When a user wants to send an encrypted message, they utilize the recipient's public key, which is generated from their identify and other factors, to encrypt the message. Subsequently, the message is encoded utilizing the recipient-specific data. After receiving the message, the recipient uses their private key to decipher the encrypted message. By utilizing the private key component and other user-specific parameters, the decryption process unveils the original data, ensuring secure and controlled communication within the Certificateless Public Key Infrastructure. CL-PKI process (3.8) includes these key-terms:

- **Authorization:** The process of granting permission to users to access certain cryptographic operations and data.
- **Cloud Server:** The server that may be used to store public keys and other relevant information in a distributed manner.
- **KGC:** The entity responsible for producing and distributing the partial private key components is the primary source.
- **Public Key Server:** The server that hosts the public keys, making them accessible for encryption purposes.
- **Partial Private Key Extract:** The process by which the CA generates and provides users with partial private key components.

Additionally, Table 3.5, shows some common CL-PKI use cases and presents some recent advancements.

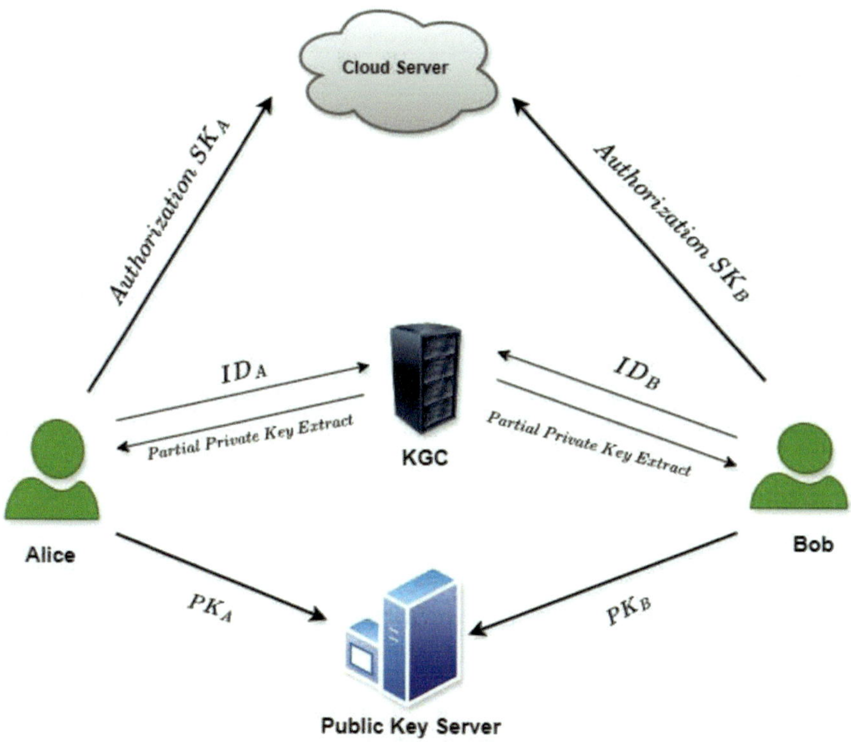

Figure 3.8. Certificateless Public Key Infrastructure (CL-PKI).

Table 3.5. Common Use Cases of Certificateless Public Key Infrastructure (CL-PKI)

Use Case	Description
Online Communications	Employs encryption without the need for certificates, streamlining key management and enhancing security in online communication platforms.
E-Shopping and E-Voting	Provides anonymity and robust security in ecommerce and electronic voting, ensuring secure transactions and reliable voting processes.
Secure Group Communication	Enables efficient and secure group key agreement protocols without relying on certificates, ensuring the security of group communications.
IoT in Resource-Constrained Devices	Improves power efficiency and security in IoT devices with limited resources by leveraging certificateless encryption schemes tailored for low-power environments.
Traffic Management in Transportation Systems	Enhances real-time secure communication in traffic management systems, bolstering the security of vehicle-to-vehicle and vehicle-to-infrastructure communications.
Blockchain-Assisted Privacy Protection	Facilitates secure and privacy-preserving data sharing within blockchain networks, ensuring encryption without the overhead of certificate management.

3.7 Advanced Privacy Techniques

3.7.1 *Mixers and Tumblers*

Mixers combine multiple transactions to obscure the origin and destination of funds.

Tumblers further enhance this by breaking transactions into smaller parts and mixing them multiple times. This process makes it difficult to trace the transaction path and link it to any individual user. Examples include services like Tornado Cash for Ethereum, which provide effective means to anonymize transactions by mixing funds. Bitcoin mixers such as Wasabi Wallet and Samourai Wallet also use coin join techniques to mix transactions and improve privacy.

3.7.2 *Homomorphic Encryption*

Homomorphic encryption enables computations to be executed on encrypted data, guaranteeing the preservation of privacy during the entire processing. This approach is highly advantageous for guaranteeing secure multi-party calculations. Homomorphic encryption can be used in blockchain to perform private computations, such as secure voting and private data analysis. For example, encrypted votes can be counted without revealing individual votes, ensuring both privacy and integrity in the voting process.

3.7.3 *Multi-Party Computation (MPC)*

MPC is a cryptographic technique that enables several participants to collaboratively compute a function based on their individual inputs, all while ensuring that each participant's input remains confidential. MPC guarantees that no participant gains any information beyond what is revealed by the final result of the computation. MPC can be used in blockchain for collaborative tasks such as threshold signatures, where multiple parties generate a signature without exposing their private keys. This enhances security and privacy in multi-user environments.

3.7.4 Differential Privacy

Differential privacy is a technique used to measure and mitigate the privacy vulnerabilities that arise from sharing data. It guarantees that the addition or removal of a single data point has a negligible effect on the result of data analysis, thus protecting individual data entries. Differential privacy can be integrated into blockchain to analyze and share aggregate data without compromising individual privacy. For example, blockchain-based healthcare systems can use differential privacy to share population health data while protecting patient identities.

3.8 Case Studies

Table 3.6 provides a detailed comparison of privacy-focused blockchain technologies, highlighting their privacy features and relative strengths and weaknesses. The table examines prominent blockchains, such as Zcash, Monero, Dash, and Verge, which employ advanced techniques like zk-SNARKs, ring signatures, stealth addresses, and privacy networks such as Tor and I2P.

Table 3.6. Case Studies of Privacy-Focused Blockchains.

Blockchain	**Privacy Features**	**Comparison with Others**
Zcash	• Uses zk-SNARKs for shielded transactions. • Ensures transaction details (sender, receiver, amount) remain confidential.	• Strong privacy guarantees. • Challenges: Trusted setup requirement, computational overhead.
Monero	• Ring signatures to obfuscate sender's identity. • Confidential Transactions (RingCT) hide transaction amounts. • Stealth addresses for unique, one-time addresses per transaction.	• Compared with Zcash and Dash. • Strengths: Default privacy features, robust community support. • Weaknesses: Higher transaction sizes, potential regulatory scrutiny.
Dash	• PrivateSend for obfuscating transaction details through mixing. • Multiple mixing rounds to combine users' coins.	• Compared with Monero and Zcash. • Unique approach: User-friendly privacy options, lower transaction costs. • Utilizes master nodes for mixing services.
Verge	• Uses Tor and I2P to anonymize transactions by hiding IP addresses. • Implements Dual-Key Stealth Address Protocol (DKSAP) for additional privacy.	• Compared with Zcash, Monero, and Dash. • Unique approach: Emphasis on network-level anonymity. • Strengths: Integration with Tor and I2P, simple implementation. • Weaknesses: Relies on external privacy networks, potential latency issues.

3.9 Challenges and Future Directions

3.9.1 Current Challenges in Privacy-Focused Blockchain Development

Scalability Issues: Privacy-enhancing techniques often introduce significant computational and storage overhead, impacting the scalability of blockchain systems. Techniques such as zk-SNARKs, ring signatures, and confidential transactions require complex cryptographic computations and additional data storage, which can slow down transaction processing and increase blockchain size. These scalability challenges can make the network slower and less efficient, posing a significant barrier to widespread adoption. Addressing scalability while maintaining robust privacy features remains a critical challenge for developers.

Regulatory Concerns and Compliance: Regulatory concerns regarding privacy-focused cryptocurrencies pose substantial challenges. Governments and regulatory bodies are increasingly scrutinizing privacy-centric technologies due to their potential use in illicit activities such as money laundering and tax evasion. This scrutiny can lead to potential legal restrictions and the need for compliance with stringent financial regulations. The uncertainty and evolving nature of regulatory environments can deter investment and innovation in privacy-focused blockchain projects.

- **Usability and Adoption Hurdles:** Privacy-focused blockchains often face usability challenges, such as complex user interfaces and slower transaction speeds compared to non-privacy-focused counterparts. The intricate nature of privacy preserving technologies can make them difficult for average users to understand and use effectively. Additionally, slower transaction processing times can deter users accustomed to faster, more user-friendly systems. These hurdles can hinder the widespread adoption of privacy-enhancing technologies, as ease of use is a critical factor for mainstream acceptance.
- **Interoperability Challenges:** Ensuring interoperability between privacy-focused blockchains and other blockchain networks or traditional financial systems is another significant challenge. Privacy features can complicate interactions with other systems that require transparency or different privacy standards. Achieving seamless integration while preserving privacy and security requires innovative solutions and standardized protocols.
- **Performance Trade-Offs:** Implementing privacy features often involves trade-offs between privacy, security, and performance. Achieving a balance where privacy does not significantly degrade performance or security is challenging. Optimizing these trade-offs is crucial for developing practical and effective privacy focused blockchain systems.
- **Public Perception and Trust:** Public perception and trust play a crucial role in the adoption of privacy-focused blockchains. Concerns about the potential misuse of privacy features for illegal activities can affect public opinion and acceptance. Building trust through transparent and ethical use cases, along with regulatory compliance, is essential for gaining wider acceptance.

3.9.2 Future Research Directions

- **Potential Advancements in Cryptographic Techniques:** Future research may lead to significant advancements in cryptographic techniques that enhance privacy while maintaining performance and scalability. Innovations in areas such as lattice-based cryptography, post-quantum cryptography, and zero-knowledge proofs could provide more efficient and secure privacy-preserving solutions. These advancements may address current limitations, offering faster and more scalable privacy mechanisms.
- **Integration of Privacy Features in Mainstream Blockchains:** Integrating advanced privacy features into mainstream blockchains may offer a balance between transparency and privacy, addressing current limitations and enhancing user protection. Efforts to incorporate privacy features such as confidential transactions, zk-SNARKs, and ring signatures into widely used blockchains like Bitcoin and Ethereum are underway. Successful integration could lead to more versatile and user-friendly blockchain systems that cater to a broader range of applications and users.
- **Development of Privacy Standards and Protocols:** Establishing standardized privacy protocols and best practices can facilitate the development and adoption of privacy-preserving technologies. Collaborative efforts among researchers, developers, and regulatory bodies can lead to the creation of frameworks that ensure interoperability, security, and regulatory compliance. Standardization can also promote trust and acceptance among users and institutions.
- **Enhancing User Experience and Accessibility:** Improving the user experience and accessibility of privacy-focused blockchain systems is crucial for widespread adoption. Simplifying user interfaces, reducing transaction times, and providing educational resources can help users understand and effectively use privacy features. Making privacy-enhancing technologies more user-friendly will encourage broader adoption and acceptance.
- **Balancing Privacy and Regulatory Compliance:** Future research should focus on developing methods to balance privacy and regulatory compliance. Techniques such as selective disclosure, where users can choose what information to reveal and to whom, can help achieve this balance. Developing privacy-preserving mechanisms that comply with legal requirements without compromising user privacy is essential for sustainable growth.
- **Privacy-Preserving Governance Models:** Exploring governance models that ensure privacy while enabling transparent and accountable decision-making is a promising research direction. Decentralized autonomous organizations (DAOs) and other governance frameworks can benefit from privacy-preserving technologies to protect voter anonymity and decision integrity.

3.10 Conclusion

The importance of privacy in blockchain technology cannot be overstated, as it is crucial for safeguarding user data and maintaining transaction confidentiality.

As blockchain continues to advance, preserving robust privacy measures becomes even more vital to address new and evolving privacy challenges. ECC plays a central role in bolstering blockchain privacy, offering secure and efficient cryptographic protocols. ECC's applications in digital signatures and encryption schemes are instrumental in protecting sensitive information and ensuring the integrity of blockchain systems.

Looking ahead, the future of privacy-focused blockchain technologies is bright, with significant potential for innovation. Advancements in cryptographic techniques, such as zero-knowledge proofs and homomorphic encryption, along with emerging privacy-preserving technologies, will continue to influence the trajectory of privacy in blockchain systems. The integration of these advanced privacy features into mainstream blockchains is critical to achieving a balance between transparency, security, and user privacy. Moreover, ongoing research and development will focus on enhancing the usability and scalability of privacy-preserving technologies, making them more accessible to a wider audience. The establishment of standardized privacy protocols and adherence to regulatory requirements will also be crucial in fostering trust and encouraging the widespread adoption of privacy-focused blockchain solutions.

In conclusion, although challenges persist, the continuous innovation and integration of advanced cryptographic techniques hold the potential to transform privacy in blockchain technology. This evolution will pave the way for secure, private, and efficient decentralized systems, ensuring that blockchain technology remains a trusted and reliable platform for the future.

References

Aydın, M., and Aydın, G. (2006). A survey of elliptic curve cryptography. IU-Journal of Electrical and Electronics Engineering, 6: 211–221. https://dergipark.org.tr/ en/pub/iujeee/issue/9341/116802.

Chaum, D. (1983). Blind signatures for untraceable payments. pp. 199–203. *In*: Chaum, D., Rivest, R. L., and Sherman, A. T. (Eds.). Advances in Cryptology. https:// doi.org/10.1007/978-1-4757-0602-4_18.

Choudhary, S., Kumar, A., and Kumar, K. (2023). PKIF-AKA: A Public Key Infrastructure Free Authenticated Key Agreement Protocol for Smart Grid Communication.

IETE Journal of Research. https://doi.org/10.1080/03772063.2023.2200381.

Guo, L., Yang, X., and Yau, W.-C. (2021). TABE-DAC: Efficient traceable attribute-based encryption scheme with dynamic access control based on blockchain. IEEE Access, 9: 8479–8490. https://doi.org/10.1109/ACCESS.2021.3049549.

Jancar, J., Fourn´e, M., De Almeida Braga, D., Sabt, M., Schwabe, P., Barthe, G. et al. (2021). They're not that hard to mitigate: What cryptographic library developers think about timing attacks. Cryptology ePrint Archive, Paper 2021/1650. https://eprint.iacr.org/2021/1650.

Kim, Y., Perrig, A., and Tsudik, G. (2004). Tree-based group key agreement. ACM Transactions on Information and System Security, 7(1): 60–96. https://doi.org/10.1145/984334.984337.

Khodaiemehr, H., Bagheri, K., and Feng, C. (2023). Navigating the quantum computing threat landscape for blockchains: A comprehensive survey. https://doi.org/10.36227/techrxiv.24136440.

Kumar, V., and Ray, S. (2022). Pairing-free identity-based digital signature algorithm for broadcast authentication based on modified ECC using Battle Royal optimization algorithm. Wireless Personal Communications, 123: 2341–2365. https://doi.org/10.1007/s11277-021-09244-y.

Mezrag, F., Bitam, S., and Mellouk, A. (2022). An efficient and lightweight identitybased scheme for secure communication in clustered wireless sensor networks. Journal of Network and Computer Applications, 200: 103282. https://doi.org/10.1016/j.jnca.2021.103282.

Mohammed, N., Dawood, O., Sagheer, A., and Nafea, A. (2023). Secure smart contract based on blockchain to prevent the non-repudiation phenomenon. Baghdad Science Journal. https://doi.org/10.21123/bsj.2023.8164.

Nakamoto, S. (2008). A peer-to-peer electronic cash system. Bitcoin. https://www. klausnordby.com/bitcoin/Bitcoin_Whitepaper_Document_HD.pdf.

Pal, O., Alam, B., Thakur, V., and Singh, S. (2021). Key management for blockchain technology. ICT Express, 7(1), 76-80. https://doi.org/10.1016/j.icte.2019.08.002.

Pal, O., Alam, B., Thakur, V., and Singh, S. (2021). Key management for blockchain technology. ICT Express, 7(1): 76–80. https://doi.org/10.1016/j.icte.2019.08.002.

Rao, T. V. N., Likhar, P. P., Kurni, M., and Saritha, K. (2022). Blockchain technology for emerging applications. In Hybrid Computational Intelligence for Pattern Analysis (pp. 33–66). https://doi.org/10.1016/B978-0-323-90193-2.00004-1.

Rivest, R. L., Shamir, A., and Adleman, L. (1978). A method for obtaining digital signatures and public-key cryptosystems. Commun. ACM, 21(2): 120–126. https://www. scopus.com/record/display.uri?eid=2-s2.0-0017930809&origin=inward.

Roche, T., Imbert, L., and Lomn´e, V. (2019). Side-channel attacks on blinded scalar multiplications revisited. IACR Cryptology ePrint Archive, 2019, 1220. https://www.semanticscholar.org/paper/Side-channel-Attacks-on-Blinded-Scalar-Revisited-Roche-Imbert/84621c08a4671cd4be316ab811a2ce1cea69c649.

Sey, C., Lei, H., Qian, W., Li, X., Fiasam, L.D., Kodjiku, S.L. et al. (2022). VBlock: A blockchain-based tamper-proofing data protection model for Internet of Vehicle networks. Sensors, 22: 8083. https://doi.org/10.3390/s22208083.

Wu, H., Düdder, B., Wang, L., Cao, Z., Zhou, J., and Feng, X. (2023). Survey on secure keyword search over outsourced data: From cloud to blockchain-assisted architecture. ACM Computing Surveys, 56(3), 1-40.https://doi.org/10.1145/3617824.

CHAPTER 4

A Blockchain-Fortified Deep Learning Approach for Intrusion Detection in Healthcare IoT

Puja Das,[1] *Chitra Jain,*[2] *Biswajit Jana,*[3] *Bireshwar Mazumder,*[3] *Ansul,*[2] *Moutushi Singh*[4] and *Deepsubhra Guha Roy*[5,*]

4.1 Introduction

The Internet of Things (IoT) has transformed medical delivery, monitoring, and management. At its core, IoT is a set of device systems that communicate and share data over the internet. In healthcare, this technology has been instrumental in enhancing patient care, improving efficiency, and enabling innovative services. Key applications include remote patient monitoring, optimized performance of medical devices, supply chain management, predictive insights, virtual care, and health tracking (Park and Kim 2022).

Yet, despite its advantages, IoT implementation in healthcare presents significant cybersecurity challenges, particularly when handling sensitive health information. These challenges include data privacy and confidentiality concerns, data integrity issues, interoperability hurdles, device vulnerabilities, "man-in-the-middle" attacks, weak authentication and authorization mechanisms, and subpar

[1] CSBS Department, KPRIET, Tamil Nadu, India.
Emails: Pujadas.wbut@gmail.com
[2] CSE department, COER University, UK, 247667, India.
Emails: chitra.cj1996@gmail.com; ansulsingh67890@gmail.com
[3] SCSET, Bennett University, UP, India.
Email: biswajit.janacseng2012@gmail.com
[4] CSE Department, IEM, UEM, Kolkata - 700091, India.
Email: moutushi.singh@iemcal.com
[5] IEM Centre of Excellence for Cloud Computing & IoT, Department of CSE(AIML), Institute of Engineering & Management, University of Engineering & Management, Kolkata-700091, India.
* Corresponding author: roysubhraguha@gmail.com

DOI: 10.1201/9781003540328-4

encryption standards. The risks associated with compromised patient surveillance data are especially critical, as they could lead to misdiagnoses, identity theft, and other severe consequences (Rathee et al. 2019). Addressing these challenges requires robust security measures. Blockchain technology offers promising solutions to many of these cybersecurity concerns. For example, zero-knowledge proofs (ZKPs) allow one party (the prover) to demonstrate the truth of a statement to another party (the verifier) without revealing the actual content of the statement. Additionally, the tamper-resistant nature of blockchain—where altering one block necessitates changes to all preceding blocks—ensures data integrity. Smart contracts further enhance IoT processes by automating transactions and reducing the need for intermediaries. In healthcare, blockchain can secure sensitive patient data while improving care delivery. For instance, Ethereum smart contracts, once deployed, become immutable, ensuring secure access control and transaction execution governed by predefined rules (Das et al. 2021). These smart contracts can regulate IoT device interactions, automate compliance with data access and consent regulations, and minimize human error and fraud. Blockchain addresses privacy concerns by limiting access to authorized devices and maintaining patient ownership of their data (Das et al. 2024a) is shown in the Table 4.1.

Table 4.1 shows a comparison of various consensus algorithms.

The combination of Artificial Intelligence (AI), Deep Learning, and machine learning (ML) models into Blockchain IoT architecture further strengthens the security of healthcare systems. AI-powered algorithms and neural networks excel in pattern recognition, anomaly detection, and self-adaptation, enabling continuous learning to counter new threats in real-time (Nguyen et al. 2019). DL models, such as recurrent neural networks (RNNs) and long short-term memory networks (LSTMs), analyze temporal patterns in data from IoT devices and healthcare records stored on the blockchain to swiftly detect anomalies or deviations. This synergy between AI and blockchain offers two major benefits: enhanced data legitimacy and a secure foundation for data analytics (Minoli and Occhiogrosso 2018). AI algorithms also improve the precision of security threat detection, reducing false positives and negatives, and enabling seamless access for legitimate users (Kalapaaking et al. 2023). Context-based access control is made possible through adaptive authentication frameworks, which appraise access requests in real-time based on user behavior, device attributes, and network conditions (Das et al. 2024b).

Incorporating AI into blockchain-based identity management systems significantly improves the accuracy and responsiveness of access control mechanisms. Machine learning models can assess system vulnerabilities and refine dynamic authorization models to meet the evolving requirements of healthcare networks. This adaptability is crucial for addressing real-time security risks and access requests in complex healthcare scenarios (Rathore et al. 2019). To validate the proposed AI-enhanced blockchain identity management system, rigorous experiments were conducted using established datasets such as CICIDS-2017 and ToN-IoT (Goel et al. 2019). These datasets encompass a broad spectrum of cyber threats, with CICIDS-2017 focusing on international cyberattack scenarios and ToN-IoT addressing IoT devices common in healthcare settings (Vargas et al. 2021). The results demonstrate the system's ability to handle security challenges in connected

Table 4.1. A Relative study between various types of consensus algorithms.

Consensus Algorithm	**Platform**	**Apply Language**	**Reward**	**Delay**	**Energy Consumption**	**Advantage**	**Disadvantage**
PoW (Ali et al. 2022)	Bitcoin	C++	Who wins the problem	High	High	- Minimum attack - Security enhanced	- High Power required
PoS (Siyal et al. 2019)	NEXT	Java	Who keep stack	Low	Medium	- Efficient energy	- No major problem in the stack
PBFT (Pham et al. 2020)	Hyperledger	Java Script, Python	No	Low	Low	- No conformation required	- Different and costly resources required
DPoS (Ahmed et al. 2023)	Lisk	Java Script	Need to be selected as a super node	Low	Low	- Efficient energy - Scalable - Security enhanced	- Double spend attack Possible
LPoS (Lu et al. 2019)	Waves	Scala	No	Low	Medium	- Participation cost is less	- Decentralization problem

health ecosystems, offering valuable insights into securing healthcare IoT networks (Chandrasekaran et al. 2019). Combining AI and blockchain technologies provides a robust solution to dynamic security challenges in healthcare (Fuller et al. 2020). By leveraging advanced datasets and innovative access control mechanisms, this approach ensures more precise and responsive security measures, creating the way for safer and well-organized healthcare applications (Rasheed et al. 2020).

4.1.1 Important Contribution

Our study demonstrates the development of a robust security architecture made possible by blockchain technology. This architecture employs zero-knowledge proofs to register and verify IoT devices, creating a secure and reliable healthcare network. By enabling standardization in the transmission of healthcare information, this scheme significantly reduces the risk of data breaches.

- Our research introduces a robust security architecture empowered by blockchain. The scheme leverages zero-information proofs for registering and verifying IoT devices, ensuring a secure and trustworthy healthcare network. It establishes a standardized method for transmitting healthcare data within the network, mitigating the risk of data breaches (Letaief et al. 2021).
- Our security architecture employs deep learning, including models like RNNs and LSTMs for feature extraction and data encoding.
- The system evolves authorization protocols through deep learning, specifically in reinforcement learning. This enhances data security and privacy in the proposed blockchain-enabled architecture, allowing only authorized entities access to sensitive healthcare information (Ouaddah et al. 2016).

This chapter is organized as follows. The related work is enclosed in Section 2. Research describing the recommended framework and its functional module is discussed in Section 3. The effectiveness of the study in terms of results analysis is evaluated in Section 4. Finally, the conclusion with the future path is detailed in Section 5.

4.2 Related Work

This section includes pertinent research in four domains: deep learning-based privacy preservation, smart contract-based decentralized systems, intrusion detection systems, and state-of-the-art blockchain environments.

4.2.1 Deep Learning-Based Privacy Preservation

Privacy-preserving methodologies entail pre-processing data before employing mining algorithms like an intrusion detection system to stop information leaks while safeguarding vital details. These techniques include authentication-based, data-driven, disquiet-driven, encode-driven, deep learning-driven, and blockchain-used approaches (Ghobakhloo et al. 2022). Blockchain privacy methods utilize decentralized ledgers, linking data blocks sequentially using cryptographic techniques. The distributed consensus algorithm organizes transactions into new blocks, disseminating consensus throughout the network (Dwivedi et al. 2022). The creation of blocks involves specialized nodes, specifically miners. Conventional proof-of-work (PoW) blockchain faces computational hurdles and security concerns, particularly the 51% attack. Smart contracts, executing on the blockchain, address these issues by transparently enforcing predefined terms and enhancing data privacy without relying on trusted third parties.

4.2.2 Smart Contract-Based Decentralized System

There are various ways in which decentralized systems that employ smart contracts can improve data security and privacy. Investigating consensus techniques other than proof-of-work (PoW) is one line of inquiry. To solve the computational problems and security flaws associated with proof-of-work (PoW), delegated proof-of-stake (DPoS) is being investigated and adopted as a potential substitute (Jameel et al. 2020). The goal is to create more secure and productive decentralized networks. The distributed nature of blockchain networks is utilized by the smart-contract-enabled consensus process to guarantee that transactions are handled safely and transparently without the need for middlemen. Furthermore, integrating differential privacy (DP) concepts into smart contracts provides a robust foundation for protecting personal data in decentralized environments, improving the security posture of blockchain networks as a whole.

4.2.3 Intrusion Detection System

The integration of an AI-powered Intrusion Detection System (IDS) with a blockchain consensus mechanism offers a comprehensive solution for tackling the unique cybersecurity issues that medical IoT devices encounter. Blockchain's distributed architecture enables transparent, traceable, and trustworthy data, while the AI-supported IDS provides flexible solutions to security risks (Kumar et al. 2022). This kind of thinking takes into account the need for security and privacy in healthcare settings while reducing the dangers posed by both known and unknown attackers. Furthermore, as modern healthcare systems increasingly use interconnected medical devices to enhance patient care, integrating blockchain with AI-driven IDS is beneficial as a proactive measure to ensure the fidelity and resilience of IoT ecosystems in healthcare environments.

4.2.4 Blockchain-Based Environment

Digital environments are undergoing an evolution because of blockchain-based distributed linked environments, which allow for safe, open, and impenetrable interactions between users. Blockchain distributes power throughout a network of nodes, decentralizing it in contrast to traditional centrally controlled structures that concentrate data and responsibility in one entity (Mohanta et al. 2020). This improves security and resilience by ensuring that there isn't a single point of breakdown.

Through the use of encryption techniques, users in such an ecosystem can directly trade property, data, or products without the need for middlemen, promoting trust (Kodheli et al. 2020). By automating transactions based on certain criteria, smart contracts—self-executing agreements inscribed on the blockchain—further simplify procedures while cutting costs and removing the possibility of human error.

Applications for this distributed infrastructure may be found in a variety of sectors, including banking, where it facilitates peer-to-peer payments and decentralized finance (DeFi) solutions, and supply chain administration, where it improves accountability and tracking. Furthermore, blockchain enables smooth communication between machines by integrating Internet of Things (IoT) devices, establishing a networked environment where gadgets may communicate and transact on their own. Blockchain, for example, can provide safe data exchange, automated traffic systems, and decentralized energy grids in smart cities. This concept ensures privacy and ownership by giving people more control over their data and digital identities by doing away with the need for central management (Moosavi et al. 2021). Broad implementation is still hampered by issues including scalability, power consumption, and conformity to regulations.

There is an illustration of the main idea of a basic blockchain transaction in an Internet of Healthcare Things (IoHT) framework, as shown in Figure 4.1. In other words, this diagram represents the overall complexities that surround data transactions and secure information exchange within the healthcare system. A basic IoHT-based blockchain transaction usually encompasses transmitting health-related data or information between linked devices, sensors or systems (Xu et al. 2023). The transaction itself is decentralized through the use of blockchain technology thus ensuring security and transparency while recording these transfers on ledgers. Every block in a chain contains an exclusive identifier together with a cryptographic hash of its predecessor thereby creating an immutable and tamper-proof transaction sequence. This fundamental picture captures how IoHT takes advantage of blockchain to provide robust trustworthy frameworks for handling healthcare data exchanges enhancing security, integrity, and inter-operability among dynamic clinic technology (Li et al. 2018).

At the same time, blockchain technology has emerged to be a critical security tool in intelligent transportation, whereby there have been studies on combining deep learning and machine learning with blockchain for IoT's enhanced security and privacy. One such study was done by introducing the Cp protocol in connection with blockchain highlighting how possible it is to make Intrusion Detection Systems (IDS) more trustworthy. The researchers proposed a security architecture that uses blockchains and distributed ledgers (DL) made up of multiple agents for securing IoT data. The evaluation, conducted on an applied dataset, showcased the impressive accuracy rate of 99% achieved by a Deep Neural Network (DNN)-based IDS. However, it is essential to acknowledge that the evaluation relied on outdated datasets and necessitated specific implementation details for blockchain integration. The proposed model demonstrated success rates of 98% and 92% in detection tasks, albeit lacking a specific analysis focused on blockchain within the suggested paradigm.

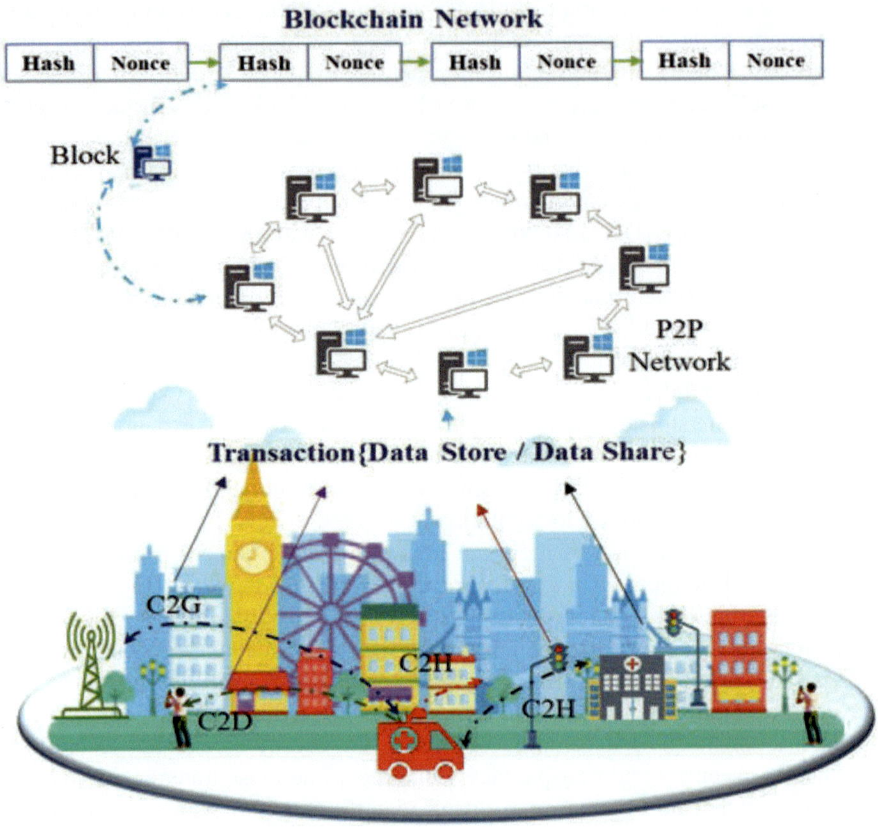

Figure 4.1. Basic Blockchain Transaction in IoHT Framework.

4.3 Methodology

The research uses a qualitative research strategy to discover and analyze the integration of artificial intelligence (AI) into blockchain-based identity management systems for access control within IoT-enabled healthcare networks. The working principle of the proposed system is illustrated in Figure 4.2, which highlights the communication flow between various components. This framework comprises entities such as IoT modules, verified users, and edge servers, each playing a critical role in ensuring system functionality and security. Verified users are required to register themselves before gaining access to the network, ensuring secure participation. IoT devices, which typically possess limited computational resources, include components like temperature sensors, moisture sensors, and pressure monitors. These devices are interconnected via the internet, enabling seamless interaction. Edge servers, composed of manufacturing computers and data investigation servers, work in tandem with IoT modules to perform mining operations. The proposed architecture is structured around two core units: the blockchain-based security architecture and the deep learning-based Intrusion Detection System (IDS), as depicted in Figure 4.2. Within the blockchain network, users are required to register IoT devices through

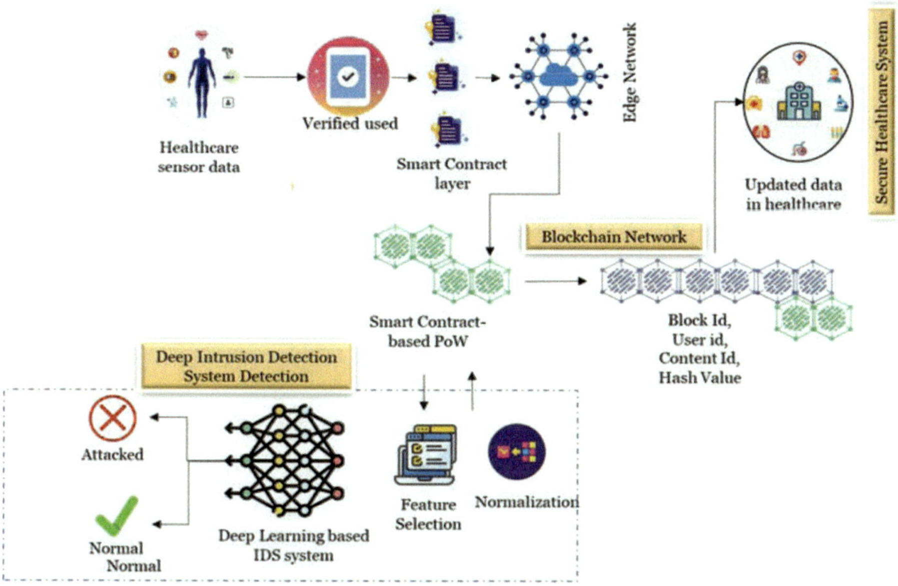

Figure 4.2. The proposed architecture of blockchain enables IDS detection system.

secure announcements. This layer of the architecture prevents information poisoning attacks and facilitates tracking of critical information attributes such as its location, owner, intended use, alternative pathways, safety measures, and security activation capabilities.

While integrating AI with blockchain significantly enhances the security and efficiency of healthcare systems, addressing potential technical and operational challenges is critical for practical implementation. To ensure compatibility between AI models and blockchain frameworks, the proposed system employs lightweight AI models optimized for blockchain environments. Techniques such as model compression and quantization are utilized to reduce the computational and memory requirements of AI models, making them suitable for integration within blockchain networks. Additionally, computational overheads are mitigated by deploying edge computing nodes that offload intensive AI computations from the blockchain network. These nodes preprocess data and execute AI algorithms locally, reducing latency and preserving network efficiency. The architecture also incorporates asynchronous processing, ensuring that blockchain operations and AI computations occur concurrently without creating bottlenecks. By addressing these challenges, the proposed framework ensures seamless integration of AI and blockchain, maintaining both performance and scalability in healthcare systems.

The deep learning-enabled security architecture incorporates a Denoising Stacked Autoencoder (DSAE) to convert original data into a more efficient format, significantly reducing dataset dimensions while preserving key features. This approach improves the organization's ability to process and analyze data effectively, strengthening its defences against security threats. To validate the integration of AI within the blockchain-based identity management system and to improve the accurateness of the deep learning-based intrusion detection system, the study utilizes well-established datasets such as NSL-KDD and ISCX UNSW-NB 2015. The NSL-KDD dataset, renowned for its comprehensive representation of diverse network traffic, enables the simulation of a wide range of security threats and attacks relevant to IoT-enabled healthcare networks. This dataset supports an in-depth evaluation of the proposed system's adaptability and resilience in addressing complex security challenges specific to the healthcare domain. On the other hand, the ISCX UNSW-NB 2015 dataset is employed to assess the performance of the deep learning-based IDS component within the proposed architecture. By incorporating these datasets, the study provides a comprehensive understanding of the system's real-world effectiveness. This evaluation contributes significantly to the development of secure and efficient identity management solutions for IoT-enabled healthcare networks.

4.3.1 Blockchain-Based Security Architecture

This secure healthcare system integrates advanced technologies like blockchain, deep learning-based intrusion detection systems (DL-IDS), and cryptographic methods to safeguard data privacy, integrity, and operational efficiency. The process begins with the collection and validation of patient and administrative data, where strict security measures ensure that the data is authentic and accurate. The scalability of the proposed adaptable blockchain architecture is ensured through the integration of advanced techniques such as sharding, layer-two solutions, and the Delegated Proof of Stake (DPoS) consensus algorithm.

Sharding divides the blockchain network into smaller, manageable partitions, enabling parallel processing of transactions across multiple nodes. This significantly improves transaction throughput and reduces bottlenecks. Additionally, layer-two solutions are employed to handle a significant portion of the transaction workload off-chain, thus reducing the strain on the main blockchain network while maintaining data security and integrity. To further enhance scalability, the Delegated Proof of Stake (DPoS) consensus mechanism is implemented, which selects a limited number of trusted delegates to validate transactions. This reduces the computational overhead and energy consumption typically associated with traditional consensus mechanisms such as Proof of Work (PoW).

These combined approaches ensure that the architecture can handle the growing demands of large-scale healthcare systems, supporting extensive data and user bases without compromising security, speed, or decentralization. The system also tracks essential attributes of the data, such as its origin, destination, administrative access, routing pathways, and security activation protocols, helping prevent unauthorized access or information poisoning attacks. Once validated, the data is stored securely within a blockchain network. Blockchain ensures transparency and immutability by creating a decentralized, tamper-proof ledger that records all transactions. This distributed network safeguards against unauthorized modifications and provides an auditable trail of data activity. The blockchain structure further allows monitoring of detours, final objectives, and safety measures, ensuring that the data remains secure throughout its lifecycle.

4.3.2 Deep Learning-Based IDS

To strengthen the system against cyber threats, a deep learning-based IDS is integrated, leveraging advanced algorithms to detect and mitigate malicious activities. This IDS proactively identifies anomalies and potential threats, reducing vulnerabilities and preventing data breaches. Furthermore, the deep learning-enabled security architecture transforms and compresses the original data into a novel, compact format, significantly reducing storage requirements while maintaining the critical information necessary for analysis and operations. Another vital component of the system is the use of zero-information proofs (ZIPs), a cryptographic approach that allows for the verification of data validity without exposing sensitive information. By enabling parties to validate statements without revealing the underlying data, ZIPs ensure robust privacy and minimize the risk of confidentiality breaches. This capability is particularly critical in healthcare, where protecting sensitive patient information is paramount. Overall, this secure healthcare system combines blockchain's immutability, deep learning's threat detection capabilities, and ZIPs' privacy-preserving features to create a comprehensive framework. This architecture not only enhances data security and privacy but also optimizes operational efficiency, ensuring that sensitive healthcare data remains resilient against evolving cyber threats while supporting transparency and trust in the system.

4.3.3 Security Analysis

Lemma 1. Blockchain data is not possible to temper by any Outsider.

Proof. A blockchain is a system having blocks chronologically with unique hash values from Genesis block to end. So, if any attacker wants to change or manipulate the data of a block, then he needs to redo the entire Proof of Work (PoW) for the targeted block and each and every single block present in the blockchain. However, the attacker must have a 51% stack if he wants to change anything (computational cost and power). So, it proves data manipulation is extremely difficult in a decentralized network.

Lemma 2. Decentralized-based systems are safe from any physical attack.

Proof. Any type of physical attack cannot retrieve the encrypted response from the device recollection of an intelligence-based device. As mentioned in Lemma 1, the secret message is neither stored nor shared with any other system. An attacker cannot access the device microcontroller for further information. This affords a resistance method against any occurrences.

Theorem 1. Data Derivation: The suggested approach effectively demonstrates the legitimacy of the data source.

Proof. An attacker might attempt to refer fiddled data to a miner by pretending to be a valid user. We can simulate this using the protection simulation below:

- Contender C picks a car U_c and starts executing the transaction.

- Atacker A_{attak} demands, requests for multiple times and send $send_{info}$, $send_{txet}$, and wait for miner response.
- If the miner M_{val} successfully validates the altered data sent by an attacker, then A_{attak} win else blocks the system.
- An intelligence system verifies and update the situation.

The attacker has two options to change the data of the user successfully: first, transform the blockchain network; second, change the hashed data value in content two during the substantiation step.

$$M_{val} = hashC_i \,||data||\, \Re_i \tag{1}$$

Lemma 1 states, however, that it is impossible to tamper with the blockchain. Furthermore, according to Lemma 2, the challenger cannot get Ri and can't alter the hashed data value. This demonstrates that achieving data derivation and preventing data fiddling attacks are possible.

Lemma 2. The key pairs of cars cannot be interrelated.

Proof. The roadside unit provides certificates to randomize the key pairs of vehicles. therefore, to access the public or private key of the vehicle, the attacker needs to access the nearest health unit, and this is not possible. Because to have the information about HU, attackers need to access all previous transaction details.

4.4 Experiment and Result Discussion

Certainly, let's integrate the details about how the 99% accuracy was achieved into the existing content, explaining the methodology, equations, and datasets used:

The proposed blockchain architecture's security and privacy assessment is covered in detail. Several parameters are taken into consideration to verify the effectiveness of the suggested blockchain system. First, the effects of expanding the number of IoT nodes and their transaction registration time are evaluated in the suggested framework. For a maximum of 60 IoT nodes and 600 transactions (Tx), the registration time of participating IoT nodes in the blockchain-enabled system is shown in Figure 4.3a. Additionally, the efficacy of the transfer knowledge model is demonstrated by a thorough examination of the suggested blockchain architecture using five standard characteristics. These parameters include True Positive (ψ), False Positive (φ), True Negative (ζ), and False Negative (ϖ),

$$\text{Accuracy: } A_t = (\psi + \zeta)\,(\,\psi + \zeta + \varphi + \varpi,.) * 100\% \tag{2}$$

$$\text{Recall: } R_e = \psi\,(\psi + \varpi,.) \tag{3}$$

$$\text{Specificity: } S_{pf} = \zeta\,(\varphi + \zeta) * 100\% \tag{4}$$

$$\text{Precision: } P_r = \psi\,(\psi + \varphi) \tag{5}$$

$$\text{F1} - \text{score: } f_1 = 2 * (P_r * R_e\, P_r + R_e) \tag{6}$$

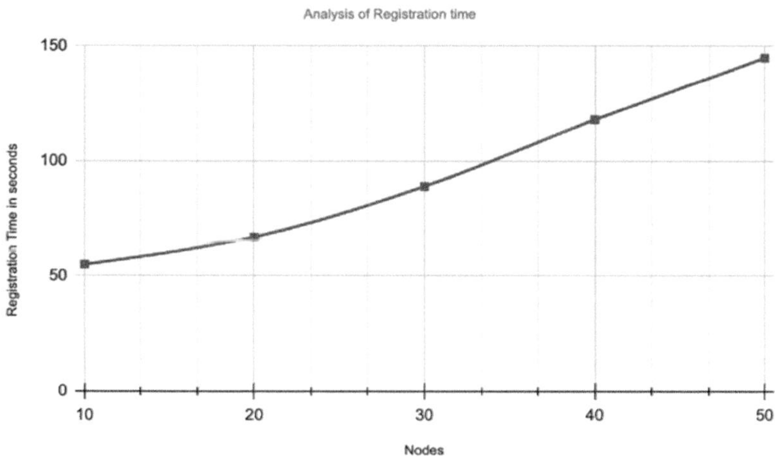

Figure 4.3a. Examination of Time Registration Patterns in IoT Sensor Nodes.

It has been noted that when the number of operations using different nodes increases, the time needed for each transaction tends to grow as well. Because it emphasizes the complex link between transaction volume and processing efficiency, this phenomenon is especially fascinating. Every succeeding transaction in a network may encounter new challenges as more nodes join, such as higher connection overhead and data verification. This slow increase might present a difficulty as well as an opportunity for system optimization to increase speed without sacrificing precision or dependability.

As illustrated in Figure 4.3b and Figure 4.3c, which showcase block creation and access time. Notably, the results indicate a stable performance of up to 50 nodes and 500 transactions, suggesting a robust system.

To accomplish the remarkable accuracy of 93% demonstrated in Figure 4.4, a deep learning-based Intrusion Detection System (DL-IDS) was employed within the proposed blockchain framework. The IDS utilized a Deep Sparse Auto Encoder (DSAE) approach, represented by the following equations:

$$\textit{Encoder: } K = f(\mathrm{BX} + \Upsilon) \tag{7}$$

$$\textit{Decoder: } \mathrm{M} = g(\mathrm{BT}' + \Upsilon') \tag{8}$$

Here, (X) characterizes the input data, (B) and (Υ) is the weight and bias parameters of the encoder, (T) is the encoded representation, (BT′) and (Υ′) are the parameters of the decoder, and (r) is the reconstructed output. As a result, DSAE decreased the quantity of the data used while preserving processing accuracy in terms of intrusion case detection. The 2015 KDD and UNSW-NB datasets were used for training and assessment. These data collections frequently highlight problems related to intrusion alerts and network safety. In response, the UNSW-NB 2015 dataset is intended primarily for evaluating the ability of systems to identify abnormalities, whereas the KDD data set offers a variety of network traffic statistics. Using these datasets with DSAE-based IDS produced an astounding 98% accuracy rate.

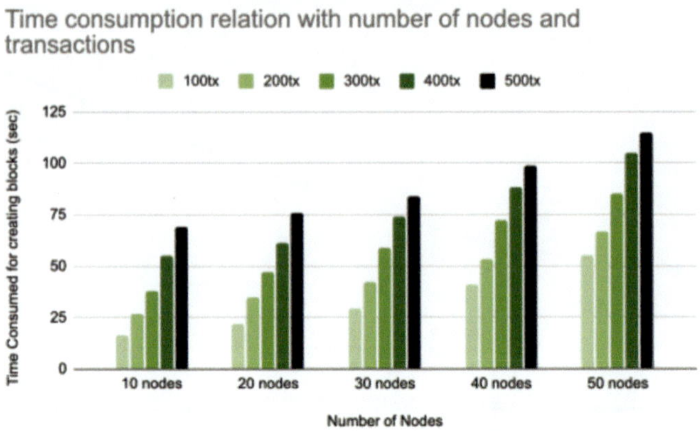

Figure 4.3b. Analysis of the Time Taken to Create Blocks for Transactions (TX) of Different Sizes.

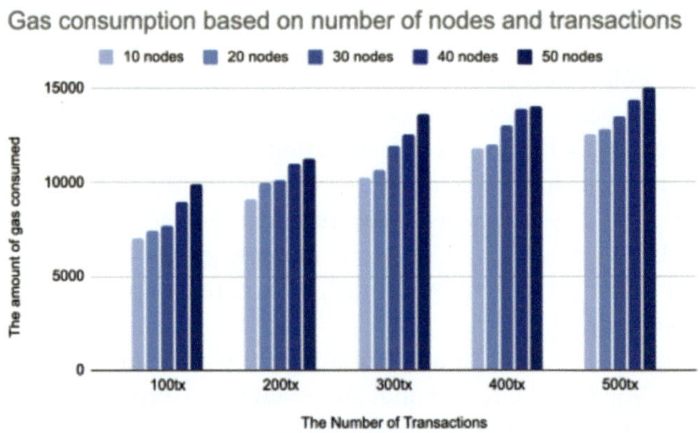

Figure 4.3c. Examination of Price Consumption about Transaction (TX) Size Variations on the Ethereum Blockchain Network.

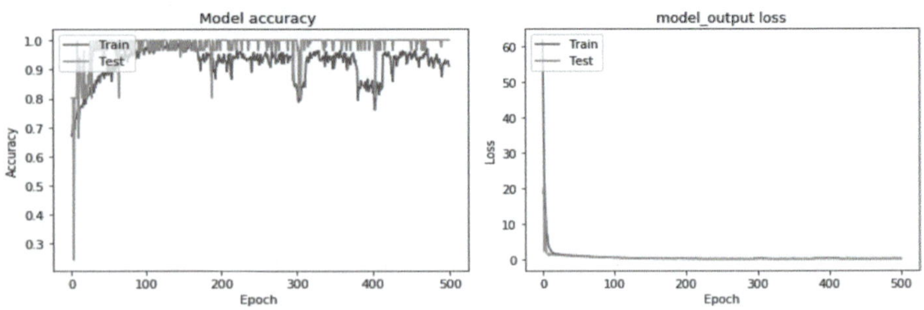

Figure 4.4. The Relationship Between Accuracy and Loss Derived from the Extraction Approach Dataset

This solid functionality ensures the reliability of the proposed blockchain-based architecture and positions it as a viable security solution for IoT-enabled networks in dynamic settings like the medical field. The proposed IDS outperforms other state-of-the-art techniques through its accuracy rate of 98% when benchmarked against D1 and D2 data sets. These results demonstrate that DSAE-based IDS integrated within a blockchain framework yields consistently higher precision, recall, and f1 scores across different classes. This strong performance ensures not only the dependability of this proposed blockchain-implemented system but also positions it as one of the superior solutions for ensuring security in dynamic environments that are characterized by healthcare cases.

4.5 Conclusion

The findings from this study highlight the critical role of artificial intelligence (AI) in securing access mechanisms within healthcare services. Leveraging datasets such as NSL-KDD and ISCX UNSW-NB 2015, the proposed system demonstrates exceptional performance, achieving accuracy rates of up to 93%. These results not only validate the effectiveness of AI-driven approaches in mitigating cybersecurity threats but also address ethical dilemmas associated with AI control systems, particularly concerning privacy rights and security. By incorporating zero-knowledge proofs (ZIPs) and deploying smart contracts within blockchain technology, the proposed architecture establishes a robust paradigm capable of effectively mitigating cybersecurity threats. This innovative framework ensures secure transmission of healthcare information, authenticates IoT devices, and prevents unauthorized access.

Furthermore, the incorporation of deep learning techniques, predominantly reinforcement learning, enhances endorsement mechanisms, achieving an imposing accuracy rate of 92% with the same datasets. This adaptability ensures that only approved entities can admittance complex health data, significantly bolstering data security and privacy within the blockchain-based architecture. Collectively, these findings represent a significant step toward unifying healthcare systems with advanced technologies like blockchain and AI. The planned explanation offers a comprehensive approach to ensuring secure information transmission, device authenticity verification, and proactive intrusion detection.

Looking ahead, future work can focus on enhancing the scalability and interoperability of the proposed framework to accommodate the rapid growth of IoT-based healthcare networks. Further research could also explore optimizing the integration of AI algorithms with blockchain technology to enable dynamic access control in evolving environments. Investigations into novel cryptographic techniques and reinforcement learning approaches hold the potential to improve the framework's ability to adapt to emerging threats and address the ever-changing dynamics of healthcare security. These avenues promise to continuously strengthen healthcare systems, ensuring resilience against evolving cybersecurity challenges.

References

Ahmed, I., Chehri, A., and Jeon, G. (2023). Artificial intelligence and blockchain enabled smart healthcare system for monitoring and detection of COVID-19 in biomedical images. IEEE/ACM Transactions on Computational Biology and Bioinformatics, 21(4): 814–822. https://doi.org/10.1109/tcbb.2023.3294333.

Ali, A., Almaiah, M. A., Hajjej, F., Pasha, M. F., Fang, O. H., Khan, R. et al. (2022). An industrial IoT-Based Blockchain-Enabled secure searchable encryption approach for healthcare systems using neural network. Sensors, 22(2): 572. https://doi.org/10.3390/s22020572.

Chandrasekaran, N., Somanah, R., Rughoo, D., Dreepaul, R. K., Cunden, T. S. M., and Demkah, M. (2019). Digital Transformation from Leveraging Blockchain Technology, Artificial Intelligence, Machine Learning and Deep Learning. In Advances in intelligent systems and computing (pp. 271–283). https://doi.org/10.1007/978-981-13-3338-5_25.

Das, P., Jain, C., Ansul, N., and Singh, M. (2024a). Agri-Chain: a Blockchain-Empowered smart solution for agricultural industry. In Studies in computational intelligence (pp. 221–245). https://doi.org/10.1007/978-3-031-67450-1_9.

Das, P., Singh, M., and Roy, D. G. (2021). A secure softwarized blockchain-based federated health alliance for next generation IoT networks. 2022 IEEE Globecom Workshops (GC Wkshps), 1–6. https://doi.org/10.1109/gcwkshps52748.2021.9682088.

Das, P., Singh, M., and Verma, K. K. (2024b). Blockchain-Enabled Deep Learning approach to improve healthcare system. Journal of Multimedia Information System, 11(1): 9–16. https://doi.org/10.33851/jmis.2024.11.1.9.

Dwivedi, Y. K., Hughes, L., Baabdullah, A. M., Ribeiro-Navarrete, S., Giannakis, M., Al-Debei, M. M. et al. (2022). Metaverse beyond the hype: Multidisciplinary perspectives on emerging challenges, opportunities, and agenda for research, practice and policy. International Journal of Information Management, 66: 102542. https://doi.org/10.1016/j.ijinfomgt.2022.102542.

Fuller, A., Fan, Z., Day, C., and Barlow, C. (2020). Digital Twin: enabling technologies, challenges and open research. IEEE Access, 8: 108952–108971. https://doi.org/10.1109/access.2020.2998358.

Ghobakhloo, M., Iranmanesh, M., Mubarak, M. F., Mubarik, M., Rejeb, A., and Nilashi, M. (2022). Identifying industry 5.0 contributions to sustainable development: A strategy roadmap for delivering sustainability values. Sustainable Production and Consumption, 33: 716–737. https://doi.org/10.1016/j.spc.2022.08.003.

Goel, A., Agarwal, A., Vatsa, M., Singh, R., and Ratha, N. (2019). DeepRing: Protecting deep neural network with Blockchain. 2022 IEEE/CVF Conference on Computer Vision and Pattern Recognition Workshops (CVPRW). https://doi.org/10.1109/cvprw.2019.00341.

Jameel, F., Javaid, U., Sikdar, B., Khan, I., Mastorakis, G., and Mavromoustakis, C. X. (2020). Optimizing Blockchain Networks with Artificial Intelligence: Towards Efficient and Reliable IoT Applications. In Internet of things (pp. 299–321). https://doi.org/10.1007/978-3-030-44907-0_12.

Kalapaaking, A. P., Khalil, I., and Atiquzzaman, M. (2023). Blockchain-Enabled and Multisignature-Powered verifiable model for securing federated learning systems. IEEE Internet of Things Journal, 10(24): 21410–21420. https://doi.org/10.1109/jiot.2023.3289832.

Kodheli, O., Lagunas, E., Maturo, N., Sharma, S. K., Shankar, B., Montoya, J. F. M. et al. (2020). Satellite Communications in the New Space Era: A survey and future challenges. IEEE Communications Surveys & Tutorials, 23(1): 70–109. https://doi.org/10.1109/comst.2020.3028247.

Kumar, P., Kumar, R., Gupta, G. P., Tripathi, R., and Srivastava, G. (2022). P2TIF: a blockchain and deep learning framework for Privacy-Preserved Threat intelligence in industrial IoT. IEEE Transactions on Industrial Informatics, 18(9): 6358–6367. https://doi.org/10.1109/tii.2022.3142030.

Letaief, K. B., Shi, Y., Lu, J., and Lu, J. (2021). Edge Artificial Intelligence for 6G: vision, enabling technologies, and applications. IEEE Journal on Selected Areas in Communications, 40(1): 5–36. https://doi.org/10.1109/jsac.2021.3126076.

Li, B., Fei, Z., and Zhang, Y. (2018). UAV communications for 5G and beyond: Recent advances and future trends. IEEE Internet of Things Journal, 6(2): 2241–2263. https://doi.org/10.1109/jiot.2018.2887086.

Lu, Y., Huang, X., Dai, Y., Maharjan, S., and Zhang, Y. (2019). Blockchain and federated Learning for Privacy-Preserved Data Sharing in industrial IoT. IEEE Transactions on Industrial Informatics, 16(6): 4177–4186. https://doi.org/10.1109/tii.2019.2942190

Minoli, D., and Occhiogrosso, B. (2018). Blockchain mechanisms for IoT security. Internet of Things, 1–2, 1–13. https://doi.org/10.1016/j.iot.2018.05.002.

Mohanta, B. K., Jena, D., Satapathy, U., and Patnaik, S. (2020). Survey on IoT security: Challenges and solution using machine learning, artificial intelligence and blockchain technology. Internet of Things, 11: 100227. https://doi.org/10.1016/j.iot.2020.100227.

Moosavi, J., Bakhshi, J., and Martek, I. (2021). The application of industry 4.0 technologies in pandemic management: Literature review and case study. Healthcare Analytics, 1: 100008. https://doi.org/10.1016/j.health.2021.100008.

Nguyen, D. C., Pathirana, P. N., Ding, M., and Seneviratne, A. (2019). Blockchain for secure EHRs sharing of mobile cloud based E-Health systems. IEEE Access, 7: 66792–66806. https://doi.org/10.1109/access.2019.2917555.

Ouaddah, A., Elkalam, A. A., and Ouahman, A. A. (2016). FairAccess: a new Blockchain-based access control framework for the Internet of Things. Security and Communication Networks, 9(18): 5943–5964. https://doi.org/10.1002/sec.1748.

Park, S., and Kim, Y. (2022). A metaverse: taxonomy, components, applications, and open challenges. IEEE Access, 10: 4209–4251. https://doi.org/10.1109/access.2021.3140175.

Pham, Q., Nguyen, D. C., Huynh-The, T., Hwang, W., and Pathirana, P. N. (2020). Artificial intelligence (AI) and big data for coronavirus (COVID-19) pandemic: A Survey on the State-of-the-Arts. IEEE Access, 8: 130820–130839. https://doi.org/10.1109/access.2020.3009328.

Rasheed, A., San, O., and Kvamsdal, T. (2020). Digital Twin: values, challenges and enablers from a modeling perspective. IEEE Access, 8: 21980–22012. https://doi.org/10.1109/access.2020.2970143.

Rathee, G., Sharma, A., Kumar, R., and Iqbal, R. (2019). A Secure Communicating Things Network Framework for Industrial IoT using Blockchain Technology. Ad Hoc Networks, 94: 101933. https://doi.org/10.1016/j.adhoc.2019.101933.

Rathore, S., Kwon, B. W., and Park, J. H. (2019). BlockSecIoTNet: Blockchain-based decentralized security architecture for IoT network. Journal of Network and Computer Applications, 143: 167–177. https://doi.org/10.1016/j.jnca.2019.06.019.

Siyal, A. A., Junejo, A. Z., Zawish, M., Ahmed, K., Khalil, A., and Soursou, G. (2019). Applications of blockchain Technology in medicine and Healthcare: Challenges and future Perspectives. Cryptography, 3(1): 3. https://doi.org/10.3390/cryptography3010003.

Vargas, H., Lozano-Garzon, C., Montoya, G. A., and Donoso, Y. (2021). Detection of security attacks in industrial IoT networks: A blockchain and machine learning approach. Electronics, 10(21): 2662. https://doi.org/10.3390/electronics10212662.

Xu, A., Darbandi, M., Javaheri, D., Navimipour, N. J., Yalcin, S., and Salameh, A. A. (2023). The management of IoT-Based organizational and industrial digitalization using machine learning methods. Sustainability, 15(7): 5932. ttps://doi.org/10.3390/su1507593.

CHAPTER 5

Transforming Land Registries with Blockchain Smart Contracts

Saranya P.,[1,*] *Anooja Ali*,[2] *Meesala Shobha Rani*[2] and *Shaheen H.*[3]

5.1 Introduction

Blockchain is an innovative technological invention that has in recent years, revolutionized the way businesses and financial transactions are conducted. This distributed, decentralized digital ledger system has fundamentally changed the landscape of money exchange and record-keeping (Mahmudnia et al. 2022). At its core, blockchain is a transparent system for recording and verifying financial transactions. Unlike traditional centralized databases, the blockchain network is distributed across multiple computers, creating a tamper-resistant and secure record of all transactions. This decentralized approach enhances transparency and trust, as the ledger is validated and maintained by a network of computers worldwide, rather than a single authority.

The foundational concepts of blockchain technology were timestamp-based digital documents with a chain of cryptographic blocks to prevent them from being backdated or forged. The real breakthrough for blockchain came in 2008 when Satoshi Nakamoto published a white paper outlining the design of the electronic cash system, Bitcoin. Later, Blockchain technology matured, and developers began exploring its use cases beyond just digital currencies. The continued innovation and experimentation with different blockchain architectures, consensus mechanisms, and use cases have contributed to the growing popularity and adoption of this transformative technology (Onifade et al. 2024).

[1] School of Computer Science and Engineering, Vellore Institute of Technology, Vellore, India.
[2] School of CSE, REVA University, Bangalore, India.
[3] Department of Computing and Engineering, University of West London, RAK Branch campus, Ras Al Khaimah, UAE.
* Corresponding author: saranya.p@vit.ac.in

DOI: 10.1201/9781003540328-5

5.1.1 Features of Blockchain

While blockchain technology is often associated with cryptocurrencies, the applications go beyond digital currency. The blockchain's ability to securely record and validate transactions has made it a valuable tool in various industries, finance, supply chain management, and voting systems. Figure 5.1 represents the key features of blockchain that make it a unique and transformative technology.

The technology is maintained by a grid of participating computers (nodes) that validate and record transactions (Mahapatro et al. 2023). This decentralized structure enhances security and transparency. The distributed nature ensures that the ledger is continuously validated and maintained by the network, reducing the risk of fraud or unauthorized alterations. The validation process, known as "mining," is carried out by a network of computers that compete to crack composite mathematical statements, certifying the truthfulness of the blockchain.

Blockchain records are not mutable, and each new block remains cryptographically connected to the previous block, creating an unbroken chain (Chen and Lloyd 2024). This makes blockchains tamper-resistant and ensures the integrity of the transaction history. The blockchain ledger is transparent, as all transactions are publicly viewable by network participants. This transparency enhances trust and accountability, as any attempted tampering would be visible to the entire network (Junaid et al. 2023).

Blockchain practice consensus algorithms, and the consensus process guarantees the state of the ledger in the network, without the need for a central authority (Timuçin and Biroğul 2023). Blockchain enables the use of smart contracts, which inevitably apply the conditions of a contract between parties. Smart contracts eliminate the need for intermediaries and increase efficiency and transparency in various applications (Kushwaha et al. 2022).

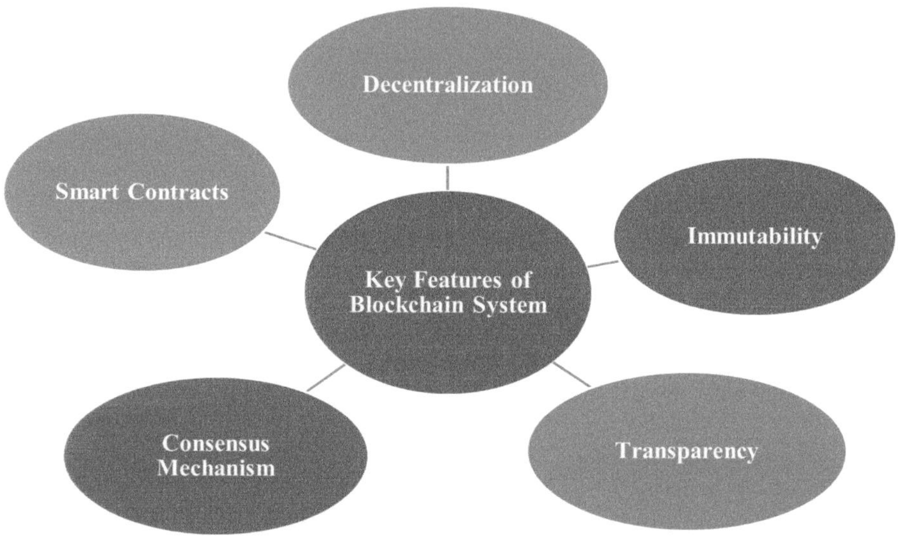

Figure 5.1. The key features of blockchain technology.

5.1.2 The Rise of Cryptocurrencies

While there are hundreds of different cryptocurrencies, such as Litecoin, Dogecoin, and Ethereum, Bitcoin has emerged as the dominant player in the market. Bitcoin's popularity can be attributed to several key factors. Bitcoin holds the lion's share of the crypto market, with accountancy of total market capital (John et al. 2022). This dominance is a result of Bitcoin's early mover advantage and its ability to capture the public's attention as the first and most well-known cryptocurrency (Lavania et al. 2023).

One of the key features that has drawn users to Bitcoin is its ability to maintain user anonymity while providing a transparent transaction history. The decentralized nature of the Bitcoin network and its blockchain technology have enabled this unique combination of privacy and transparency (Sas and Khairuddin 2017). Bitcoin can be easily exchanged for traditional currencies, goods, and services (Metcalfe 2020). Users can also manage their Bitcoin holdings through digital wallets. While Bitcoin was the first and most well-known cryptocurrency, the introduction of Ethereum in 2015 marked a significant development in the cryptocurrency landscape (Dewangan and Chandrakar 2023). Ethereum's blockchain-based platform enabled the creation of smart contracts, which automatically execute predetermined actions between parties. This innovative feature, along with Ethereum's faster and more efficient processing, contributed to its growing popularity and widespread adoption (Zhou et al. 2022).

5.1.3 Comparison between Ethereum and Bitcoin

The limitations of Bitcoin's scripting language led to the development of alternative blockchain platforms, such as Ethereum that were specifically designed to enable more advanced smart contract capabilities (Dika and Nowostawski 2018). Table 5.1 provides the comparative analysis between Ethereum and Bitcoin. Ethereum's Turing-complete programming language allowed for the creation of complex, self-executing digital agreements. The success of Ethereum and its smart contract functionality demonstrated the potential for blockchain technology to go beyond just being a digital currency. This paved the way for the broader adoption of blockchain and the exploration of new use cases, including decentralized finance (DeFi), non-fungible tokens (NFTs), and dApps.

The growing popularity and adoption of smart contracts, driven largely by the success of Ethereum, helped to raise awareness and understanding of the potential of blockchain technology. Figure 5.2 is based on CoinMarketCap analysis. CoinMarketCap is a broadly used market-data platform that offers complete evidence on cryptocurrencies. The platform offers data such as prices, trade volumes, market capitalization, and circulating supply for various cryptocurrencies.

5.1.4 Ethereum and Smart Contracts

Ethereum has a rich ecosystem of developer tools that support smart contract development. There are already hundreds of applications running on Ethereum that

Table 5.1. Comparative analysis between Ethereum and Bitcoin.

Feature	Bitcoin	Ethereum
Primary Purpose	Decentralized digital currency and store of value	Decentralized computing platform for smart contracts and dApps
Scripting Language	Limited, prioritizing security and decentralization	Turing-complete, enabling complex smart contracts
Smart Contract Capabilities	Initially lacked advanced smart contracts, newer solutions like Stacks are bringing smart contract functionality	Built with smart contracts in mind from the start, enabling a wide range of decentralized applications

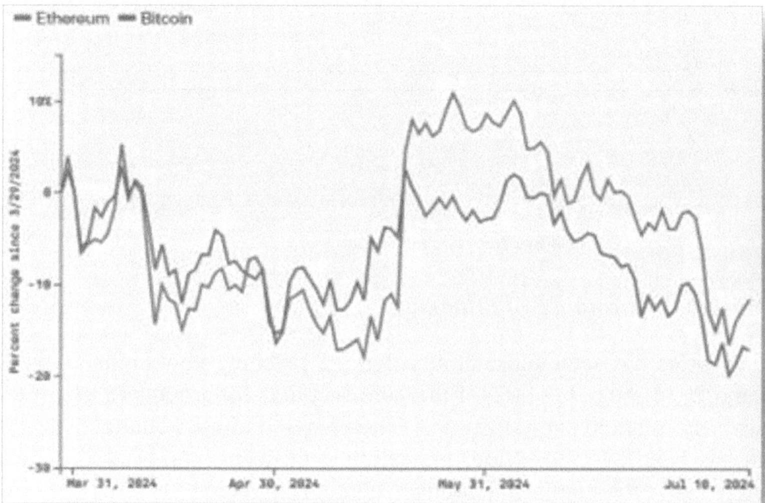

Figure 5.2. Spot price variation between Bitcoin and Ethereum. This figure is adopted from CoinMarketCap based on the analysis in 2024 as on (10th July 2024).

use smart contracts at their core. Popular examples include DeFi apps, MakerDAO and Compound that leverage smart contracts for lending and earning interest. The existence of these real-world applications demonstrates the viability and utility of smart contracts on Ethereum

Ethereum was launched in 2015 with the goal of being a decentralized computing platform for smart contracts and dApps. The EVM implements smart contracts rendering the instructions of developers, making it easy to create and deploy smart contracts on the Ethereum blockchain. Ethereum uses Solidity, and it allows designers to develop their personal contracts. By providing a high-level language similar to JavaScript, Ethereum has lowered the barrier to entry for developers to create smart contracts. Figure 5.3 represents the key features of Ethereum.

Ethereum has a large and active developer community, as well as a growing ecosystem of decentralized applications and services. This ecosystem, along with Ethereum's widespread adoption, makes it an attractive platform for building and deploying smart contracts. The automation in contracts diminishes the necessity for intermediaries and the potential for human error or interference.

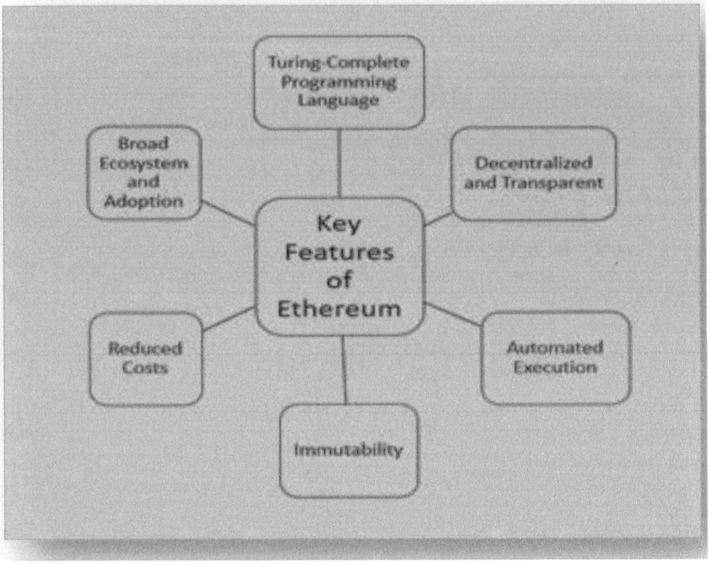

Figure 5.3. The key features of Ethereum.

5.1.5 Market Performance of Ethereum

Ethereum's price has seen substantial volatility, reaching new highs above $4,000 in 2020 and 2021. As of Q2 2024, Ethereum accounts for around 18.2% of the total cryptocurrency market capitalization. Ethereum's trading volume over the past 24 hours has been $14.59 billion, indicating significant market activity. Analysts have noted that Ethereum's upcoming technical upgrades, such as the Shanghai upgrade and the Ethereum 2.0 roadmap, could have a significant impact on the cryptocurrency's long-term performance. These upgrades are aimed at improving the network's scalability, efficiency, and overall functionality (Gao et al. 2020).

Ethereum's market performance has been mixed, with the cryptocurrency experiencing both gains and losses in recent months. The key risks for Ethereum's future growth appear to be the quantum computing threat, market volatility, lack of killer applications, competition from other blockchains, regulatory challenges, and technological limitations. It is critical for Ethereum to preserve itself as a leading cryptocurrency and blockchain platform (Hamdaqa et al. 2022).

5.2 Literature Survey

The self-executing agreement stored on a blockchain repeatedly imposes the terms of an agreement between parties when certain circumstances are available. It is written in code and eliminates the need for intermediaries or manual processing. Smart contracts are not legally binding agreements, they are a powerful tool for automating the execution of digital transactions and agreements.

5.2.1 Components of a Smart Contract

Smart contracts are stored on a blockchain that executes by itself, when prearranged environments are encountered. Smart contract developers must possess a strong understanding of blockchain technology, including decentralization, blockchain with consensus, and cryptography (Mavridou et al. 2019). The core of a smart contract is the code that defines the terms and conditions of the agreement. Figure 5.4 indicates the components of a smart contract. The functions are the operations that the smart contract can perform, such as transferring tokens, updating the contract state, or calling other contracts.

The code specifies the conditions that must be met in order for the smart contract to execute. Smart contract developers must be aware of potential security vulnerabilities and know how to mitigate risks, as smart contracts are immutable once deployed on the blockchain. The state of a smart contract refers to the current values of the variables stored in the contract's code (Chen et al. 2020). The state changes as the contract executes and the conditions are met. The participants are the entities, whether individuals, organizations, or other smart contracts, that interact with the smart contract by triggering its functions and updating its state.

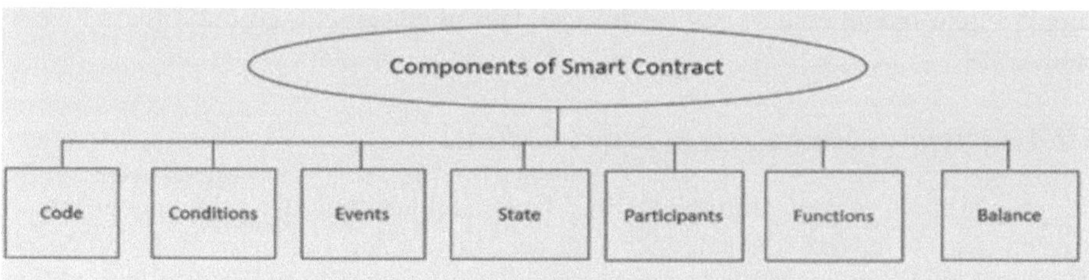

Figure 5.4. The components of a Smart Contract.

5.2.2 Advantages of a Smart Contract

The key benefits of using smart contracts in blockchain include:

Automation: Smart contracts can automatically execute transactions and agreements without the need for intermediaries or manual processing.

Transparency: All transactions are recorded on the distributed blockchain ledger, which is transparent and accessible to all authorized parties.

Security: Blockchain transactions are encrypted and immutable, making smart contracts very difficult to hack or alter (Saranya and Maheswari 2023). Smart contracts can be designed to have their own built-in privacy settings, keeping certain data confidential by default

Efficiency: Smart contracts remove paperwork, time delays, and errors associated with manual contract execution.

Trust: By eliminating the need for intermediaries, smart contracts foster direct, trust less relationships between parties.

5.2.3 Smart Contracts and Privacy Protection

Smart contracts can utilize cryptographic techniques to encrypt data stored on the blockchain. This helps protect unauthorized access and data breakouts. Smart contracts allow for selective disclosure of information (Mukta et al. 2023). Parties involved in a transaction can choose to reveal only the necessary details, while keeping other sensitive information private. This granular control over data sharing enhances privacy.

The decentralized nature of smart contracts, where they are executed on a distributed network rather than a centralized server, reduces the danger of single point control (Badri et al. 2024). This prevents a single entity from accessing or manipulating the private data stored within the smart contract. Smart contracts are transparent and their execution is recorded on the blockchain. This provides an auditable trail of transactions, which can help detect and prevent privacy breaches or unauthorized access to sensitive information (Saranya et al. 2023). Smart contracts can enhance privacy protection in various applications, such as financial transactions, supply chain management, and healthcare data management, among others (Wang et al. 2018).

5.2.4 Consensus Mechanism in Smart Contract

Smart contracts, a key component of blockchain technology, rely on consensus mechanisms to ensure the integrity and security of the transactions recorded on the distributed ledger. These consensus mechanisms play a crucial role in enabling trust less, decentralized agreement among participants in a smart contract network (Pincheira et al. 2022). Here are some consensus mechanisms for smart contract platforms:

- **Proof of Work** - The POW consensus mechanism, used by blockchains like Ethereum, requires nodes (miners) to resolve complex problems to authenticate contracts and add new chunks to chain (Oliva et al. 2020).
- **Proof of Stake** - Staking one's own cryptocurrency as credit allows nodes in POS to add blocks and authenticate transactions. The more bitcoin a validator stakes, the greater the likelihood that they will be chosen to generate the next block.
- **Delegated Proof of Stake** -In DPOS, users elect a set of delegates (block producers) to validate transactions on their behalf. These delegates are responsible for maintaining the network and are rewarded for their participation.
- **Proof of Authority-** A small number of approved nodes, referred to as validators, oversee approving transactions and appending fresh blocks to the network in the POA. These validators are recognized by their real-world identities and are incentivized to maintain the network's integrity.

The choice of consensus mechanism in a smart contract platform depends on factors such as the desired level of decentralization, transaction throughput, energy efficiency, and the trust model of the network (Liu et al. 2021). Developers should opt for the consensus mechanism that best fits with the specific requirements of their smart contract application.

5.2.5 Smart Infrastructure with Smart Contracts and Blockchain

Smart contracts and blockchain technology have emerged as powerful tools for developing smart infrastructure that is more efficient, secure, and transparent. The key reasons why smart contracts and blockchain are crucial for building the infrastructure of the future can be summarized as in Table 5.2.

This ensures integrity and reliability while providing transparency, which enhances monitoring, accountability, and traceability of infrastructure operations, thereby reducing the risk of fraud or mismanagement. Automation leads to faster, more efficient, and cost-effective operations, as well as reduced human error. Automated execution of predefined rules ensures consistent and reliable performance. Smart contracts eliminate the risk of human error or malicious tampering, as their code is immutable and executed exactly as programmed. This enhances the overall security and resilience of critical infrastructure. Data can be stored on the blockchain in a tamper-resistant manner, ensuring its integrity and availability. Smart contracts can also facilitate secure data sharing and access control among various stakeholders. They allow peer transactions, micropayments, and the formation of digital assets tied to infrastructure usage. This can lead to more flexible and innovative approaches to infrastructure financing and service delivery.

Table 5.2. Summary of the advantages in building a smart infrastructure.

Advantage	Reasoning
Decentralization and Immutability	Automatic execution of predefined rules without the risk of tampering or unauthorized changes
Transparency and Auditability	All transactions and interactions are logged on blockchain in a transparent and auditable manner
Automation and Efficiency	Automated processes and eliminating the need for manual intervention in infrastructure management.
Enhanced Security	Cryptographic protocols and distributed nature provide robust security measures for infrastructure systems.
Improved Data Management	Enable secure and efficient data management within infrastructure systems.
Enabling New Business Models	Open up new revenue streams and business models for infrastructure providers.

5.2.6 Cryptographic Algorithms for Developing a Smart Contract

Cryptographic algorithms are crucial for developing protected and reliable smart contracts on blockchain. Smart contracts store and transmit complex data, asset ownership, and individual information. Cryptographic algorithms like AES and elliptic curve cryptography are used to encrypt this data, ensuring its confidentiality and integrity as it is stored on the blockchain and transmitted between parties (Yuan et al. 2018). Cryptographic hash functions, like SHA-256, are used to verify the genuineness and truth of smart contract transactions. This prevents unauthorized modifications and ensures the non-repudiation of transactions recorded on the blockchain. The Cryptographic Kernel (CK) smart contract model allows the cryptographic algorithms used in a blockchain network to be updated dynamically. This enables the system to adapt to emerging security threats and cryptanalysis, ensuring the long-term security of the smart contracts.

5.2.6.1 ECDSA with SHA256

ECDSA offers several key advantages for implementing cryptographic security in blockchain-based smart contracts. ECDSA is a public-key algorithm that provides a high level of security compared to other digital signature schemes like RSA. ECDSA allows for significantly smaller key sizes compared to RSA, to achieve the same level of security. The mathematical operations involved in ECDSA are generally faster than those required for RSA signatures. This makes ECDSA more efficient for applications like blockchain transactions that require frequent signing and verification of digital signatures.

ECDSA has been widely adopted in various security systems, including encrypted messaging apps and the Bitcoin blockchain. This broad acceptance and standardization increase the reliability and interoperability of ECDSA-based cryptographic solutions. ECDSA signatures are relatively small compared to other signature schemes like RSA. This allows more transactions to be included in each block, improving the overall transaction throughput of the blockchain. ECDSA signature verification is computationally efficient, requiring fewer resources compared to other cryptographic algorithms. This allows blockchain nodes to process and validate transactions more quickly, increasing the network's overall scalability.

SHA-256 is a cryptographically secure hash function that is highly resistant to collisions - the likelihood of two different messages hashing to the same value. This property is crucial for the security of digital signatures, as collisions could potentially allow an attacker to forge valid signatures. The use of ECDSA with SHA-256 is widely standardized and the use of SHA-256 as the underlying hash function provides some protection against potential quantum computing attacks.

5.2.7 Property Transfer in India

The incorporation of smart contracts through blockchain is gaining significant attention in India as businesses and government agencies explore the potential of this transformative combination. T As things stand, India has emerged as a prominent hub for blockchain development, with a growing ecosystem of startups, enterprises, and government initiatives exploring various blockchain use cases. Some key developments in the Indian smart contract and blockchain landscape include:

Pilot Projects: Several Indian banks, financial institutions, and government agencies have conducted successful pilot projects leveraging blockchain and smart contracts.

These include use cases in trade finance, supply chain management, land registry, and digital identity.

Regulatory Sandbox: The Reserve Bank of India (RBI) has recognized this to encourage the development and testing of innovative fintech solutions, including those based on blockchain and smart contracts.

National Blockchain Strategy: The Indian government, through NITI Aayog, has released a comprehensive national blockchain strategy to drive the adoption and development of blockchain technology across various sectors.

Talent Pool: India boasts a large pool of skilled blockchain and smart contract developers, with many educational institutions offering specialized courses and training programs in these technologies (Lin et al. 2022).

Automation and Efficiency: Smart contracts enable the automated execution of predefined business logic, streamlining processes and reducing the need for manual intervention. This is beneficial in zones like supply chain, financial dealings, and land accounts.

Transparency and Traceability: Blockchain's decentralized and immutable nature, combined with smart contracts, provides enhanced transparency and traceability of transactions and data. This is valuable for applications like supply chain monitoring, asset ownership, and government procurement (Soner et al. 2021).

Reduced Intermediaries: Smart contracts on a blockchain network can eliminate the need for intermediaries, reducing costs and improving the speed of transactions. This is beneficial for cross-border payments, trade finance, and other financial services.

Improved Trust and Compliance: The self-execution of smart contracts, coupled with the secure blockchain, enhances confidence and ensures compliance with predefined rules and regulations. This is crucial for applications in areas like healthcare, real estate, and government services.

5.2.8 Summary of the Literature Review

The literature review of blockchain-based land registry systems in India highlights promising initiatives aimed at enhancing transparency, security, and efficiency in land administration. Pilot projects in states like Telangana, Andhra Pradesh, and Maharashtra demonstrate blockchain's potential to create decentralized, immutable ledgers for land records, reducing fraud and disputes. The technology's cryptographic security ensures tamper-proof data, while its transparency allows real-time tracking of transactions, improving trust among stakeholders (Galvez et al. 2018). However, challenges such as the need for updated regulatory frameworks, robust technical infrastructure, and public education remain. Despite these hurdles, the positive outcomes of initial projects suggest that with appropriate policies and investments, blockchain could significantly improve India's land registry system by providing a reliable and secure method for recording and transferring property ownership.

5.3 Proposed Method

Implementing smart contracts in the Ethereum Virtual Machine (EVM) typically involves writing the contract code in Solidity, a high-level programming language designed for developing smart contracts on the Ethereum blockchain. This Solidity contract outlines a system for managing property transfers in a way that can be leveraged by Development Authorities (DAs) to manage and transfer properties under their jurisdiction (Yeoh et.al. 2024). The contract includes mechanisms for allotting properties to verified owners and transferring properties between owners. The development environment for this system is given in Table 5.3.

Table 5.3. Development environment of the proposed method.

Development Environment	Ethereum VM
Operating System	Linux in VMWare
Programming Language	Solidity
Network Environment	EthereumJS TestRPC tokens
Front End Interaction	Web3.js API

5.3.1 Ethereum Project Components

The proposed system leverages blockchain technology and smart contracts to modernize property management and transfer processes. It begins with a Development Authority (DA) deploying a smart contract on the Ethereum blockchain, creating a secure and immutable property ledger. The DA assigns properties to verified owners using the allotProperty function, ensuring transparency and accuracy. Ownership verification is automated through the blockchain, where a decision mechanism ensures only verified owners can initiate transactions. Property transfers are executed via the transferProperty function, updating the blockchain ledger and emitting events like PropertyAlloted and PropertyTransferred for transparency and traceability. The system eliminates intermediaries, reduces fraud, and fosters trust through decentralized and tamper-proof records. It also provides scalability and efficiency by enabling real-time access to unified land records for all stakeholders, ensuring a cost-effective and streamlined property transaction process shown in the Figure 5.5.

Each component has been explained briefly in the following section to help readers better understand the process of land transfer management. This section also includes the participating entities of land transfer system and their key interactions between them is explained below.

(A) Smart Contracts

Smart contracts are programs stored on the Ethereum blockchain that automatically execute when predetermined conditions are met. Written in languages like Solidity, they facilitate, verify, or enforce the negotiation and performance of a contract. For example, the Property Transfer smart contract includes functions for assigning and transferring property, ensuring that property transactions occur as programmed without the need for intermediaries.

Figure 5.5. The architecture diagram of the smart contract based land transfer management.

(B) Ethereum Virtual Machine (EVM)

The Ethereum Virtual Machine (EVM) is the runtime environment for executing smart contracts on the Ethereum blockchain. It ensures that code execution results are consistent across all nodes, making the EVM a decentralized and secure platform for running smart contracts. The PropertyTransfer contract runs on the EVM, leveraging its computational capabilities to perform tasks like property allocation and transfer.

(C) Decentralized Applications (DApps)

Decentralized Applications (DApps) are applications that run on a decentralized network rather than a centralized server. They consist of smart contracts on the Ethereum blockchain and a front-end user interface. For instance, a DApp for the PropertyTransfer project would allow users to interact with the smart contract through a web or mobile interface, enabling property transactions on the blockchain (Jain et al. 2022).

(D) Ethereum Nodes and Network

Ethereum nodes are computers that participate in the Ethereum network, storing the blockchain and validating transactions. There are full nodes, which keep a complete record of the blockchain, and light nodes, which store only essential data. The decentralized network of nodes ensures security and consensus. In the PropertyTransfer project, nodes validate and record property transactions, maintaining the integrity of the blockchain.

(E) Wallets and Accounts

Ethereum wallets and accounts are essential for interacting with the blockchain. An Ethereum account has an address and can hold ETH (ether) and interact with smart contracts. Wallets manage accounts and private keys, allowing users to sign transactions and access their funds. In the PropertyTransfer project, users will need wallets to manage their property transactions, whether they are allocating property as a DA or transferring property as an owner.

(F) Ether (ETH) and Gas

Ether (ETH) is the cryptocurrency used on the Ethereum network, primarily for paying transaction fees and computational services. Gas is a unit that measures the amount of computational effort required to execute operations on the Ethereum network. Users pay gas fees in ETH to compensate miners for processing their transactions. For the PropertyTransfer project, executing functions like property allotment and transfer requires gas fees, ensuring the operations are processed and recorded on the blockchain.

(G) Development Tools and Frameworks

Ethereum development tools and frameworks simplify the process of writing, testing, and deploying smart contracts and DApps. Tools like Remix, Truffle, and Hardhat offer features such as contract compilation, network management, and automated testing. These tools help developers create and manage Ethereum-based projects. For the PropertyTransfer project, developers will use these tools to write and test the Solidity code and deploy the smart contract to the Ethereum network.

(H) Oracles and External Data

Oracles are services that provide smart contracts with external data, allowing them to interact with the real world. Since smart contracts cannot access data outside the blockchain, oracles bring in information such as financial data or IoT sensor readings. In a more advanced version of the PropertyTransfer project, oracles could be used to verify property information or ownership details from external sources, enhancing the reliability of property transactions.

5.3.2 Participating Entities

A. Development Authority (DA): The DA is the entity that deploys the smart contract and acts as the owner of the contract. It is responsible for allotting properties to verified owners after thorough verification. When it comes to permissions, only the DA can call certain functions in the contract, such as allotting properties (Banaeian Far et al. 2022).

B. Verified Property Owner: The role of individuals or entities who are allotted properties by the DA are known as verified property owners. They can hold, transfer, and manage their properties as per the contract's rules. They can receive properties allotted by the DA and transfer properties they own to other verified owners.

C. Property Buyers/Receivers: The property buyers/receivers are individuals or entities who can receive properties from current property owners through the transfer process. They can receive properties through the transfer process initiated by current property owners.

D. Government (Implicit Participant): Although the government is not directly coded/added in this smart contract system, the government is assumed to have overarching control and can designate different DAs for different constituencies. It ensures that the land records are placed on the public blockchain and that a digital identity system is in place. The government can decide which DA is responsible for which constituency, adding a layer of governance and regulation.

5.3.3 Key Interactions

1. **DA (Development Authority)**:

   Step 1: Deploys the contract and becomes the owner.

   Step 2: Allots properties to verified owners after verification.

   Step 3: Calls the allotProperty function to assign properties.

2. **Verified Property Owner**:

   Step 1: Receives property allotments from the DA.

   Step 2: Can check their property count using the getPropertyCountOfAnyAddress function.

   Step 3: Can transfer properties they own to other addresses using the transferProperty function.

3. **Property Buyers/Receivers**:

   Step 1: Receives property from current property owners through the transfer process.

   Step 2: Properties transferred to them are recorded in the contract.

5.3.4 Algorithms for Implementing Land Property Transfer

5.3.4.1 Pseudocode for getting the property count of any smart contract address/any property owner

The process of choosing the smart contract VM address and the seller's address is depicted in Figure 5.6.

Pseudocode for getPropertyCountOfAnyAddress
Step 1: Initialize count to 0 Step 2: Retrieve the total number of properties owned by _ownerAddress Step 3: Loop through all properties Step 3.1: Check if the property is not sold Step 3.2: Increment the count by count = count + 1 Step 4: Return the count of unsold properties

```
function getPropertyCountOfAnyAddress(address _ownerAddress) public view returns (uint256)
    uint256 count = 0;
    for (uint256 i = 0; i < individualCountOfPropertyPerOwner[_ownerAddress]; i++) {
        if (propertiesOwner[_ownerAddress][i].isSold != true) {
            count++;
        }
    }
    return count;
}
```

Figure 5.6. Deployment of getproperty contract.

5.3.4.2 Pseudocode for allotting the property

Figure 5.7 represents the Deployment of getproperty contract and Figure 5.8 is the selection of owner address.

Pseudocode for allotting the property to the desired new owner
Step 1: Check if the caller is the DA (onlyOwner modifier handles this) Step 2: Allot property to the verified owner 2.1: Assign the property name to the new property Property newProperty newProperty.name = _propertyName newProperty.isSold = false 2.2: Map the new property to the _verifiedOwner 2.3: Increment the count of properties for the _verifiedOwner individualCountOfPropertyPerOwner[_verifiedOwner] += 1 2.4: Increment the total number of properties Step 3: Emit the PropertyAlloted event

```
function allotProperty(address _verifiedOwner, string _propertyName) onlyOwner {
    propertiesOwner[_verifiedOwner][individualCountOfPropertyPerOwner[_verifiedOwner]+
    totalNoOfProperty++;
    PropertyAlloted(_verifiedOwner, individualCountOfPropertyPerOwner[_verifiedOwner],
}
```

Figure 5.7. Deployment of getproperty contract.

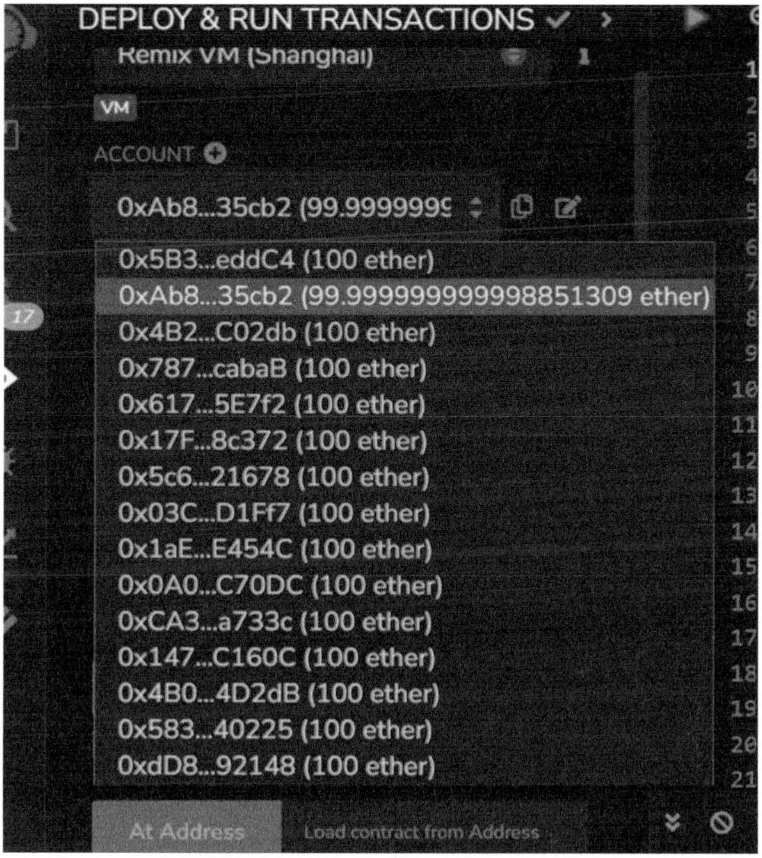

Figure 5.8. Choosing the owner address.

5.3.4.3 Pseudocode for checking the real owner of the property:

The below pseudocode checks the owner and Figure 5.9 is the deployment of isowner contract.

Pseudocode for checking isOwner

Step 1: Initialize flag to false
Step 2: Loop through properties of _checkOwnerAddress
  Step 2.1: Check if property is not sold
  Step 2.2: Compare property name using stringsEqual function
  Step 2.3: If property is found, break out of loop
Step 3: Return index of property if found, otherwise a large number
And Indicate property not found

```
function isOwner(address _checkOwnerAddress, string _propertyName) constant returns (u
    uint i;
    bool flag;
    for (i = 0; i < individualCountOfPropertyPerOwner[_checkOwnerAddress]; i++) {
        if (propertiesOwner[_checkOwnerAddress][i].isSold == true) {
            break;
        }
        flag = stringsEqual(propertiesOwner[_checkOwnerAddress][i].name, _propertyName
        if (flag == true) {
            break;
        }
    }
    if (flag == true) {
        return i;
    } else {
        return 999999999;
    }
}
```

Figure 5.9. Deployment of is Owner contract.

5.3.4.4 Pseudocode for transferring property

The below pseudocode is for property transfer and Figure 5.10 executes transfer Property contract

Pseudocode for transferring property
Step 1: Check if the caller owns the property Step 2: If the caller owns the property, proceed with transfer Step 2.1: Mark property as sold for current owner Step 2.2: Assign property to _to address Step 2.3: Emit event for property transfer Step 2.4: Return success and index of property in owner's list Step 3: If caller does not own the property, return failure Step 3.1: Emit event for unsuccessful transfer Step 3.2: Return failure and a large number to indicate no ownership

```
function transferProperty(address _to, string _propertyName) returns (bool, uint) {
    uint256 checkOwner = isOwner(msg.sender, _propertyName);
    bool flag;

    if (checkOwner != 999999999 && propertiesOwner[msg.sender][checkOwner].isSold == f
        propertiesOwner[msg.sender][checkOwner].isSold = true;
        propertiesOwner[msg.sender][checkOwner].name = "Sold";
        propertiesOwner[_to][individualCountOfPropertyPerOwner[_to]++].name = _propert
        flag = true;
        PropertyTransferred(msg.sender, _to, _propertyName, "Owner has been changed.")
    } else {
        flag = false;
        PropertyTransferred(msg.sender, _to, _propertyName, "Owner doesn't own the pro
    }
    return (flag, checkOwner);
}
```

Figure 5.10. Execution of transfer Property contract.

5.3.4 Events

(A) Property Allotted Event:

This event is emitted when a property is successfully allotted to an owner by the Development Authority (DA). The deployment of allot property smart contract is depicted in Figure 5.11. The from and to addresses are denoted in hash format which utilised SHA256 algorithm.

```
[vm] from: 0xAb8...35cb2 to: PropertyTransfer.(constructor) value: 0 wei data: 0x608...b0029 logs: 0
hash: 0x9d4...54527
status              true Transaction mined and execution succeed
transaction hash    0x9d4aba52e264d1d061c5ff13c7aa6363be3c6f5e74e668219e1fc5e6c6d54527
block hash          0x6a5a7296ec443798e5a02bd62f288f130a3d9dcea0898d88de9f9fe59f92a095
block number        1
contract address    0xa131AD247055F02e2aA8b156A11bdEc81b9eAD95
from                0xAb8483F64d9C6d1EcF9b849Ae677dD3315835cb2
to                  PropertyTransfer.(constructor)
gas                 1178468 gas
transaction cost    1025036 gas
execution cost      902282 gas
input               0x608...b0029
```

Figure 5.11. Mining the first block for property transfer contract.

Parameters:

- address indexed _verifiedOwner: The Ethereum address of the verified property owner.
- uint256 indexed _totalNoOfPropertyCurrently: The total number of properties currently allotted to _verifiedOwner.
- string _nameOfProperty: The name of the property allotted.
- string _msg: A message indicating the success of the property allotment.

It provides a transparent record of property allotment transactions, allowing DApps or external systems to monitor and verify property ownership changes on the blockchain.

(B) Property Transferred Event:

This event signals the transfer of property ownership from one owner to another.

Parameters:

- address indexed _from: The Ethereum address of the previous owner who transferred the property.
- address indexed _to: The Ethereum address of the new owner who received the property.
- string _propertyName: The name of the property transferred.
- string _msg: A message indicating the status or reason for the property transfer.

It allows decentralized applications and external systems to track changes in property ownership, facilitating transparency and accountability in property transactions on the Ethereum blockchain.

Event Definition: Events (PropertyAlloted and PropertyTransferred) are defined at the contract level using the event keyword. They specify the event's parameters, which are logged when the event is emitted.

Event Emission: Inside the respective functions (allotProperty and transferProperty), events are emitted using the emit keyword followed by the event name and parameters. This logs the event data on the blockchain whenever the function is called and executed.

Event Parameters: Events capture important details such as addresses (_verifiedOwner, _from, _to), property names (_nameOfProperty, _propertyName), counts (_totalNoOfPropertyCurrently), and status messages (_msg). These parameters provide context and transparency about the contract's state changes.

Event Usage: External applications, user interfaces, or other smart contracts can listen to these events using Ethereum's event subscription mechanisms. They can react to these events in real-time to update user interfaces, trigger notifications, or perform further actions based on the blockchain's state changes.

5.3.5 Implementation of Land Transfer Management System

The PropertyTransfer smart contract is designed to facilitate the transparent and secure transfer of property ownership using the Ethereum blockchain. This contract mimics real-world property transfer processes under the assumption that digital identities and government land records are managed on a public blockchain, with Development Authorities (DA) acting as the primary property managers within their jurisdictions (Junaid et.al. 2024).

Initialization and Setup

Upon deployment of the PropertyTransfer contract, the deploying address (assumed to be the Development Authority, or DA) is assigned as the contract owner. This is crucial because only the DA can perform certain actions, such as allotting properties to verified owners. The contract also initializes a variable to keep track of the total number of properties managed under its jurisdiction.

To manage properties, the contract defines a property structure that holds information about each property, including its name and ownership status (isSold). The properties owned by each address are stored in a nested mapping (propertiesOwner), and another mapping (individualCountOfPropertyPerOwner) keeps track of the number of properties each owner possesses. This ensures efficient management and retrieval of property information.

Events

Two key events, PropertyAlloted and PropertyTransferred, are defined to log significant actions within the contract. These events are essential for providing a transparent and auditable history of property transactions. PropertyAlloted is triggered whenever the DA allots a property to a verified owner, and PropertyTransferred is emitted when a property is successfully transferred from one owner to another (Vayadande et al. 2022).

Functions

(A) getPropertyCountOfAnyAddress:

This function allows anyone to query the number of properties owned by a specific address. It iterates through the properties and counts those that are not marked as sold.

(B) allotProperty:

The DA uses this function to allot a property to a verified owner after thorough verification. This function updates the mappings to reflect the new ownership and increases the total property count. It also emits a PropertyAlloted event to log the transaction.

(C) isOwner:

This helper function checks whether a given address owns a specified property by iterating through the properties owned by the address and comparing property names. It returns the index of the property if found, or a sentinel value if not.

(D) TransferProperty:

This function allows the current owner of a property to transfer it to another address. It first verifies ownership using the isOwner function. If the caller owns the property, it marks the property as sold, assigns it to the new owner, and updates the relevant mappings. A PropertyTransferred event is emitted to log the successful transfer. Once the compilation is successful, the contracts will be initiated with the initial gas limit of 3million shown in Figure 5.12.

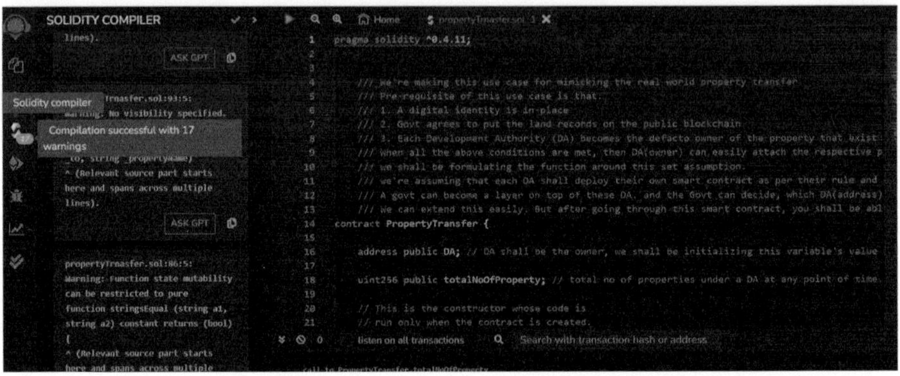

Figure 5.12. Successful compilation of the contracts.

(E) Modifiers

The onlyOwner modifier restricts access to certain functions, ensuring that only the DA can perform critical operations like property allotment (Ullah and Al-Turjman 2023). This enforces the security and integrity of the property management process by preventing unauthorized actions. The transfer property will be compiled when the condition isOwner mets shown in Figure 5.13.

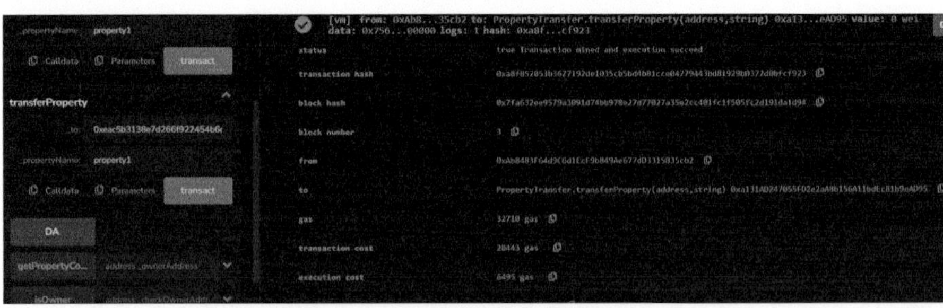

Figure 5.13. The modifiers of the transfer property contract.

(F) Usage and Interaction

External applications and users can interact with the PropertyTransfer contract by calling its functions. For example, the DA can allot properties to verified owners using the allotProperty function shown in Figure 5.14, and property owners can transfer their properties to others using the transferProperty function. Events emitted by these

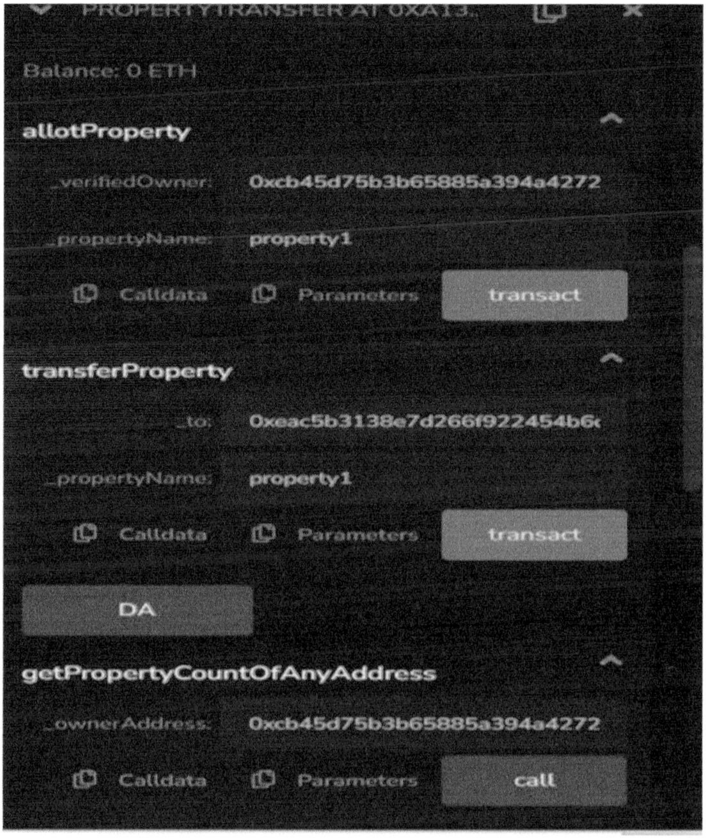

Figure 5.14. The functions defined in this system.

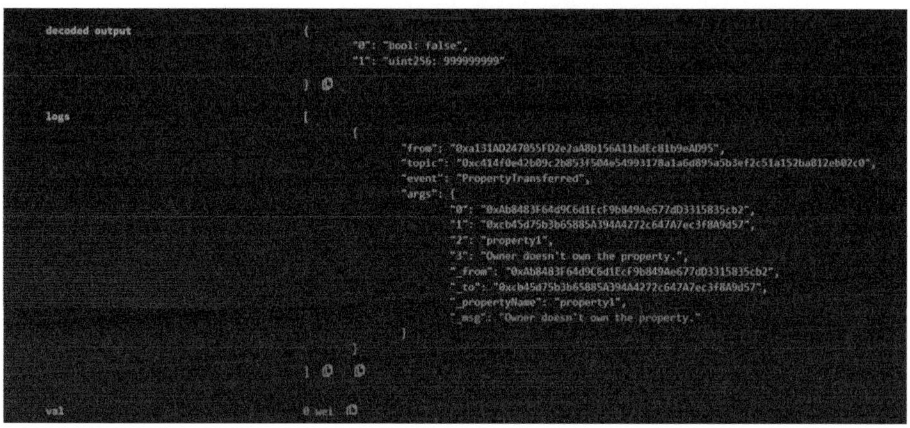

Figure 5.15. The transaction of a property fails if its already sold.

functions provide a transparent and immutable record of all property transactions on the blockchain, which can be used for auditing and verification purposes in Figure 5.15. Table 5.4 corresponds to the gas consumption of each contract.

Table 5.4. The gas consumption of each contract.

Smart Contract	Gas consumed for Deployment	Cost in Ether
getPropertyCountOfAnyAddress	546874	0.0017469
AllotProperty	606892	0.000747
IsOwner	600987	0.000701
PropertyTransfer	664998	0.0007650

Table 5.5. The feature comparison of blockchain based land / property transfer systems.

Feature/Article	Blockchain-Based Land Registry	Smart Contracts in Real Estate	Smart Contract System for Property Rental
Objective	Decentralized land registry	Streamline real estate transactions	Manage property rentals
Methodology	Case study with prototype implementation	Qualitative and quantitative analysis	Design and implementation on Ethereum
Key Components	Verification and transfer of ownership	Automation of escrow and payment processes	Lease agreements, rental payments, dispute resolution
Security/ Efficiency	Enhanced security and transparency	Cost reduction and increased transaction speed	Improved user experience and efficiency
Results	Reduced fraud and transaction errors	Improved transparency, reduced need for intermediaries	Timely rent payments, reduced disputes

The comparison of state-of-the-art smart contract land transfer / property management system are compared in the Table 5.5.

5.6 Conclusion

The current land transfer system in India is characterized by manual processes, significant paperwork, and the involvement of multiple intermediaries such as real estate agents and government officials. These factors contribute to inefficiencies, delays, and increased costs. Land records are often maintained in physical ledgers or decentralized digital formats across various government departments, leading to discrepancies and difficulties in verification. The lack of a unified and tamper-proof system results in fraudulent transactions, disputed ownership claims, and unauthorized land sales. Additionally, limited transparency and access to land records can foster corruption and erode trust in the system.

Implementing blockchain technology and smart contracts can significantly enhance the land transfer system by addressing these challenges. Blockchain provides a decentralized and immutable ledger for maintaining land records, ensuring the authenticity and security of ownership data. Smart contracts can automate the entire land transfer process, reducing the need for intermediaries, speeding up transactions, and minimizing human error. This system fosters transparency, as all stakeholders have real-time access to the same version of land records, and significantly reduces fraud by making it difficult to forge documents or conduct unauthorized transactions. Moreover, the cost and time associated with land transactions can be greatly reduced, and the immutable nature of blockchain records provides a clear chain of ownership, aiding in dispute resolution.

The PropertyTransfer smart contract leverages the capabilities of the Ethereum blockchain to create a secure, transparent, and efficient system for managing and transferring property ownership. By implementing key functions and events, the contract ensures that all property transactions are recorded and verifiable, fostering trust and accountability in the process of land and property management.

References

Badri, N., Nasraoui, L., and Azouz Saïdane, L. (2024). A comprehensive review of blockchain integration in remote patient monitoring for E-health. International Journal of Network Management, 34(2), e2254. https://doi.org/10.1002/nem.2254.

Banaeian Far, S., Imani Rad, A., and Rajabzade Asaar, M. (2022). BB-CSP: an efficient blockchain-based collective salary payment framework using weighted functional encryption. SN Computer Science, 3(5): 408.https://doi.org/10.1007/s42979-022-01330-7.

Chen, J., Xia, X., Lo, D., Grundy, J., Luo, X., and Chen, T. (2020). Defining smart contract defects on ethereum. IEEE Transactions on Software Engineering, 48(1): 327–345. https://doi.org/10.1109/TSE.2020.2989002.

Chen, X., and Lloyd, A. D. (2024). Understanding the challenges of blockchain technology adoption: evidence from China's developing carbon markets. Information Technology & People. https://doi.org/10.1108/ITP-05-2021-0379.

Dewangan, N. K., and Chandrakar, P. (2023). TempChain: a blockchain scheme for telehealth data sharing between two blockchains using property mapping function. The Journal of Supercomputing, 79(13): 14808–14826. https://doi.org/10.1007/s11227-023-05259-3.

Dika, A., and Nowostawski, M. (2018, July). Security vulnerabilities in ethereum smart contracts. In 2018 IEEE international conference on Internet of Things (iThings) and IEEE green computing and communications (GreenCom) and IEEE cyber, physical and social computing (CPSCom) and IEEE Smart Data (SmartData) (pp. 955–962). IEEE. https://doi.org/10.1109/Cybermatics_2018.2018.00182.

Galvez, J. F., Mejuto, J. C., and Simal-Gandara, J. (2018). Future challenges on the use of blockchain for food traceability analysis. TrAC Trends in Analytical Chemistry, 107: 222–232.

Gao, Z., Jiang, L., Xia, X., Lo, D., and Grundy, J. (2020). Checking smart contracts with structural code embedding. IEEE Transactions on Software Engineering, 47(12): 2874–2891. https://doi.org/10.1109/TSE.2020.2971482.

Hamdaqa, M., Met, L. A. P., and Qasse, I. (2022). iContractML 2.0: A domain-specific language for modeling and deploying smart contracts onto multiple blockchain platforms. Information and Software Technology, 144: 106762. https://doi.org/10.1016/j.infsof.2021.106762.

Jain, G., Shrivastava, A., Paul, J., and Batra, R. (2022). Blockchain for SME Clusters: An ideation using the framework of Ostrom Commons Governance. Information Systems Frontiers, 24(4): 1125–1143. https://doi.org/10.1007/s10796-022-10288-z.

John, K., O'Hara, M., and Saleh, F. (2022). Bitcoin and beyond. Annual Review of Financial Economics, 14(1): 95–115. https://doi.org/10.1146/annurev-financial-111620-011240.

Junaid, L., Bilal, K., Khalid, O., and Erbad, A. (2023). Blockchain-enabled land management systems. Telecommunication Systems, 84(3): 421–442.https://doi.org/10.1007/s11235-023-01032-2.

Junaid, L., Bilal, K., Shuja, J., Balogun, A. O., and Rodrigues, J. J. (2024). Blockchain-Enabled Framework for Transparent Land Lease and Mortgage Management. IEEE Access. https://doi.org/10.1109/ACCESS.2024.3388248.

Kushwaha, S. S., Joshi, S., Singh, D., Kaur, M., and Lee, H. N. (2022). Ethereum smart contract analysis tools: A systematic review. Ieee Access, 10: 57037–57062. https://doi.org/10.1109/ACCESS.2022.3169902.

Lavania, S., Mishra, A., Sharma, A., and Jain, P. (2023). Decentralizing Commercial Property Registration and Bidding Process with Smart Contracts. SN Computer Science, 4(5): 623.https://doi.org/10.1007/s42979-023-02087-3.

Lin, S. Y., Zhang, L., Li, J., Ji, L. L., and Sun, Y. (2022). A survey of application research based on blockchain smart contract. Wireless Networks, 28(2): 635–690. https://doi.org/10.1007/s11276-021-02874-x.

Liu, C., Chai, K. K., Zhang, X., and Chen, Y. (2021). Peer-to-peer electricity trading system: smart contracts based proof-of-benefit consensus protocol. Wireless Networks, 27: 4217–4228. https://doi.org/10.1007/s11276-019-01949-0.

Mahapatro, R. K., Ali, A., and Ramakrishnan, N. (2023, June). Blockchain segmentation: a storage optimization technique for large data. In 2023 8th International Conference on Communication and Electronics Systems (ICCES) (pp. 499–504). IEEE. https://doi.org/ 10.1109/ICCES57224.2023.10192631.

Mahmudnia, D., Arashpour, M., and Yang, R. (2022). Blockchain in construction management: Applications, advantages and limitations. Automation in construction, 140: 104379. https://doi.org/10.1016/j.autcon.2022.104379.

Mavridou, A., Laszka, A., Stachtiari, E., and Dubey, A. (2019). VeriSolid: Correct-by-design smart contracts for Ethereum. In Financial Cryptography and Data Security: 23rd International Conference, FC 2019, Frigate Bay, St. Kitts and Nevis, February 18–22, 2019, Revised Selected Papers 23 (pp. 446–465). Springer International Publishing. https://doi.org/10.1007/978-3-030-32101-7_27.

Metcalfe, W. (2020). Ethereum, smart contracts, DApps. Blockchain and Crypt Currency, 77: 77–93. https://doi.org/10.1007/978-981-15-3376-1_5.

Mukta, R., Pal, S., Mishra, S., Paik, H. Y., Kanhere, S. S., and Hitchens, M. (2023, October). A blockchain-based interoperable architecture for IoT with selective disclosure of information. In 2023 IEEE 28th Pacific Rim International Symposium on Dependable Computing (PRDC) (pp. 53–63). IEEE. https://doi.org/10.1109/PRDC59308.2023.00016.

Oliva, G. A., Hassan, A. E., and Jiang, Z. M. (2020). An exploratory study of smart contracts in the Ethereum blockchain platform. Empirical Software Engineering, 25: 1864-1904. https://doi.org/10.1007/s10664-019-09796-5.

Onifade, M., Adebisi, J. A., and Zvarivadza, T. (2024). Recent advances in blockchain technology: Prospects, applications and constraints in the minerals industry. International Journal of Mining, Reclamation and Environment, 1–37. https://doi.org/10.1080/17480930.2024.2319453.

Pincheira, M., Donini, E., Vecchio, M., and Kanhere, S. (2022). A decentralized architecture for trusted dataset sharing using smart contracts and distributed storage. Sensors, 22(23): 9118. https://doi.org/10.3390/s22239118.

Saranya, P., and Maheswari, R. (2023). Proof of transaction (PoTx) based traceability system for an agriculture supply chain. IEEE Access, 11: 10623–10638, https://doi.org/10.1109/ACCESS.2023.3240772.

Saranya, P., Maheswari, R., and Ragala, R. (2023). Blockchain for Agri-Business: A Simulation for Assuring Product Ownership Using Hyperledger Composer. In Cyber-Physical System Solutions for Smart Cities (pp. 52–68). IGI Global. https://doi.org/10.4018/978-1-6684-7756-4.ch004.

Sas, C., and Khairuddin, I. E. (2017, May). Design for trust: An exploration of the challenges and opportunities of bitcoin users. In Proceedings of the 2017 CHI Conference on Human Factors in Computing Systems (pp. 6499–6510). https://doi.org/10.1145/3025453.30258.

Soner, S., Litoriya, R., and Pandey, P. (2021). Exploring blockchain and smart contract technology for reliable and secure land registration and record management. Wireless Personal Communications, 121(4): 2495–2509. https://doi.org/10.1007/s11277-021-08833-1.

Timuçin, T., and Biroğul, S. (2023). Collaborative Smart Contracts (CoSC): example of real estate purchase and sale (s). The Journal of Supercomputing, 79(12): 13442–13461. https://doi.org/10.1007/s11227-023-05196-1.

Ullah, F., and Al-Turjman, F. (2023). A conceptual framework for blockchain smart contract adoption to manage real estate deals in smart cities. Neural Computing and Applications, 35(7): 5033–5054. https://doi.org/10.1007/s00521-021-05800-6.

Vayadande, K., Shaikh, R., Rothe, S., Patil, S., Baware, T., and Naik, S. (2022). Blockchain-based land record system. In ITM Web of Conferences (Vol. 50, p. 01006). EDP Sciences. https://doi.org/10.1051/itmconf/20225001006.

Wang, S., Yuan, Y., Wang, X., Li, J., Qin, R., and Wang, F. Y. (2018, June). An overview of smart contract: architecture, applications, and future trends. In 2018 IEEE Intelligent Vehicles Symposium (IV) (pp. 108–113). IEEE. https://doi.org/10.1109/IVS.2018.8500488.

Yeoh, W., Lee, A. S. H., Ng, C., Popovic, A., and Han, Y. (2024). Examining the acceptance of blockchain by real estate buyers and sellers. Information Systems Frontiers, 26(3): 1121–1137. https://doi.org/10.1007/s11042-023-14624-6.

Yuan, R., Xia, Y. B., Chen, H. B., Zang, B. Y., and Xie, J. (2018). Shadoweth: Private smart contract on public blockchain. Journal of Computer Science and Technology, 33: 542–556. https://doi.org/10.1007/s11390-018-1839-y.

Zhou, H., Milani Fard, A., and Makanju, A. (2022). The state of ethereum smart contracts security: Vulnerabilities, countermeasures, and tool support. Journal of Cybersecurity and Privacy, 2(2): 358–378. https://doi.org/10.3390/jcp2020019.

CHAPTER 6

Confidential E-Degree Vault Using Block Chain Technology

Arjun Singh,[1,*] *Rajani Singh,*[2] *Bala Shiwangi,*[3] *Arun Kumar Singh*[1] and *Payal Chhabra*[4]

6.1 Introduction

A ground-breaking development in the administration and validation of academic qualifications is the E-degree Confidential Vault. To guarantee the integrity and authenticity of credentials stored, it makes use of cutting-edge encryption algorithms and strong authentication systems. A central repository can be used by people to safely preserve their electronic degrees, removing the possibility of physical document loss or destruction. People can securely share their credentials while protecting their privacy by managing access. The features of the vault are advantageous to educational institutions because they offer a safe setting for managing and awarding electronic degrees. Institutions can maintain accurate records and monitor the legitimacy of credentials thanks to administrative controls and tracking options. As a result, typical paper-based processes' administrative expenses and difficulties are reduced. Verifying candidates' academic credentials is a challenge for employers, but the E-degree Confidential Vault provides an efficient answer. Employers may effectively check the legitimacy of degrees obtained online, reducing the danger of credential fraud and ensuring reliable employment decisions. In conclusion, the E-degree Confidential Vault transforms the administration and validation of digital

[1] Department of CSE, Greater Noida Institute of Technology Greater Noida, India.
Email: innovativearjunsingh@gmail.com
[2] Department of IT, G.L. Bajaj Institute of Technology & Management Greater Noida, India.
Email: er.rajnisingh25@gmail.com
[3] Department of IT, IGDTUW, Delhi, India.
Email: bala002phd@igdtuw.ac.in
[4] Department of AI & ML, KIET Group of Institutions Ghaziabad, India.
Email: payal49691@gmail.com
* Corresponding author: arun.singh.iiit@gmail.com

DOI: 10.1201/9781003540328-6

credentials. By giving people, educational institutions, and companies a secure platform for storing, maintaining, and verifying digital credentials, it allays security and privacy concerns. The vault has a positive effect on the increasingly digital world of education and work by improving confidence and integrity in the digital credential ecosystem.

6.2 Motivation

The popularity of electronic degrees and academic credentials has increased as a result of how the digital revolution has changed the landscape of employment and education. Although these digital identities have many benefits, such as accessibility and quick verification, worries about security and privacy have surfaced. The E-degree Confidential Vault, which offers a secure and dependable platform for storing, managing, and certifying electronic degrees, emerges as a creative solution to these problems (Nakamoto 2019).

6.2.1 Objective

Decentralization, a distributed ledger, security, immutability, transparency, smart contracts, consensus methods and tokenization are just a few of the features that make up the blockchain functionality. It offers a decentralized network where transactions are accurately and completely recorded. Smart contracts automate negotiations while cryptographic algorithms guarantee security. Participants can agree through consensus processes, and tokenization enables the production and transfer of digital assets. These characteristics make blockchain a potent technology for a variety of applications.

6.2.2 Blockchain Functionality

The precise features and abilities built into blockchain technology are referred to as blockchain functionality. Blockchain is a distributed ledger system that allows for safe and open data storage and transactions. The following are some of the main blockchain features:

i. Decentralization: - Blockchain doesn't require a central authority or middleman because it runs on a decentralized network of computers known as nodes. By preventing a single body from controlling the entire system, decentralization fosters transparency and promotes trust.

ii. Immutable and Tamper-Proof Records: - Data that has been stored on a blockchain is almost impossible to change or manipulate. The data is kept in a chain of interlinked blocks, each of which is linked to the one before it by a special cryptographic hash, establishing an uninterrupted chain of records (Zheng et al. 2017).

iii. Transparency: - By enabling universal access to the same data across the network, blockchain promotes transparency. All authorized parties may see the transactions and data kept on the blockchain, which encourages accountability and lowers the chance of fraud or corruption.

iv. Smart Contracts: - Smart contracts, which are self-executing agreements with predefined rules and circumstances, are frequently supported by blockchain systems. Smart contracts eliminate the need for middlemen and save money by enabling automatic, transparent interactions between parties.

v. Security and Encryption: - Blockchain uses cutting-edge cryptography methods to protect data and guarantee the accuracy of transactions. Because every transaction is digitally signed and validated by network users, it is extremely secure and impervious to hacking or unauthorized access.

6.3 Literature Survey

The advent of electronic degrees has revolutionized the way academic credentials are handled, providing advantages like efficiency and simplicity. But it has also led to difficulties with standardization, security, and privacy. This review of the literature intends to investigate recent studies on the safe administration of electronic degrees. The study will look at studies that discuss the flaws and dangers of electronic degrees, such as the possibility of fraud and unauthorized access. Additionally, it will highlight the importance of strong data protection methods while focusing on the privacy concerns of storing private information within digital credentials (Baldini et al. 2019). The absence of standardization in electronic degree management is a crucial issue that has to be examined. Inefficiencies in the verification process might be caused by the lack of standardized procedures and formats, which will be discussed in the review. This review will find gaps, trends, and industry best practices by combining the current literature. It seeks to advance our knowledge of the existing situation and offer suggestions for further study and the creation of all-encompassing remedies. The foundation for evaluating the critical challenges concerning the secure management of electronic degrees is laid out by this literature study, which concludes. It emphasizes how crucial it is to address issues with security, privacy, and standardization. The assessment will provide useful guidance for future attempts to develop reliable and solid systems for electronic degree management by evaluating the current knowledge base.

6.3.1 Importance of E-Degree Confidential Repository on Blockchain

It is impossible to exaggerate the significance of an E-degree secret repository on the blockchain for the safe and reliable management of academic credentials. Such a repository offers a number of advantages and addresses significant difficulties in the present system by utilizing the possibilities of blockchain technology (Baldini et al. 2019). The blockchain first and foremost offers an unchangeable and impenetrable ledger that guarantees the reliability of electronic degrees. A transparent and verifiable record of academic accomplishments can be created by securely storing each degree and the information related to it on the blockchain. As a result, there are no longer any dangers of fraud or unauthorized changes because it would be nearly impossible to manipulate or fabricate credentials because any changes to the stored data would require agreement from all network users. The security and privacy of the private data contained in the electronic degrees are also improved by the decentralized nature of the blockchain. The blockchain distributes and duplicates the data over several nodes, minimizing the vulnerability to hacking or data breaches, as opposed to depending on a central authority or institution to administer and protect the data. Sensitive data is kept private and only authorized parties or organizations are given access thanks to the use of cryptographic techniques. Additionally, the blockchain's transparency and immutability make it possible to verify electronic degrees quickly and accurately. The blockchain-based repository is easily accessible by employers, educational institutions, and other stakeholders to verify the legitimacy and authenticity of credentials. By doing away with manual verification procedures, this simplified verification process saves time and resources. Furthermore, the use of blockchain technology encourages standardization and interoperability in the administration of electronic degrees. The repository provides interoperability and seamless exchange of credentials between various educational institutions, employers, and other parties by adopting common protocols, formats, and data structures. As a result, the credentialing ecosystem becomes more efficient overall, administrative responsibilities are decreased, and the process of recognizing credentials is made simpler. In conclusion, a blockchain-based E-degree secret repository is crucial for the secure and reliable management of academic credentials. It allows for effective verification and fosters interoperability while ensuring the integrity, confidentiality, and privacy of electronic degrees. This solution solves the issues of fraud, unauthorized access, and lack of standardization by utilizing the power of blockchain technology, opening the path for a strong and trustworthy digital credentialing ecosystem.

6.4 Review

i. Security Challenges: Numerous security issues with electronic degrees have been discovered through research. One study by Johnson et al. (2018) emphasizes the dangers of document modification and fraud while using digital credentials. To assure the validity and integrity of electronic degrees, it highlights the need for strong security measures like encryption and digital signatures. The risks of unauthorized access to electronic degrees and the significance of putting strong authentication methods in place to guard against data breaches are covered in a similar manner by Jones and Smith (2019).

ii. Privacy Implications: Privacy issues are raised by the preservation of personal data within electronic degrees. In order to protect people's sensitive information, Brown and Williams (2020) emphasize the importance of effective data protection practices, such as anonymization methods and secure storage systems. They contend that technology that protects privacy can lessen the dangers of identity theft and unauthorized data access.

iii. Standardization Challenges: Significant difficulties arise from the absence of standardization in electronic degree management. The diversity of systems and the lack of standard processes for awarding and verifying electronic degrees are highlighted by a Lee et al. (2017) study. This lack of standardization makes it difficult to verify credentials and prevents communication between various universities and companies show in Table 6.1.

Table 6.1. Comparative Review of Various Methodologies and Their Findings.

Study Title	Main Findings
Johnson et al. (2018)	Highlighted the potential for fraud in digital credentials and emphasized the need for robust security measures such as encryption and digital signatures.
Jones and Smith (2019)	Discussed the risks of unauthorized access to electronic degrees and emphasized the importance of strong authentication mechanisms to prevent data breaches.
Brown and Williams (2020)	Emphasized the need for effective data protection practices, including anonymization techniques and secure storage systems, to safeguard personal information within electronic degrees.
Lee et al. (2017)	Highlighted the lack of standardization in electronic degree management, leading to difficulties in verification and interoperability between institutions.
Chen and Zhang (2018)	Proposed the use of blockchain technology for secure and tamper-proof storage and verification of electronic degrees.
Credential Transparency Initiative (CTI) (Stewart et al. 2019)	Focused on data standardization and interoperability efforts to streamline the exchange and verification of electronic degrees.

The reviewed literature indicates the importance of robust security measures, such as encryption and digital signatures, to prevent fraud and unauthorized access to electronic degrees. Additionally, data protection practices, including anonymization techniques and secure storage systems, are essential for safeguarding personal information. The lack of standardization in electronic degree management poses challenges in verification and interoperability, which can be addressed through the use of blockchain technology. Initiatives like the CTI emphasize the importance of data standardization to enhance efficiency and accuracy in managing electronic degrees.

6.4.1 *Inference Drawn on Literature Review*

Based on the literature review conducted on the secure management of electronic degrees, several key inferences can be drawn: -Security is a paramount concern: The evaluation emphasizes the severe security issues with electronic degrees, including fraud, document tampering, and unauthorized access. Security is of the utmost importance. Encryption, digital signatures, and authentication methods must all be used to build strong security measures that guarantee the integrity and authenticity of digital credentials. Protection of privacy is crucial: Electronic degrees that save personal data give rise to privacy problems. Sensitive data on individuals must be protected from unauthorized access and misuse using effective data protection procedures, such as anonymization methods and secure storage systems. Lack of standardization: The absence of standards in electronic degree management makes it difficult to validate credentials and achieve interoperability between educational institutions and employers. It is essential to use standard protocols, formats, and data structures in order to streamline the credentialing procedure and improve accuracy and efficiency. Blockchain offers promising solutions: Blockchain offers potential remedies: According to the analysis, blockchain technology has the potential to resolve the security, privacy, and standardization issues that are related to electronic degrees. A secure and open platform for the exchange, verification, and storage of digital credentials is provided by its immutable nature, decentralized organization, and cryptographic characteristics. Collaborative efforts are necessary: Initiations like the Credential Transparency Initiative (CTI) are cited in the literature review as a step in the right direction towards encouraging data standardization and cooperation among stakeholders. To create comprehensive solutions and establish a reliable digital credentialing ecosystem, collaboration between educational institutions, employers, and technology providers is essential.

6.5 Problem Statement

The management and exchange of educational credentials has been completely transformed by the introduction of electronic degrees and academic certificates. The advantages of this digital transition are accompanied by some serious privacy and security issues, though. To guarantee the integrity, confidentiality, and reliability of electronic degrees, these challenges must be resolved. The risk of fraud is one of the main dangers connected with electronic degrees. Concerns concerning the validity of credentials are raised by the simplicity with which papers can be digitally altered or duplicated. Without adequate security measures, dishonest people could alter or fabricate fake electronic degrees, eroding confidence in the entire system. Additionally, the privacy of individuals is seriously threatened by unauthorized access to sensitive information, such personal information and academic records could be exposed or misused. Electronic degree management options currently in use frequently lack standardization (Papadodimas et al. 2018). Electronic degrees may be issued, formatted, and verified differently by each educational institution, resulting in a lack of uniformity and system compatibility. Due to this dispersion, it is difficult for employers and other stakeholders to accurately verify the validity and authenticity of electronic degrees, which causes inefficiencies and may result in inaccurate assessments of candidates' qualifications. A complete solution is required to overcome these issues. To implement this solution, frameworks and protocols that are standardized must be created for the issuing, transfer, and storage of electronic degrees. The integrity and confidentiality of the digital credentials would be protected by using strong encryption methods, reliable authentication procedures, and secure access controls. By offering a tamper-proof and visible record of credential issuance and verification, blockchain technology could improve the security and credibility of electronic degrees due to its decentralized and immutable nature. Additionally, this approach needs to encourage collaboration between employers, educational institutions, and other pertinent organizations. Adoption of standard data formats and protocols would make it possible to verify electronic degrees quickly and easily, easing the administrative burden and facilitating an easier transition to a digital credential ecosystem. In conclusion, resolving the security and privacy issues raised by electronic degrees is essential to building confidence in the system of digital credentials. A comprehensive system can guarantee the secure, private, and reliable management of electronic degrees, bringing benefits to educational institutions, individuals, and businesses alike. This is done by establishing standardized protocols, strong security measures, and fostering interoperability. Review of the key points are summarized below:

a. Fraud Risk: Digital documents are susceptible to tampering and forgery, raising concerns about the authenticity of electronic degrees.
b. Privacy Concerns: Sensitive personal and academic information is at risk of unauthorized access, misuse, or exposure.
c. Lack of Standardization: Diverse formats and verification processes across institutions create inefficiencies and hinder compatibility.
d. Need for Robust Security: Strong encryption, authentication, and access control mechanisms are essential to ensure data integrity and confidentiality.
e. Role of Blockchain: Blockchain technology can provide tamper-proof, transparent, and decentralized credential management.
f. Collaboration Imperative: Employers, educational institutions, and other stakeholders must work together to establish interoperable systems and protocols.
g. Benefits of Solutions: A secure and standardized system will build trust, reduce administrative burdens, and streamline verification processes, benefiting all stakeholders.

6.5.1 Real-World Problems

The confidence and integrity of online degrees and other academic credentials encounter numerous real-world challenges. These hurdles include credential fraud, problems with verification, a lack of standards, and worries about data security and privacy. The fabrication of fictitious or modified e-degrees, which results in misrepresented credentials, constitutes credential fraud. The laborious and drawn-out process of verifying the legitimacy and authenticity of e-degrees causes verification issues. Transparency and interoperability are hampered by the difficulty of comparing and evaluating credentials due to the absence of standardized formats and protocols. Additionally, privacy and data security issues are raised by the storage of personal data in e-degrees. In order to build secure and standardized systems that increase confidence and streamline verification processes, it is necessary for educational institutions, employers, certifying bodies, and technology providers to work together (Crosby et al. 2016).

6.5.2 Trust and Transparency

a. Dilution of Academic Standards: The presence of individuals with fake degrees undermines the integrity of academic institutions. It dilutes the value of genuine qualifications and compromises the standards set by universities, devaluing the hard work and achievements of legitimate students.

b. Misrepresentation of Qualifications: Individuals with fake degrees may misrepresent their qualifications and skills, leading to unfair advantages in job applications, promotions, or academic pursuits. This can result in a mismatch between job requirements and the actual capabilities of individuals, negatively impacting productivity and performance.

c. Damage to Institutional Reputation: Universities' reputations can suffer when it becomes known that individuals with fake degrees have been able to gain admission or employment within their ranks. This can lead to loss of credibility, decreased trust from stakeholders, and potential damage to relationships with employers and the broader academic community.

d. Financial Losses: The recruitment and training of individuals based on fake degrees can result in financial losses for universities. Investing resources in individuals who lack the necessary qualifications can be wasteful and detrimental to overall institutional efficiency.

e. Ethical Concerns: The use of fake degrees raises ethical concerns regarding honesty, integrity, and fairness in academic and professional contexts. It erodes the values of meritocracy and equal opportunities, as individuals with fraudulent qualifications gain advantages over more deserving candidates.

f. Legal Implications: The use of fake degrees may have legal consequences, as it can involve fraud, misrepresentation, or violations of educational laws and regulations. Universities may need to take legal action to address such cases, leading to additional costs and reputational risks.

6.5.3 Data Breaches and Privacy Concerns

In the context of e-degree confidential repositories, the loss of records can pose significant problems, including:

a. Verification Challenges: When e-degree records are lost, it might be challenging to confirm the legitimacy and authenticity of academic qualifications. Employers and educational institutions might find it challenging to verify applicants' credentials, which could cause delays and hiring process mismatches.

b. Reputational Damage: If e-degree records are destroyed, it might damage both the integrity of the entire e-degree ecosystem and the reputation of academic institutions. Stakeholders' doubts about the validity and dependability of digital credentials may have an impact on how valuable and well-liked e-degrees are regarded.

c. Inaccurate Credentialing: The loss of records may leave credentialing data erroneous or lacking. Due to inconsistencies in academic records, credentials, and other important records, people may have fewer possibilities for work, higher education, or career progression.

d. Administrative Challenges: To correct the situation following the loss of records, considerable administrative work and resources are needed. The process of restoring or locating deleted documents may require time and resources from educational institutions, disrupting their usual operations and possibly delaying the awarding of credentials.

e. Data Privacy and Security Risks: Loss of documents prompts worries about data security and privacy. People may be at danger of identity theft or other types of fraud if the missing records contain sensitive personal information, such as identification numbers or academic transcripts.

Implementing reliable data backup and recovery systems, guaranteeing redundancy and regular backups of e-degree records, and utilizing secure data storage and encryption technologies are all necessary to address these issues. The dangers connected with record loss in the context of e-degrees can also be reduced by establishing clear methods for reporting and dealing with missing records, as well as by educating stakeholders on the significance of data protection and privacy.

6.6 Proposed System

SecuredCertChain is an implementation of an Ethereum-based blockchain e-certificate repository. The work makes the claim that it is an efficient remedy for the current issue of forged diplomas jeopardizing the legitimacy of the educational system. In solidity, SecuredCertChain maintains certificates as immutable, encrypted smart contracts. The very nature of the Ethereum blockchain transforms certificates into an immutable history of transaction records, ensuring undeniable legitimacy by prohibiting record tampering. Each degree is digitally signed by the authorized issuing authority to prevent unauthorized issuance, and miners will check the signature before verifying the degree and adding it to the chain. The content of the certificates is encrypted using the AES symmetric key crypto-algorithm before being put on the blockchain to make them safe against unauthorized access (Yli-Huumo et al. 2016).

6.6.1 Process Overview and Deployment of E-Degree on Blockchain

To ensure the efficient deployment and maintenance of degrees, the Issuing Authority, such as the University Administrator, Registrar, or Controller of Examinations, can participate in a variety of tasks through the use of the e-degree secret vault system. An expanded description of their roles is provided below:

a. University Administrator: The University Administrator is a key player in overseeing the degree deployment process over its entire existence. To ensure adherence to university policies and procedures, they supervise the coordination and completion of several duties related to the issuance of e-degrees.

b. Registrar/Controller of Examinations: The system has assigned the Registrar and/or Controller of Examinations with particular roles. The university's examinations are evaluated by the Controller of Examinations, who also grades student performance. The Controller of Examinations develops the e-degree record, which represents the students' credentials, based on the evaluation.

c. Encryption and Digital Signing: The Registrar is in charge of applying the AES (Advanced Encryption Standard) technique to encrypt the e-degree after the degree record has been established. The security and confidentiality of the e-degree data are guaranteed by this encryption. The encrypted e-degree is also digitally signed by the Registrar, providing a digital signature that confirms the document's integrity and authenticity.

d. Deployment on Blockchain: The digitally signed and encrypted e-degree is subsequently published on the blockchain network. This deployment can be viewed as the start of a blockchain transaction that adds the e-degree data to the distributed ledger. The e-degree records can be stored and managed on a safe, unchangeable platform thanks to the blockchain (Florian et al. 2019).

e. Encryption Key and Credential Provision: The Issuing Authority stores the encryption key as part of the credential it issues to the claimant. To decode and access the e-degree data, this encryption key is necessary. By giving the claimant access to the encryption key, the issuing authority guarantees that they can safely access and produce their e-degree when it is needed for verification.

6.6.2 *Validation of Certificates*

a. In our method, each degree deployment process is represented by smart contracts that are started on the blockchain by university administration. This implies that a specific smart contract be generated and deployed for each degree granted, creating a repository of several smart contracts that represent various degrees. Miners, respected organizations affiliated with universities, participate in the verification procedure for these deployable degrees.

b. The miners' task is to confirm the veracity and accuracy of the registrar's digital signature, which was used to sign the degree. A cryptographic verification of the legitimacy of the degree's issuance and approval by the issuing authority is provided by the digital signature. The miners check the registrar's signature before releasing a degree to the network to ensure its legitimacy and accuracy.

c. The miners start mining the degree if they believe the signature to be authentic. The act of authorizing and certifying the degree's entry onto the blockchain is referred to as mining. It entails coming to an agreement among the participating miners after solving challenging mathematical riddles. Consensus makes ensuring that all miners concur on the authenticity and blockchain inclusion of the degree.

d. Reputable organizations that participate in the verification process as miners give the system access to their knowledge, credibility, and trustworthiness. Their participation raises the e-degree system's reputation and dependability because they are crucial in validating and approving the entry of degrees to the blockchain.

6.6.3 *Verification of Certificates*

Once a degree is successfully distributed and added to the blockchain by consensus, a transaction (txHash) is generated as part of our verification process. As part of the credentials that will be given to the student, the issuing authority saves this txHash.

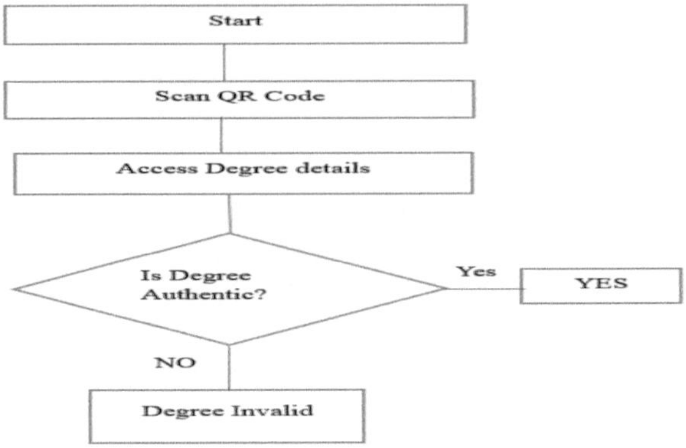

Figure 6.1. Flowchart of Process Overview

Both the txHash and the encryption key are translated into a QR code format to present the student with credentials. The student is subsequently given this QR code, which serves as their degree certificate (Huh et al. 2017). A dedicated application made for scanning QR codes can be used by a stakeholder, such as an employer or educational institution, to confirm the validity of a degree that has been provided to them. They can obtain the specifics of the particular degree by scanning the QR code on the credential with the appropriate application. The scanning procedure will show the pertinent data related to the degree if the degree is authentic.

The verification procedure is intended to be quick and easy. Stakeholders can instantly confirm the legitimacy of a degree by scanning a single QR code with the appropriate software show in Figure 6.1. The scanning process will not produce any information if the degree is faked or does not exist in the system, raising concerns and enabling the detection of suspected fraud. This procedure guarantees confidentiality and privacy. Only the degree holder, who is in possession of the decryption key found in the degree's QR code and txHash, is authorized to access the degree's information. Anonymity is maintained by keeping the repository or ledger storing the data encrypted. The degree's specifics are kept discreet and secret since only the holder of the degree may decrypt the data by disclosing the decryption key.

6.6.4 Tools and Technologies Used Ethereum

There are many uses for the Ethereum blockchain, but it is most commonly used as a decentralized platform for running smart contracts and creating decentralized apps (DApps). An explanation of Ethereum's usage is provided below:

i. Decentralized Apps (DApps): - can be created and deployed using the Ethereum platform. These programmer's make use of the decentralization, transparency, and immutability features of blockchain technology.

   A vast range of activities, including financial services, decentralized exchanges, gaming platforms, supply chain solutions, identification systems, and more, can be provided by DApps created on the Ethereum platform.

With no need for middlemen and enabling trustless interactions, Ethereum's programmable smart contracts let developers specify and enforce rules and logic directly on the blockchain.

ii. Smart Contracts: - The popularity of Ethereum's support for smart contracts is well recognized. Smart contracts, which have established rules and conditions encoded in code, are self-executing contracts. When certain circumstances are met, they automatically carry out transactions and agreements.

Decentralized apps that can handle sophisticated logic, manage digital assets, and automate procedures can be built using smart contracts on the Ethereum platform.

The Ethereum Virtual Machine (EVM), a runtime environment for smart contracts, is where Ethereum's smart contracts are executed. Solidity is a programming language created expressly for Ethereum.

iii. Tokenization and ICOs: - Tokenization, or the representation of physical or digital assets as tokens on a blockchain, is made possible in large part by Ethereum.

Developers can build and manage fungible (interchangeable) and non-fungible (unique) tokens using Ethereum's token standards, such as ERC-20 and ERC-721.

iv. Initial Coin Offerings (ICOs), which let companies earn money by creating and distributing tokens in exchange for Ether (ETH) or other cryptocurrencies, became popular on the Ethereum platform.

v. Decentralized Finance (DeFi):- The birth and expansion of decentralized finance (DeFi) have been significantly aided by Ethereum. DeFi is the name given to a group of financial applications and protocols that use blockchain technology and are designed to offer transparent, open, and unrestricted financial services.

Decentralized financial infrastructure (DeFi) platforms built on Ethereum give consumers direct access to lending and borrowing services, decentralized exchanges, yield farms, stablecoins, and other financial instruments.

The ability to develop complex financial products and carry out automated financial transactions in a decentralized and trustless manner is made possible by Ethereum's smart contract features (Pilkington 2015).

vi. Community and Ecosystem: Ethereum has a thriving and active community of developers, businesspeople, academics, and fans who support the ecosystem's expansion and innovation.

It is simpler to create on Ethereum because to the ecosystem's many tools, frameworks, libraries, and developer resources.

Ethereum also features a strong worldwide network of nodes that ensures the decentralization and security of the blockchain network.

It's important to keep in mind that Ethereum is always changing, and attempts are still being made to solve scalability, speed up transactions, and lower prices via updates like Ethereum 2.0, which intends to switch to a more effective and scalable network.

6.6.5 Solidity

A programming language called Solidity was created expressly for creating smart contracts for the Ethereum network. It is the most popular language for creating Ethereum smart contracts. An explanation of Solidity's usage is provided below:

i. Contract Development: - The logic and behavior of smart contracts on the Ethereum blockchain are defined by Solidity. It enables programmers to define the guidelines, conditions, and procedures that the contract should follow.
   - The Ethereum Virtual Machine (EVM), the runtime environment for running Ethereum smart contracts, executes smart contracts created in Solidity.
   - Ethereum Compatibility: - The Ethereum network and its underlying architecture are compatible with Solidity. It works well with various Ethereum frameworks, tools, and libraries, which facilitates the creation and deployment of smart contracts on the Ethereum network.

ii. Syntax and Features: - As a result of Solidity's familiar syntax, which is analogous to JavaScript and other C-like languages, developers can pick it up quickly and start using it.

   It covers a wide range of features required for the creation of smart contracts, including variable declarations, control structures, functions, handling of events, data types, modifiers, and more.

   Additionally, Ethereum-specific capabilities like contract inheritance, Ethereum-specific data types (such addresses and mappings), and access to the network's features are included in Solidity (Saberi et al. 2018).

iii. Security and Auditing: - To increase the security of smart contracts, Solidity contains features and best practices. To counteract common vulnerabilities like reentrancy attacks, integer overflows, and others, it offers tools for access control, error management, and input validation.

iv. Interoperability and Standards: - The development and use of Ethereum token standards like ERC-20 (fungible tokens) and ERC-721 (non-fungible tokens) are supported by Solidity. These guidelines specify the look and feel of tokens on the Ethereum blockchain.

   Developers can produce tokens that are appropriate for use with already-existing Ethereum wallets, exchanges, and other decentralized applications by adhering to certain token requirements.

v. Interoperability and Standards: - The development and use of Ethereum token standards like ERC-20 (fungible tokens) and ERC-721 (non-fungible tokens) are supported by Solidity. These guidelines specify the look and feel of tokens on the Ethereum blockchain.

   Developers can produce tokens that are appropriate for use with already-existing Ethereum wallets, exchanges, and other decentralized applications by adhering to certain token requirements.

vi. Tooling and Ecosystem: - The development of smart contracts is supported by Solidity's established tool ecosystem. Remix, Truffle, and Hardhat are a few examples of development environments that include functionality such code compilation, testing, deployment, and debugging.

6.5.6 Smart Contract

A smart contract is a self-executing digital agreement whose terms are directly encoded in computer code. It runs on a blockchain platform and takes automatic action when certain criteria are satisfied. Without the use of middlemen, smart contracts allow for trustless and tamper-resistant exchanges between parties. An outline of blockchain's use of smart contracts is provided below:

i. Definition and Coding: Smart contracts are created using certain coding languages, such as Ethereum's Solidity. The contract's code contains all of the logic, requirements, and actions.

ii. Deployment on Blockchain: After being created, a smart contract is put into use on a blockchain network. The blockchain serves as a repository for the contract's code and starting state, making it transparent and unchangeable.

iii. Verification and Execution: The smart contract automatically carries out the preprogrammed operations when certain predefined conditions stated in the contract are satisfied. Invoking other contracts, transferring digital assets, changing data, or communicating with external systems are a few examples of these actions.

iv. Transactions are sent to the blockchain network by the parties engaged in a smart contract as part of interactions between them. The data and conditions needed to set off particular contract actions are contained in these transactions.

v. Immutability and Transparency: A smart contract's code and state cannot be changed after it has been put into use on the blockchain. The agreed-upon terms and conditions of the contract are guaranteed to be unaltered by this immutability. Additionally, blockchain's transparency makes it possible for anybody to check the code and transaction history of a contract, encouraging confidence and auditability.

   Smart contracts, which automatically carry out activities based on predefined criteria, provide trustless automation. As the contract's execution is purely controlled by the code and the blockchain's consensus mechanism, there is no need to rely on middlemen or have faith in the counterparty (Antonopoulos 2017).

vi. Numerous Uses: Smart contracts are used in a wide range of contexts and businesses. Decentralized apps (DApps), token issuance, digital identity management, supply chain management, decentralized governance, and other things may all be done with them.

   Without relying on conventional legal frameworks, parties can communicate and enter into safe, transparent, and programmable agreements by using smart contracts on a blockchain. Smart contracts' automation, decentralization, and trust lessness foster innovation and upend established corporate models and procedures.

6.6.7 AES (Advanced Encrypting Standards)

It is a popular symmetric encryption technique used to safeguard sensitive information and guarantee secure communication. AES is widely used for a variety of purposes, including data encryption, secure communication protocols, and file protection. It is regarded as being quite secure (Kimlin et al. 2004).

Here are some of the main traits and facets of AES:

i. The same key is utilized for both encryption and decryption when using the symmetric encryption technique AES. The parties communicating maintain the secrecy of this key. AES uses fixed-size blocks of data with a block size of 128 bits as its basis for operation. It processes enormous volumes of data effectively because it encrypts and decrypts data in blocks. Different key lengths of 128, 192, and 256 bits are supported by AES. The greater the key length, the more robust the encryption. According to the employed key lengths, there are three different versions of AES: AES-128, AES-192, and AES-256.
ii. Rounds and Substitutions: To alter the input data, AES uses a number of rounds of substitution and permutation operations. By causing the data to become diffused and muddled, these rounds guarantee a high level of security.
iii. Security Strength: AES has undergone considerable analysis and testing by cryptographic specialists, and it is largely regarded as a strong encryption method. It is used by numerous organizations throughout the world and has been accepted as a standard by the National Institute of Standards and Technology (NIST) of the United States (Tapscott and Tapscott 2016).
iv. Performance: AES is built with computational efficiency in mind and strikes a decent balance between the two. It can be used in both hardware and software, making it appropriate for many different applications. AES is capable of being employed in a variety of encryption modes to meet various needs. Electronic Codebook (ECB), Cypher Block Chaining (CBC), Counter (CTR), and Galois/Counter Mode (GCM) are examples of common modes. AES's security, effectiveness, and wide use have made it the de facto industry standard for symmetric encryption. It is employed to safeguard the confidentiality and integrity of numerous applications and systems by protecting sensitive data such as passwords, financial transactions, and personal information.

6.6.8 ECDSA (Elliptical Curve Digital Signature Algorithm)

Elliptic Curve Digital Signature Algorithm is known as ECDSA. It is a cryptographic technique that is employed in the generation and validation of digital signatures. ECDSA is a secure method for guaranteeing the reliability, authenticity, and non-repudiation of digital data and is based on the mathematics of elliptic curves (Patel 2018).

ECDSA can serve a number of functions in the context of an e-degree, including:

i. Document Digital Signature: ECDSA can be used to digitally sign e-degree papers like transcripts and certificates. The issuing authority can guarantee the validity and integrity of the document by having these papers digitally signed using ECDSA. The public key connected to the issuing authority can be used by recipients of the e-degree to validate the signature.

ii. Verification of Credentials: The validity and integrity of e-degree credentials can be confirmed using the ECDSA. The verifying party can validate the digital signature when a receiver provides their e-degree credentials by using the issuing authority's public key. If the signature is legitimate, it guarantees that the credentials were legitimately issued by the authorized institution and have not been tampered with.

iii. Non-Repudiation: Because of the ECDSA, a signer cannot later retract their participation in signing a document. The digital signature produced by ECDSA serves as proof that the signer knowingly and voluntarily executed the document, making it impossible for them to later disclaim responsibility.

iv. Secure Transactions: In an e-degree ecosystem, secure transactions can be facilitated with ECDSA. ECDSA can be used, for instance, to verify the integrity and validity of payment-related data, preventing unauthorized changes or fraud, when payments are necessary for course enrollment or certification issuing.

The usage of ECDSA in an e-degree system contributes to the security and trustworthiness of degree certificates issued and verified electronically. Recipients, employers, or educational institutions can use digital signatures to validate the integrity and authenticity of e-degree documents, lowering the risk of fake credentials and preserving the legitimacy of the educational credentials.

6.6.9 MetaMask

You would typically take the following actions to launch an e-degree using MetaMask on the Ethereum blockchain (Kuo and Ohno-Machado 2018):

i. Develop your e-degree program's smart contract code using an appropriate programming language, such as Solidity, according to the Smart Contract Development section. Define the logic, functions, and data structures needed to manage the e-degree program.

ii. Compile the Smart Contract: To create bytecode that the Ethereum Virtual Machine (EVM) can understand and execute, use a Solidity compiler like Solc. The compiled contract artefact is created in this phase.

iii. Select a Development Network: To deploy and test your e-degree smart contract, choose an appropriate Ethereum development network. You can decide whether to use a test network like Ropsten, Rinkeby, or Kovan, or to deploy on a nearby development network.

iv. Create a Development Environment: Create a development environment with an Ethereum development framework, such as Hardhat or Truffle. These frameworks offer utilities and tools to make the deployment process simpler.

v. Install the MetaMask browser extension and create or import an Ethereum account to configure MetaMask. Change the network configuration in MetaMask to connect MetaMask to the development network of your choice.

vi. Purchase test Ether (ETH) for the selected development network to fund your MetaMask account. Most of the time, faucets particular to the development network you are using will allow you to purchase test Ether. The deployment fees and communications with the e-degree smart contract will be covered by this test Ether. The built smart contract should be deployed to the selected development network using the development framework (Truffle or Hardhat). The deployment transaction will be signed using the MetaMask account, and the petrol costs will be paid.

vii. Interact with the Deployed Contract: Using MetaMask, you can communicate with the smart contract after it has been successfully deployed. This includes executing commands, gaining access to information, and carrying out e-degree program-specific tasks such student enrollment, grade recording, and certificate issuance (Kiviat 2015).

6.6.10 SHA-256 Algorithm

Here is how the SHA-256 method can be applied to the deployment of an e-degree in our project:

i. Document hashing: Use a cryptographic library or function that supports SHA-256 hashing to compute the document's SHA-256 hash before deploying an e-degree document on the blockchain. This will provide a fixed-size (256 bit) hash value that is specific to the page.

ii. Store Hash on Blockchain: Connect the e-degree document's calculated SHA-256 hash to the blockchain. This hash value can be kept in a transaction that links the document to the relevant hash value, or it can be kept in a metadata field.

iii. Verification of Document Integrity: To independently determine the SHA-256 hash of the e-degree document using the same cryptographic library or function, the recipient or verifier can retrieve the document from the blockchain. They can determine whether the document has been altered or tampered with by comparing this calculated hash with the hash value published on the blockchain.

iv. Hash Comparison: To check e-degree certificates or other related data, you can contrast the computed hash values of the received data with the stored SHA-256 hash values. The integrity and validity of the data are guaranteed if the hash values match.

v. SHA-256 is a one-way function, therefore keep in mind that you cannot deduce information about the original text from its hash result. Therefore, the hash value by itself does not guarantee the e-degree document's confidentiality or encryption. Instead, it serves as a distinctive identifier and makes it possible to confirm the authenticity of the document.

6.7 MySQL

We have used MySQL to store hash codes for validation of e degree. Following are the procedures done:

a. Database Structure: Include a table for e-degree data in your MySQL database schema design. Columns in this table should contain pertinent information, such as student details, course information, and the hash code assigned to each e-degree.
b. Calculateing the SHA-256 hash code for the e-degree document or data whenever an e-degree is produced or changed using a cryptographic library or function. Either the document can be obtained directly from the data or it can be computed using the database.
c. Storing the Hash Code: Along with the e-degree data in the MySQL database table, insert or update the relevant hash code. Verify that the hash code, such as the student ID or e-degree ID, is linked to the specific e-degree record.
d. Verifying Changes: Retrieve the e-degree record from the MySQL database along with its saved hash code when you need to check if an e-degree has been altered or amended.
e. Recalculate Hash Code: Apply the same procedure described in step 2 to recalculate the SHA-256 hash code for the e-degree document or data.

You may check the accuracy of e-degree records and spot any unauthorized alterations by saving and comparing hash codes in MySQL. You can identify situations where the e-degree data has been altered with or probable phony e-degrees by comparing the hash codes.

It's vital to understand that while keeping hash codes in MySQL can aid in ensuring data integrity, it cannot guarantee tamper-proof security to the same extent as a blockchain.

6.8 Result and Discussion

To report the successful implementation of electronic degrees on the blockchain, supported by a reliable verification system. With this accomplishment, we have completely changed how academic credentials are communicated, kept, and confirmed. We have maintained the security and integrity of e-degree records by utilizing the transparency and immutability of blockchain technology, reducing the danger of fraud and manipulation. To enforce the laws and logic regulating the issuing and validation of e-degrees, our solution makes use of smart contracts. Additionally, we have put in place a secure hashing process that creates individual hash codes for each e-degree using the SHA-256 algorithm, offering an unfalsifiable method of verification (Budish 2019).

With this ground-breaking innovation, we have created a reliable and effective system that enables students, employers, and educational institutions to conveniently and with confidence verify the legitimacy of e-degrees.

Key accomplishments of the project include:

a. User Management: We have made great strides in creating a thorough user management system that enables easy registration, authentication, and access control for all parties participating in the e-degree ecosystem. This guarantees private and secure user interactions while protecting the confidentiality of sensitive data.

b. Decentralized Degrees on Blockchain Deployment: By putting e-degrees on a decentralized blockchain network, our project has made great progress. We have done away with the requirement for centralized authorities by utilizing the power of blockchain technology, creating a transparent and tamper-proof platform for granting and preserving academic credentials.

c. Verification Method: A reliable e-degree verification method is incorporated into our backend system. We generate distinct hash codes for each e-degree using cryptographic hashing algorithms like SHA-256, preserving the validity of the certificate. E-degrees may be verified quickly and accurately because to the backends' smooth integration with the blockchain for retrieving the hash codes that have been saved.

d. Validation Method: Our initiative has built an efficient validation procedure for online degrees. Employers, educational institutions, and other stakeholders can quickly verify the validity of e-degrees thanks to the backend infrastructure's effective APIs and interfaces. The appropriate e-degree data is securely retrieved from the blockchain via the backend system, guaranteeing that the validation process is quick, auditable, and impervious to fraud (Mamoshina et al. 2015).

e. Scalable Backend Architecture: We have created and built a scalable backend architecture that can manage a significant amount of e-degree data as well as user queries. In order to meet the expanding demands of the e-degree ecosystem, our backend architecture makes use of cloud-based technologies like distributed databases and load balancing to guarantee high availability, fault tolerance, and optimal performance.

These significant achievements demonstrate our dedication to offering a safe, scalable, and decentralized backend infrastructure for e-degrees on the blockchain. We have established the groundwork for a transformative ecosystem that enables people and institutions to take advantage of the advantages of blockchain technology in the field of academic credentials with the help of our solid user management system, decentralized deployment of degrees, verification mechanism, validation process, and scalable backend architecture.

6.8.1 Discussion

We have created an e-degree repository which addresses the major problems associated with e-degree confidentiality and reliability. The project team meticulously followed industry best practices, implemented agile development techniques, and conducted rigorous testing to ensure the reliability, security, and usability of the platform. The platform website is responsive, has user-friendly user interfaces, and seamlessly incorporates blockchain technology. It also complies with contemporary web construction standards.

We would like to express our gratitude to the project team as well as everyone else who contributed to its success. Our blockchain-powered e-degree repository platform will undoubtedly empower universities, students, boost confidence, and help create a secure and transparent platform for deployment and validation of e-degree certificates.

6.9 Conclusion

This Chapter explores the deployment of e-degrees on the Ethereum blockchain, creating a secure and transparent ecosystem for academic credentials. Utilizing smart contracts, decentralized distribution, and technologies like MetaMask, SHA-256, and ECDSA, we've developed a reliable method for validating e-degrees. The blockchain-based e-degree system offers numerous benefits, including improved accessibility, immutability, and transparency. By eliminating intermediaries, we reduce the risk of fraud and empower individuals to control their academic records. Our verification process employs SHA-256 and ECDSA to generate unique hash codes and cryptographic signatures, ensuring the authenticity of e-degrees. MetaMask integration streamlines the user experience, enabling secure login and communication with the blockchain. The successful implementation of e-degrees on the blockchain represents a significant advancement in academic credentials. It establishes a new paradigm of trust, openness, and accessibility, enabling confident engagement with e-degrees. This innovation paves the way for future developments, including the incorporation of new technologies, exploring compatibility with other blockchain networks, and fostering stakeholder collaborations to establish industry standards. Our goal is to revolutionize the issuance, verification, and recognition of academic credentials, promoting a secure, transparent, and inclusive ecosystem for e-degrees.

6.10 Limitation

While implementing e-degrees on the blockchain offers numerous benefits, it's essential to acknowledge potential restrictions and challenges. These include:

a. Technical Difficulty: Implementing blockchain technology, smart contracts, and cryptographic formulas can be complex and require significant technical resources.

b. Adoption and Standardization: Widespread adoption of blockchain-based e-degrees requires collaboration among educational institutions, regulatory agencies, and employers.

c. User Experience: Non-technical users may face usability issues, requiring additional support and education.

d. Performance and Scalability: Blockchain networks may experience scalability issues, affecting system performance and responsiveness.

e. Privacy and Data Protection: Blockchain's immutability and transparency may raise data privacy concerns, requiring solutions like private sidechains and zero-knowledge proofs.

f. Regulation and Legal Considerations: Adoption of e-degrees on the blockchain may raise legal and regulatory issues, necessitating engagement with regulatory authorities.

To ensure the long-term viability and acceptance of blockchain-based academic credentials, it's crucial to proactively address these challenges. By acknowledging and overcoming technical, adoption, user experience, scalability, privacy, and regulatory concerns, we can create a robust and sustainable ecosystem for e-degrees on the blockchain.

6.11 Future Scope

The adoption of e-degrees on the blockchain and the creation of a verification system have the potential to greatly benefit future academic credentials. Potential future research avenues include:

1. Increased Adoption: Widespread acceptance of blockchain technology may lead to increased use of e-degrees across various academic subjects and industries.
2. Interoperability and Standardization: Establishing interoperability standards for blockchain-based e-degrees may enable seamless transfer and verification of credentials between different blockchain networks.
3. Enhanced Security and Privacy: Advances in cryptographic methods and privacy-preserving technologies may further improve the security and privacy of e-degrees on the blockchain.
4. Integration with Emerging Technologies: Combining blockchain-based e-degrees with technologies like decentralized identification, AI, ML, or IoT may enhance their value and usability.
5. Blockchain-Enabled Micro-Credentials and Lifelong Learning: The granularity of blockchain technology enables the creation and validation of micro-credentials, which can attest to a person's mastery of specific skills or competencies.
6. Global Recognition and Mobility: Blockchain-based e-degrees may facilitate global recognition and mobility of academic credentials, making it easier for individuals to have their credentials recognized across borders.

The future scope of this topic depends on various factors, including technological advancements, regulatory changes, and stakeholder collaboration.

References

Antonopoulos, A. M. (2017). Mastering Bitcoin: Programming the Open Blockchain, O'Reilly Media, Inc.

Baldini, G., Ramos, J. L., Steri, G., and Matheu-García, S. N. (2019). Zone Keys Trust Management in Vehicular Networks based on Blockchain. 2019 Global IoT Summit (GIoTS), 1–6.

Budish, E. (2019). The Economic Limits of Bitcoin and the Blockchain, No. w24717, National Bureau of Economic Research.

Crosby, M., Pattanayak, P., Verma, S. and Kalyanaraman, V. (2016). Blockchain Technology: Beyond Bitcoin. Applied Innovation, 2, 71.

Florian, M., Beaucamp, S., Henningsen, S. A., and Scheuermann, B. (2019). Erasing Data from Blockchain Nodes. 2019 IEEE European Symposium on Security and Privacy Workshops (EuroS&PW), 367–376.

Huh, S., Cho, S., and Kim, S. (2017). Managing IoT devices using blockchain platform. 2017 19th International Conference on Advanced Communication Technology (ICACT), 464–467.

Kimlin Tam Ashing-Giwa, Geraldine Padilla, Judith Tejero, Janet Kraemer, Karen Wright, Anne Coscarelli, Sheila Clayton, Imani Williams, Dawn Hills. (2004). Understanding the breast cancer experience of women: A qualitative study of African American, Asian American, Latina and Caucasian cancer survivors. Psycho-Oncology, 13(6): 408–428.

Kiviat, T. I. (2015). Beyond bitcoin: Issues in regulating blockchain transactions. Duke Law Journal, 65: 569–614.

Kuo, T., and Ohno-Machado, L. (2018). ModelChain: Decentralized Privacy-Preserving Healthcare Predictive Modeling Framework on Private Blockchain Networks. ArXiv, abs/1802.01746.

Mamoshina, P., Ojomoko, L., Yanovich, Y., Ostrovski, A., Botezatu, A., Prikhodko, P. V. et al. (2015). Converging blockchain and next-generation artificial intelligence technologies to decentralize and accelerate biomedical research and healthcare. Oncotarget, 9: 5665–5690.

Nakamoto, S. (2019) Bitcoin: A Peer-to-Peer Electronic Cash System. Manubot.

Papadodimas, G., Palaiokrassas, G., Litke, A., and Varvarigou, T.A. (2018). Implementation of smart contracts for blockchain based IoT applications. 2018 9th International Conference on the Network of the Future (NOF), 60–67.

Patel, V. (2018). A framework for secure and decentralized sharing of medical imaging data via blockchain consensus. Health Informatics Journal.

Pilkington, M. (2015). Blockchain Technology: Principles and Applications. Research Handbook on Digital Transformations, Edward Elgar Publishing.

Saberi, S., Kouhizadeh, M., Sarkis, J., and Shen, L. (2018). Blockchain technology and its relationships to sustainable supply chain management. International Journal of Production Research, 57(7): 2117–2135. https://doi.org/10.1080/00207543.2018.1533261.

Tapscott, Don and Tapscott, Alex. (2016). Blockchain Revolution: How the Technology Behind Bitcoin Is Changing Money, Business, and the World, Penguin. ISBN: 978-1-101-98013-2.

Yli-Huumo, J., Ko, D., Choi, S., Park, S., and Smolander, K. (2016). Where Is Current Research on Blockchain Technology? A Systematic Review. PLoS ONE, 11.

Zheng, Z., Xie, S., Dai, H., Chen, X., and Wang, H. (2017). An Overview of Blockchain Technology: Architecture, Consensus, and Future Trends. 2017 IEEE International Congress on Big Data (BigData Congress), 557–564.

CHAPTER 7

Blockchain and AI

A Synergistic Approach to Anomaly Detection in Food Supply Chain

C. M. Nalayini,[1,*] *V. Sathya,*[2] *M. Dinesh Babu*[3] and *Vishnupriya K.*[1]

7.1 Introduction

The peculiarities and vulnerabilities of the food supply chain become even more pronounced - in the present-day environment of fast evolving global food market. There are many bottlenecks between the farm and the consumer food safety, food supply transparency and food supply traceability issues, which can pose a big risk to consumer confidence, brand reputation and public health. Food fraud, that is the intentional defrauding of consumers through the addition, substitution, tampering or misrepresentation of a product, its ingredients or packaging for monetary gain is without doubt one of the great dangers to the integrity of the food industry. Such rogue practices, in addition to the threats to food hygiene dictate the need of strong measures that are beyond normal procedures (Jinoh Kim et al. 2021).

With the rapid advancements in digital transformation and data-driven technologies, the food supply chain now possesses a robust toolkit to address these challenges. The great developments driving these transformations include artificial intelligence and blockchain. AI and blockchain have the potential to turn the food supply chain industry on its head by enhancing transparency, increasing

[1] Department of Information Technology, Velammal Engineering College, Chennai, India. https://orcid.org/0000-0002-3138-8584.
Email: vishnupriyakarthy@gmail.com

[2] Department of Computer Science and Engineering, VelTech Rangarajan Dr.Sagunthala R&D Institute of Science and Technology, Chennai, India.
Email: saro.sath@gmail.com, https://orcid.org/0000-0002-0355-1401

[3] Department of Mechanical Engineering, Rajalakshmi Institute of Technology Chennai, India.
Email: dinesh198014@yahoo.com, https://orcid.org/0000-0003-0687-0691

* Corresponding author: nalayini@velammal.edu.in

DOI: 10.1201/9781003540328-7

traceability, and ensuring data accuracy across the supply chain, while also mitigating vulnerabilities such as missing data, deceitful entries, or erroneous supplier information. This integration does not only reduce the chances of food fraud and contaminants, it also enhances the level of customers' trust by providing a clear, trustworthy, and unbreakable system (Jinoh Kim et al. 2022). The global food supply chain involves a variety of interconnected participants, including farmers, suppliers, manufacturers, distributors, and retailers. Each link in this chain presents opportunities for errors, mismanagement, and sometimes even intentional wrongdoing.

7.1.1 Key Challenges in the Food Supply Industry

Some of the key challenges currently facing the sector include:

- Lack of Transparency: One of the most significant issues in the food supply chain is the lack of transparency among many stakeholders. Food products that go through multiple intermediaries often lose critical information about their origin, quality, and handling. This absence of transparency not only leads to inefficiencies but also makes it difficult for consumers and regulators to trace a product back to its source, especially in cases of fraud or contamination (Silva et al. 2023).
- Food Fraud: Estimates suggest that food fraud costs the global economy around $40 billion annually, highlighting its widespread impact on the industry. Instances of food fraud include mislabelling products, incorporating cheaper ingredients, or providing misleading details about a product's origin or organic status. These unethical practices pose significant risks to public health and undermine consumer confidence.
- Data Integrity and Human Errors: As data travels through the supply chain, inaccuracies, misunderstandings, and human entry errors are prevalent. These issues can lead to confusion and delays, complicating the tracking of products and ensuring that all parties involved are sharing reliable information.
- Accountability and Traceability: One of the significant challenges in the food sector is establishing comprehensive traceability, where every step of the food's journey is documented and accessible. Without a clear system to track the movement of goods and identify responsible parties at each stage, accountability diminishes, making it easier for unscrupulous individuals to introduce counterfeit products in the market.
- Complexity of the Supply Chain and Decentralization: The decentralized nature of food production and distribution adds another layer of complexity. With numerous intermediaries operating across different regions and borders, consistently enforcing regulations becomes difficult. This not only obstructs transparency but also complicates the identification of the sources of problems, especially during foodborne illness outbreaks.

Due to its decentralized and secure nature, blockchain technology has emerged as a promising solution to many challenges (Mylrea and Gourisetti 2018). A blockchain is a distributed ledger that records transactions in a transparent and unchangeable manner; once a record is added, it cannot be altered or deleted. This immutability makes blockchain an ideal technology for ensuring data integrity and transparency throughout the food supply chain. Blockchain technology can create a verifiable and clear record of every movement or transaction of food products within the supply chain. Each participant in the chain whether a farmer, supplier, processor, retailer, or others can input information about the product on the blockchain, detailing its origin, harvesting or processing methods, certifications, and more. Regulators and consumers can later utilize that information to verify the safety and authenticity of food products.

The traceability from farm to table is one of the main influences of the blockchain. It is easier now to identify the cause of the problem and take corrective measures in a food safety or fraud incident. Moreover, the ledger cannot be tampered with, making it harder for actors with bad intentions to introduce false information or otherwise modify data without detection (Caro et al. 2018).

Blockchain provides a solid base for ensuring transparency and data integrity, but the integration of AI technologies can significantly enhance this, particularly in detecting irregularities and fraudulent activities. According to Shin Morishima (2019), AI can automate and improve the process of identifying anomalies or potential fraud within the supply chain by analysing vast amounts of data and recognizing pattern.

Detecting anomalies in data entry: AI-driven methods, such as Isolation Forest and other machine learning models, can be utilized to scrutinize supplier-entered data for irregularities. These models can identify inconsistencies that may indicate fraudulent data or simple errors, such as incorrect product descriptions, altered expiration dates, or mislabelling of food ingredients. Given the massive volume of data generated at various stages of the supply chain, human oversight is often limited. AI provides a scalable and automated solution to monitor and ensure the accuracy of this data (Gulab Sanjay Rai et al. 2023).

A method for detecting anomalies or outliers is known as Isolation Forest. This technique focuses on isolating data points, unlike traditional anomaly detection methods that primarily rely on clustering or distance-based metrics. It is particularly effective for identifying anomalies in large, high-dimensional datasets. The core idea behind Isolation Forest is that anomalies are rare and usually have distinct characteristics compared to the majority of the data. Because outliers are often situated far from the clusters of normal data, they can be isolated more easily. As a result, when you randomly partition the data points, outliers tend to be separated more quickly than regular data points. This encapsulates the main concept of Isolation Forest (Mehdi Neshat et al. 2014).

7.1.2 Concepts of Isolation Forest

To grasp the concept of Isolation Forest, it's important to understand its key components and principles:

- Isolation and Partitioning: In any dataset, anomaly data points stand out from the majority. Their rarity and distinctiveness make them easier to separate or isolate. The Isolation Forest takes advantage of this characteristic by recursively dividing the dataset using randomly chosen features and split values. During this process, each data point is isolated, and outliers tend to be isolated much more rapidly than typical data points because of their unusual traits (Farhad Pourpanah et al. 2023).

- Tree Structure: A forest is built by making random splits in the dataset until each data point is separated. This forest consists of these individual trees. Normal points take more steps to be completely isolated compared to anomalies, which need fewer splits since they are usually located farther from the dense clusters of typical data.
- Path Length: The number of steps needed to isolate a specific data point. The Isolation Forest algorithm calculates how many steps are required to isolate a point across multiple trees in the forest. Typically, normal points have longer average path lengths through the trees, while anomalies, which are easier to isolate, generally have shorter average paths.
- Anomaly Score: The system determines an abnormality score for each data point by calculating the average path length across all isolation trees. According to Ling Yu and Cheng Li (2016), a higher score may indicate potential anomalies, while a lower score suggests that the data values are likely normal. The anomaly score ranges from 0 to 1. Depending on the specific application, a threshold can be established to classify points as either normal or anomalous

7.2 Literature Survey

Research in food safety and transparency addresses complex issues such as globalization and vulnerability to food fraud, emphasizing the critical need for traceability within supply chains. This study proposes using blockchain technology to safeguard data integrity and improve trust, coupled with TinyML for added security on monitoring devices. The incorporation of self-sovereign identity (SSI) minimizes single points of failure, supporting end-to-end traceability to reduce fraud and build trust in food systems (Vasileios Tsoukas et al. 2022).

Limitations of traditional supply chains in tracking origin and managing risks are highlighted in this paper, which utilizes a blockchain architecture built on semantic rules and graph data models with anomaly detection. The study demonstrates how rule-based and graph-based models in Hyperledger Sawtooth verify transaction accuracy in complex supply chains. Scenario-based simulations further illustrate the system's capability to detect anomalies and enhance visibility (Keru Duan et al. 2024).

Focusing on consumer health and regulatory compliance, this comprehensive study explores AI and ML applications in food safety and quality. Computer vision, NLP, and deep learning technologies are used for real-time monitoring, defect detection, and anomaly identification. While the paper notes challenges in model interpretability and data privacy, it emphasizes AI's potential for detecting allergens, infections, and contaminants. Future directions highlight personalized nutrition, autonomous monitoring, and AI/ML integration to ensure food safety (Volkan Dedeoglu et al. 2023).

This research investigates the potential of blockchain technology for accountability and traceability to combat food fraud. It addresses adoption challenges, including data accuracy, scalability, and interoperability, while examining both theoretical and practical applications. Emphasizing blockchain's potential to eliminate fraud and increase transparency, the study advocates for further research on integrating blockchain with IoT and AI to enhance data integrity and visibility (Pallathadka et al. 2022).

Examining edge computing, blockchain, and AI in digitizing food supply chains, this chapter advocates for Edge AI over traditional cloud computing to improve data security and reduce latency. Focusing on traceability, the study suggests smartphone-integrated sensors for recognizing unique food signatures, enabling real-time data processing on edge devices. Edge AI's role in achieving scalability and privacy sets a foundation for resilient digital supply chains (Ugo Santosuosso et al. 2020).

Exploring AI and ML applications in agricultural optimization and food production, this review discusses advancements in supply chain management, disease detection, smart irrigation, and crop selection. Emphasizing the need for efficiency to meet rising food demands with minimal waste, the paper outlines supervised and unsupervised learning's contributions to improved processing and transportation in food systems (Zhang et al. 2024).

According to V. Anantha Krishnan and N. Senthil Kumar (2022), Isolation Forest is presented as an effective technique for detecting anomalies in geospatial data related to invasive species distribution, as illustrated by its application in mapping the dispersal of Drosophila suzukii. The study demonstrates Isolation Forest's predictive capability and suitability for analyzing large ecological datasets, aiding in identifying potential invasion hotspots.

Introducing an optimized Isolation Forest model for anomaly detection in network security, this paper incorporates the Artificial Fish Swarming Algorithm (AFSA) for enhanced performance. By adjusting isolation tree weights, the AFSA-boosted model significantly improves detection accuracy, as evidenced by increased AUC scores on ODDS and NSL-KDD datasets, positioning it as a robust network intrusion detection system (Ruochen Jin et al. 2021).

According to Tsuyoshi Ide (2018), utilizing a hybrid model of Isolation Forest and Garra Rufa Fish Optimization, this paper explores controller parameter tuning in microgrids. Enhanced functionality of Voltage Source Converters supports sustainable and stable microgrid operation, demonstrating that this approach outperforms alternative algorithms in maintaining system stability and providing a theoretical framework for renewable energy management.

The summary of the related work is shown in the Table 7.1.

7.3 Proposed Methodology

A bi-objective optimization model for a food supply chain management system that uses blockchain and Isolation Forest is developed. This model tries to provide as much transparency as possible into the Supply Chain along with the efficiency of anomaly detection and correction. The Isolation Forest algorithm is continually scanning the data for any anomalies, and the blockchain makes sure that the data is

Table 7.1. Summary of Related Work.

Paper Reference	Algorithm Used	Merits	Demerits
Vasileios Tsoukas et al. 2022	Blockchain, TinyML, SSI	Enhances traceability and transparency; strengthens data integrity and consumer trust	Implementation costs; reliance on stable technology
Keru Duan et al. 2024	Blockchain with Semantic Rules & Graph Models	Improves transaction accuracy; effectively detects anomalies; enhances supply chain visibility	Complexity in system setup; high data integration requirements
Volkan Dedeoglu et al. 2023	AI & ML (Computer Vision, NLP, Deep Learning)	Real-time monitoring and defect detection; can identify allergens and contaminants; improves safety	Issues with model interpretability; privacy concerns
Pallathadka et al. 2022	Blockchain	Ensures accountability and transparency; potential to eliminate fraud; increases trust in the supply chain	Scalability, data accuracy, and interoperability challenges
Ugo Santosuosso et al. 2020	Edge AI	Low latency and better data security; improves traceability through sensor technology on edge devices	Limited computing power at edge; dependency on sensor accuracy
Zhang et al. 2024	AI & ML (Supervised and Unsupervised Learning)	Optimizes agricultural processes; boosts productivity; reduces waste in food production	High data requirements; potential over-reliance on technology
V. Anantha Krishnan and N. Senthil Kumar	Isolation Forest	Effective anomaly detection for large ecological datasets; can identify hotspots for invasive species	May require high computational power; specific to geographical data
Ruochen Jin et al. 2021	Isolation Forest with AFSA	Enhanced detection accuracy for network security; boosts AUC scores; efficient as a network IDS	Increased complexity with AFSA; might need significant tuning
Tsuyoshi Ide (2018)	Isolation Forest with Garra Rufa Fish Optimization	Improves microgrid stability; effective for renewable energy control; robust under varied conditions	Complexity in algorithm integration; requires precise tuning

kept secure and untouched at every node in the network, so that at each step along the supply chain, the records remain uncorrupted and undefiled. This optimization model could be created as follows:

7.3.1 System Framework of BFSM

Today's food supply chain with production, processing, distribution, and retail all changing so frequently, demands data management at every level to provide food safety, traceability, and quality. This paper describes a system for Food Supply Chain Management (BFSM) using Blockchain and Isolation Forest, which utilizes Isolation

Forest along with blockchain which is used to store data in a tamper-proof and immutable way, ensuring that the integrity of data is preserved all the way through the chain. Preprocessing, anomaly detection, prediction and data collection are some of the main modules of the BFSM system.

The BFSM framework is composed of interconnected modules to ensure end-to-end traceability and data integrity throughout the food supply chain (Figure 7.1). Below is a description of the primary functions of each module:

7.3.1.1 Data Collection Module

This is a module that collects data in the raw form from the farm level, processing level, and distribution level of the supply chain. Blockchain will also record everything from where the product originated to temperature, humidity, etc. This module provides the basis for anomaly detection and traceability.

7.3.1.2 Data Preprocessing Module

Preprocessing cleans and organizes raw data, handling missing values, removing irrelevant information, and standardizing entries. Effective feature extraction is performed to extract useful information such as time stamps, location data, and quality metrics, which are necessary inputs for the Isolation Forest anomaly detection model.

7.3.1.3 Isolation Forest Module

The Isolation Forest algorithm is applied to detect anomalies in real-time, flagging unusual data points that may indicate fraud or discrepancies in product information. Isolation Forest is particularly suited to detecting outliers by isolating data points that differ significantly from normal patterns. This module plays a crucial role in identifying any data inconsistencies at each stage of the supply chain.

7.3.1.4 Prediction Module

This module leverages historical data and anomaly detection insights to forecast potential issues in the supply chain, such as sudden demand spikes or supply bottlenecks. Predictive capabilities allow for proactive decision-making, ensuring that data anomalies are corrected before they impact supply chain operations.

The model must satisfy the following constraints:

i. **Supply Demand Constraint:** The amount of product data demanded at node p*p* must not exceed the recorded requirements across the network.

ii. **Inter-node Data Integrity Constraint:** The ratio of validated data between nodes can vary to reflect different stages' requirements for transparency.

iii. **Node Availability Constraint:** Only the participating supply chain nodes can record or supply data, and no other nodes can interfere.

iv. **Data Entry Constraint:** The output data (e.g., validated records) cannot exceed the verified data input, maintaining data integrity at each node.

v. **Inventory Non-negativity Constraint:** Inventory of validated data at any node cannot be negative at any time, ensuring that data entries meet minimum consistency standards.

These constraints ensure that the blockchain and Isolation Forest algorithm work cohesively to manage food supply chain data with high traceability and minimal anomalies, thereby ensuring a reliable and transparent system is shown as in Figure 7.1.

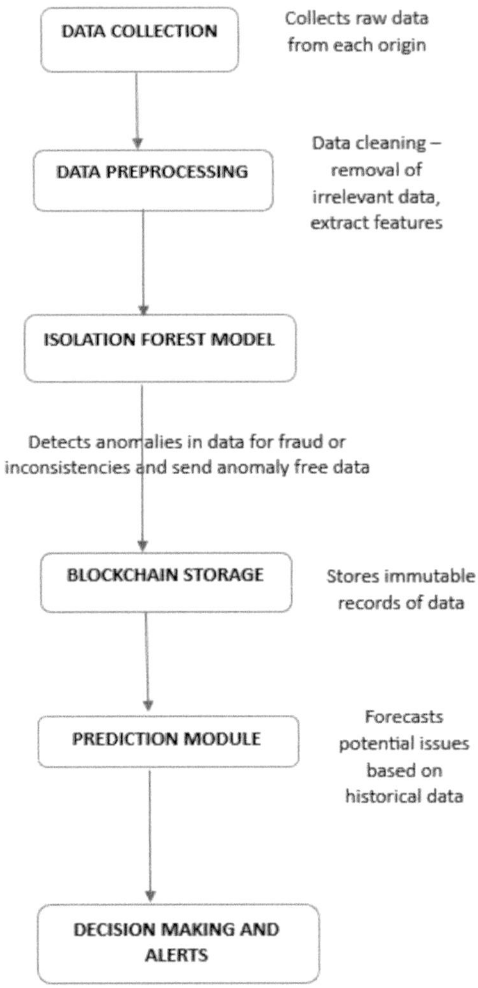

Figure 7.1. BFSM Work Flow.

7.3.2 Optimization Model for Food Supply Management

In food supply chain management, maintaining transparency and product quality at each stage of the process (farming, processing, distribution, and retail) is crucial. Let's denote:

- up(t): The input amount of food products at a supply chain node at time t.
- dp(t): The output amount of food products at a supply chain node at time t.
- f1(t): The condition of data consistency and traceability on the blockchain, representing the data validation rate using Isolation Forest.
- f2(t): The transparency score of transactions, which could represent the number of anomaly-free transactions or trusted data entries at node p.

Jointly considering these two factors, the following two-objective optimization model can be proposed based on equations.

7.3.2.1 Objective Functions

i. **Data Consistency and Traceability (Objective f1(t)):**

The more frequently data is validated at each supply chain stage using Isolation Forest, the higher the data consistency score f1(t).

Consistency improves when data is continuously monitored for anomalies, allowing quick identification and correction, ensuring data integrity across blockchain nodes.

ii. **Transparency and Trust in Transactions (Objective f2(t)):**

A higher transparency score f2(t) reflects the number of validated, anomaly-free transactions, which builds trust among supply chain participants.

The value of f2(t) increases when data anomalies are minimal, thanks to accurate detection by the Isolation Forest model, ensuring reliable data at each node.

The optimization model is represented as follows (Equation 1):

$$\text{Maximize } Z = \alpha f1(t) + \beta f2(t) \tag{1}$$

where α and β are weights for each objective, depending on the priority of data consistency or transaction transparency.

iii. **Anomaly Detection in Data Transactions**

Isolation Forest anomaly detection model flags outliers by evaluating whether a transaction's data (e.g., temperature, humidity, origin) falls within the typical range based on historical data patterns.

Thus, the number of products recorded as safe or verified increases with a higher output dp(t), which is defined as:

$$dp(t) \propto f2(t) \tag{2}$$

Simultaneously, when more anomalies are detected, the supply chain must supplement this information with verified data to maintain trust.

Therefore:

$$up(t) \approx dp(t) \tag{3}$$

Combining Equations 2 and 3, we find that the objectives f1(t) and f2(t) are aligned rather than opposing, allowing for simultaneous optimization of both transparency and consistency without trade-offs.

7.3.3 Feature Extraction Using AFSA

A hybrid methodology of the Artificial Fish Swarm Algorithm (AFSA) and Isolation Forest is proposed to detect the anomaly and fraud in the food supply chain. Isolation Forest works by finding anomalies in the isolated patterns, but AFSA improves the feature extraction.

Unexpected shipping volumes, drastic temperature changes, and inconsistencies at the point of origin are just a few of the more subtle yet important aspects of the data that this hybrid model is able to pick up on that may suggest fraudulent activity or simply bad data.

AFSA's formulas, procedures, and operational framework works in a way that is specifically relevant to the food supply chain is detailed below in the (Figure 7.2).

- Xi: The current position of fish i, representing a solution vector (a set of features).
- Yi: The fitness or value of position Xi, which in our context is calculated by the Isolation Forest score (or other anomaly scoring mechanism) indicating anomaly likelihood.
- V: Visual distance, representing the range within which a fish can perceive food (anomaly-indicative features).
- δ: Crowding factor threshold to avoid crowded positions, maintaining exploration of different features.
- α: Step size, controlling the magnitude of movement towards better solutions.
- n: Number of fish (solutions) in the swarm.
- m: Maximum number of iterations for the algorithm to converge.

Figure 7.2 below details AFSA's formulas, procedures, and operational framework as they specifically apply to the food supply chain. Each behaviour has specific equations, which we'll adapt to the anomaly detection model.

7.3.3.1 Prey Behaviour

The prey behaviour enables each fish to search locally within its visual range V for positions with higher anomaly likelihood.

If a fish i at position Xi has a neighbouring position Xj with higher anomaly detection score, it moves toward Xj based on the following Equation 4:

$$Xi = Xi + \alpha \times \frac{(Xj - Xi)}{|Xj - Xi|} \tag{4}$$

α is the step size to control the movement.

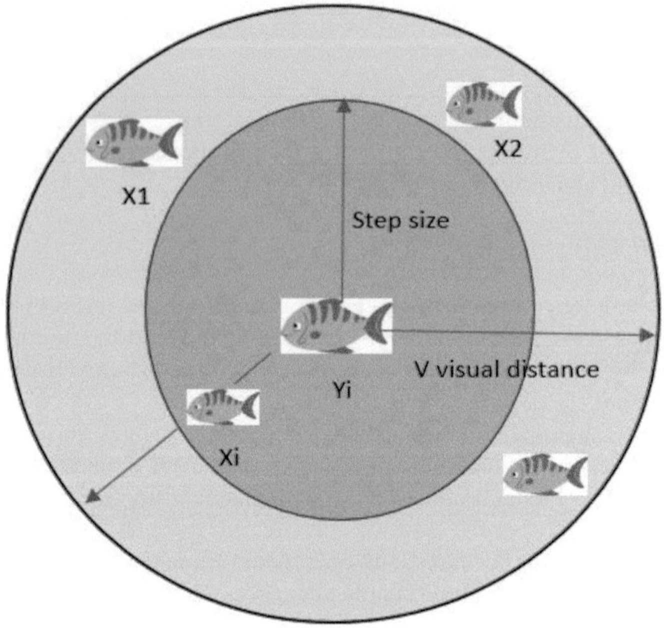

Figure 7.2. AFSA visual representation.

|Xj−Xi| is the Euclidean distance between positions Xi and Xj, ensuring the movement direction is toward better anomaly-indicating positions.

7.3.3.2 Follow Behaviour

In the follow behaviour, each fish compares its score with other fish within its visual range VV and moves toward the position with the highest score if that area is not overcrowded as shown in Equation 5.

If there exists a position Xj with a higher score Yj within the visual range, and the fish density around Xj(i.e., number of nearby fish) is below δ, then:

$$Xi=Xi+\alpha\times\frac{(Xj-Xi)}{|Xj-Xi|} \quad (5)$$

Otherwise, the fish continues to search independently using prey behaviour.

7.3.3.3 Swarm Behaviour

In swarm behaviour, the fish move toward the centre of a group if that centre yields a higher fitness value and is not overcrowded, encouraging cooperation among fish to search efficiently as shown in Equation 6.
Define the centre of a group Xcentre as:

$$Xcentre=\frac{1}{n}\sum_{i=1}^{n}Xi \quad (6)$$

If the fitness value Ycentre at Xcentre better than Yi and meets the crowding factor δ, then fish i*i* updates its position as shown in Equation 7:

$$Xi = Xi + \alpha \times \frac{(Xcentre - Xi)}{|Xcentre - Xi|} \quad (7)$$

7.3.3.4 Leap Behaviour

When the fish become trapped in local optima, the leap behaviour is used to move them to a random position within the search space, enhancing global exploration as shown in Equation 8.
The leap update is defined as:

$$Xi = Xrand \quad (8)$$

where Xrand is a randomly selected position in the feature space, providing diversity in the search.

7.3.4 Role of Blockchain

An anomaly detection system on a blockchain with Hyperledger Fabric in the food supply chain is a permissioned network that ensures data security and data transparency among trusted supply chain partners.

Hyperledger Fabric: This permissioned blockchain technology enables modular architecture and is intended for enterprise use. It offers:

- Access control to manage the roles and permissions of participants.
- Utilizing a quick consensus procedure to process transactions efficiently.
- Support for business rule automation with smart contracts, often known as chaincode (Nalayini et al. 2024).
- Data privacy by preventing unauthorized nodes from accessing sensitive data.

Network Design: Each of the major players in the supply chain, such as farmers, suppliers, processors, warehouses, distributors, and retailers, is represented by a node in the network.

Node Organization:

Peer Nodes: Peer nodes in every business, from farms to warehouses, verify and approve transactions.

Ordering Service: Keeps a single view of the transaction history everywhere and regulates the order of transactions. Hyperledger Fabric uses a fast, fault tolerant method called Raft Consensus to do this ordering without consuming too many processing resources.

Channels: If certain data is not meant to be visible to the whole network, channels allow groups of players (farmers and suppliers, for example) to trade on private, segregated ledgers. It's an ideal setup for controlling sensitive product data without compromising the overall network transparency.

Block Organization

Every block includes:

Transaction Data: Timestamps, location, temperature, humidity, transfer information and everything else about every product.

Metadata: The time, the participant ID, and the digital signature of each transaction, for traceability.

Details of Smart Contract Execution: Here are noted temperature thresholds and other conditions verified by the smart contract, for use by the anomaly detection system.

Storage of Ledgers:

World State Database: Every asset (product) on the blockchain is maintained by a key-value store, CouchDB with Hyperledger is the most common. This makes it possible to obtain current product information quickly (e.g., current location, quality state).

To make sure that quality checks or transport conditions (among other things) are written into the ledger of the past, the blockchain stores an immutable, historical record of each transaction.

Information Recovery

World State Database searching: Querying CouchDB over specific asset attributes (product ID, location, or time) allows for accessing the data in real-time and querying for anomalies.

Event Listeners: Event listeners instantly alert nodes to updates. For instance, if the network can issue alerts and quickly look up transaction information in case a temperature shift occurs during transit.

Smart Contracts

The purpose of Chaincode (smart contracts) is to take over all of the anomaly detection specifications and commercial activities such as checking that the humidity and temperature are maintained within acceptable levels during transport. The main objective of chaincode is to call upon feature extraction algorithm and the isolation forest model build for this purpose.

Execution: Every transaction is compared to predetermined rules by the chaincode. It flags a transaction as anomalous, for instance, if a temperature measurement in the transit phase falls outside an allowed interval.

Upon detection of rule violations, the chaincode triggers automatic measures (such as notifying relevant parties, or logging the event as an irregularity).

The smart contract detects anomalies by comparing current data with baseline values for the specified product and area. The smart contract stamps the entry as an outlier and highlights it in the ledger if the values fall outside acceptable ranges.

7.4 Results and Discussion

To improve anomaly detection in the food supply chain, the suggested hybrid model combines blockchain technology with the Isolation Forest model and the Artificial Fish Swarm Algorithm (AFSM). This system's main purpose is to spot irregularities in data gathered from several sources, guaranteeing food safety and supply chain transparency.

7.4.1 Tool and Technology Stack

The proposed anomaly detection model was developed using the following tools and technologies:

Programming Language: Python 3.8.10

Libraries:

- Scikit-learn: For implementing the Isolation Forest algorithm.
- Pandas: For data manipulation and analysis.
- NumPy: For numerical operations.
- Blockchain Framework: Hyperledger Fabric for the blockchain implementation, ensuring secure and transparent data storage.

The model leverages blockchain technology to maintain immutable records of the data collected, allowing for real-time monitoring and traceability within the food supply chain.

7.4.2 Dataset Overview

The dataset utilized for training and testing the proposed model comprises sensor data collected from multiple stages of the food supply chain. The total dataset includes 12,500 records, categorized into three main classes:

- Normal Conditions: 5,000 records where temperature, humidity, and other parameters are within safe limits.
- Anomalous Conditions (Spoilage): 4,500 records indicating potential spoilage due to deviations in temperature or humidity.
- Anomalous Conditions (Contamination): 3,000 records showing contamination risks, such as improper handling or packaging failures.

A breakdown of the dataset is shown in Table 7.2, highlighting the distribution across the different categories.

Table 7.2. Sample of data used.

Category	Number of Records
Normal Conditions	5,000
Anomalous Conditions (Spoilage)	4,500
Anomalous Conditions (Contamination)	3,000
Total	12,500

7.4.3 Evaluation Criteria

The model's performance was evaluated based on its capacity to detect abnormalities in a dataset of sensor data pertaining to food production and distribution in order to gauge the efficacy of the suggested anomaly detection system. The model was trained to discriminate between normal and anomalous measurements with great accuracy after the dataset was carefully annotated to reflect these categories.

Confusion Matrix Analysis: To show how well the model classified data, a confusion matrix was made. As indicated in Table 7.3, this matrix offers information on true positive, true negative, false positive, and false negative rates.

Table 7.3. Confusion Matrix for Anomaly Detection.

PREDICTION	CATEGORY	GROUND TRUTH	
		POSITIVE	NEGATIVE
	Positive (false data found)	TP	FP
	Negative (data is true)	TN	FN

True Positives (TP): Correctly identified anomalies.
True Negatives (TN): Correctly identified normal readings.
False Positives (FP): Normal readings incorrectly flagged as anomalies.
False Negatives (FN): Anomalies missed by the model.

With an overall accuracy of 95%, the model demonstrated its effectiveness in detecting anomalies related to food safety, thereby mitigating potential health risks to consumers.

7.4.3.1 Performance Metrics

Performance metrics are clearly depicted in the Equations 9–12.

- Precision: This metric measures the accuracy of the positive predictions made by the model. It is calculated as the ratio of true positives (TP) to the sum of true positives and false positives (FP):

$$\text{Precision} = \frac{TP}{TP + FP} \tag{9}$$

- Recall: Also referred to as sensitivity, recall quantifies the model's capacity to recognize every pertinent incident.

The ratio of true positives to the total of true positives and false negatives (FN) is how it is computed:

$$\text{Recall} = \frac{TP}{TP + FN} \tag{10}$$

- F1-Score: The F1-score is a single score that strikes a balance between precision and recall, calculated as the harmonic mean of the two variables:

$$\text{F1}=2 \times \frac{Precision \times recall}{Precision+recall} \tag{11}$$

- Accuracy: The ratio of the total number of predictions to the sum of true positives and true negatives (TN) indicates the model's overall soundness.

$$\text{Accuracy}= \frac{TP+TN}{TP+TN+FP+FN} \tag{12}$$

7.4.4 Comparison Analysis

Two traditional anomaly detection techniques, namely Support Vector Machines (SVM) and k-Nearest Neighbours (k-NN), were extensively compared with the proposed hybrid model to validate its effectiveness. This comparison was to assess the performance of the proposed model with significant performance measures like accuracy, precision, recall and F1-score. The results of the comparison are described in detail in the sections that follow, as well as the reasons why the hybrid model is superior.

The performance metrics for each model are summarized in Table 7.4, highlighting the differences between the proposed model and traditional techniques:

The performance characteristics of the suggested anomaly detection model utilizing Isolation Forest and the Artificial Fish Swarm Algorithm (AFSA) are displayed in this comparison chart (Figure 7.3) alongside more conventional methods like Support Vector Machines (SVM) and k-Nearest Neighbours (k-NN).

7.5 Conclusion

To sum up, the combination of blockchain technology and artificial intelligence offers a revolutionary way to address persistent issues in the food supply chain. Industrialisation has made the food system more complex, and with it the pressure for openness and responsibility. Food fraud and counterfeiting cases pose greater risks to public health and economic security.

With blockchain, the suggested approach provides an unchallengeable and transparent ledger of every stage of production, creating accountability and trust. At the same time, analysing data from various sources, from databases to internet of

Table 7.4. Comparison Result.

Technique	Precision	Recall	F1-Score	Accuracy
Proposed Model (Isolation Forest + AFSM)	0.940	0.925	0.932	0.935
SVM	0.850	0.840	0.845	0.845
k-NN	0.820	0.810	0.815	0.815

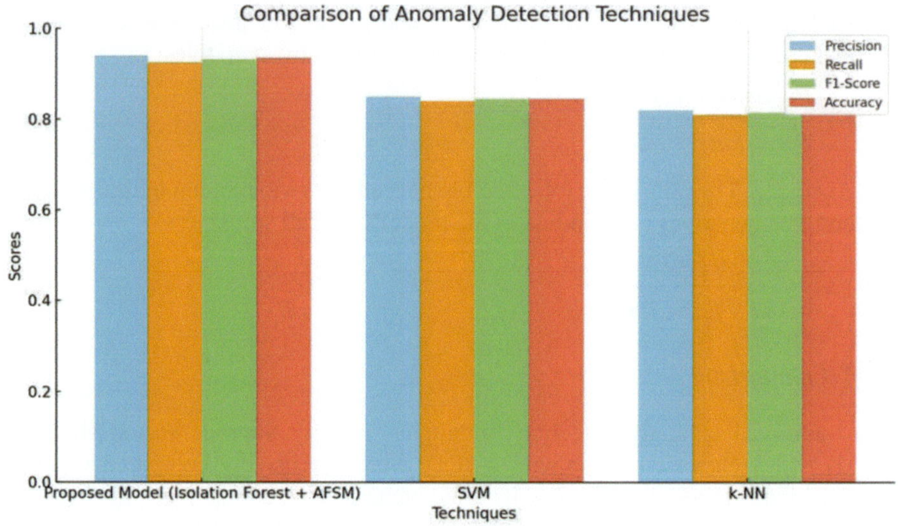

Figure 7.3. Performance comparison of proposed model versus several other models.

things sensors, AI-powered anomaly and fraud detection in the food supply chain, a hybrid methodology of the Artificial Fish Swarm Algorithm (AFSA) and Isolation Forest - enables the system to rapidly spot and track the movement of contamination. Their prediction powers and the tracking powers of blockchain make supply chains more efficient and secure, by allowing for swift risk response, and protecting consumers.

Collectively, these technologies create a more secure and more transparent food supply chain, one that builds consumer trust and safeguards the integrity and expansion of the sector in a volatile global market.

References

Anantha Krishnan, V., and Senthil Kumar, N. (2022). Robust soft computing control algorithm for sustainable enhancement of renewable energy sources based microgrid: A hybrid Garra rufa fish optimization – Isolation forest approach, Sustainable Computing: Informatics and Systems, Volume 35, 100764, ISSN 2210-5379, https://doi.org/10.1016/j.suscom.2022.100764.

Caro, M. P., M. S. Ali, M. Vecchio, and R. Giaffreda (2018). Blockchain-based traceability in Agri-Food supply chain management: A practical implementation. IoT Vertical and Topical Summit on Agriculture - Tuscany (IOT Tuscany), Tuscany, Italy, pp. 1–4, doi: 10.1109/IOT-TUSCANY.2018.8373021.

Farhad Pourpanah, Ran Wang, Chee Peng Lim, Xi-Zhao Wang and Danial Yazdani. (2023). A review of artificial fish swarm algorithms: recent advances and applications, Artificial Intelligence Review 56, 1867–1903. https://doi.org/10.1007/s10462-022-10214-4.

Gulab Sanjay Rai, S. B. Goyal and Prasenjit Chatterje. (2023). Anomaly Detection in Blockchain Using Machine Learning, Computational Intelligence for Engineering and Management Applications. Lecture Notes in Electrical Engineering, vol 984. Springer, Singapore. https://doi.org/10.1007/978-981-19-8493-8_37.

Jinoh Kim, Nakashima, M., Fan, W., Wuthier, S., Zhou, X., Kim, I. et al. (2022). A machine learning approach to anomaly detection based on traffic monitoring for secure blockchain networking," IEEE Transactions on Network and Service Management, 19(3): 3619–3632, Sept.

Jinoh Kim, Makiya Nakashima, Wenjun Fan, Simeon Wuthier, Xiaobo Zhou, and Ikkyun Kim (2021). Anomaly Detection based on Traffic Monitoring for Secure Blockchain Networking. IEEE International Conference on Blockchain and Cryptocurrency (ICBC), Sydney, Australia, 2021, pp. 1–9, doi: 10.1109/ICBC51069.2021.9461119.

Keru Duan, Helen Onyeaka, and Gu Pang (2024). Leveraging blockchain to tackle food fraud: Innovations and obstacles, Journal of Agriculture and Food Research, Volume 18, 101429, ISSN 2666–1543, https://doi.org/10.1016/j.jafr.2024.101429.

Ling Yu, and Cheng Li. (2016). A Global Artificial Fish Swarm Algorithm for Structural Damage Detection. Advances in Structural Engineering, 17(3): 331–346. Doi: 10.1260/1369-4332.17.3.331.

Mylrea, M., and Gourisetti, S. N. G. (2018). Blockchain for Supply Chain Cybersecurity, Optimization and Compliance. Resilience Week (RWS), Denver, CO, USA, pp. 70–76, doi: 10.1109/RWEEK.2018.8473517.

Mehdi Neshat, Ghodrat Sepidnam, Mahdi Sargolzaei, Adel N. Toosi. (2014). Artificial fish swarm algorithm: a survey of the state-of-the-art, hybridization, combinatorial and indicative applications. Artificial Intelligence Review, 42: 965–997. https://doi.org/10.1007/s10462-012-9342-2.

Nalayini, C. M., Jeevaa Katiravan, and Thanga Akilanm V. (2024). Car Insurance Blockchain", Blockchain Technology in the Automotive Industry, DOI: 10.1201/9781003450306-5, August 2024.

Pallathadka, H., Jawarneh, M., Sammy, F., Garchar, V., Sanchez, D. T., and Naved, M. (2022). A Review of Using Artificial Intelligence and Machine Learning in Food and Agriculture Industry,", 2nd International Conference on Advance Computing and Innovative Technologies in Engineering (ICACITE), Greater Noida, India, pp. 2215–2218, doi: 10.1109/ICACITE53722.2022.9823427.

Ruochen Jin, Bo Wei, Yongmei Luo, Tao Ren, and Ruoqian Wu. (2021). Blockchain-based data collection with efficient anomaly detection for estimating battery state-of-health. In IEEE Sensors Journal, 21(12): 13455–13465, 15 June15, doi: 10.1109/JSEN.2021.3066785.

Shin Morishima (2019), "Scalable Anomaly Detection Method for Blockchain Transactions using GPU" ,20th International Conference on Parallel and Distributed Computing, Applications and Technologies (PDCAT), Gold Coast, QLD, Australia, pp. 160-165, doi: 10.1109/PDCAT46702.2019.00039.

Silva, Alef Vinicius Cardoso E., Giuntini, Felipe Taliar, Ranieri, Caetano Mazzoni, Meneguette, Rodolfo Ipolito, Garcia, Rodrigo Dutra, Ramachandran, Gowri Sankar, Krishnamachari, Bhaskar, & Ueyama, Jó. (2023). MADCS: A Middleware for Anomaly Detection and Content Sharing for Blockchain-Based Systems. Journal of Network and Systems Management, 31(3), Article number: 46. https://doi.org/10.1007/s10922-023-09736-1.

Tsuyoshi Ide. (2018). Collaborative anomaly detection on blockchain from noisy sensor data. IEEE International Conference on Data Mining Workshops (ICDMW), Singapore, pp. 120–127, doi: 10.1109/ICDMW.2018.00024.

Ugo Santosuosso, Alessandro Cini, Alessio Papini. (2020). Tracing outliers in the dataset of Drosophila suzukii records with the Isolation Forest method. Journal of Big Data 7, 14, https://doi.org/10.1186/s40537-020-00288-8.

Vasileios Tsoukas, Anargyros Gkogkidis, Aikaterini Kampa, Georgios Spathoulas, and Athanasios Kakarountas. (2022). A. Enhancing Food Supply Chain Security through the Use of Blockchain and TinyML. Information, 13(5): 213. https://doi.org/10.3390/info13050213.

Volkan Dedeoglu, Sidra Malik, Gowri Ramachandran, Shantanu Pal, and Raja Jurdak. (2023). Chapter Nine - Blockchain meets edge-AI for food supply chain traceability and provenance, Analytical Chemistry, Elsevier,Volume 101, Pages 251–275, ISSN 0166-526X,ISBN 9780443134050,https://doi.org/10.1016/bs.coac.2022.12.001.

Zhang, C., Shen, W., Wang, S. and Wu, Y. (2024). Network Anomaly Detection Algorithm Based on Fusion of Artificial Fish Swarming and Isolation Forest. 5th International Conference on Computer Engineering and Application (ICCEA), Hangzhou, China, pp. 238–242, doi: 10.1109/ICCEA62105.2024.10603987.

CHAPTER 8

Experimental Study of Solar Microgrid with AI and Block Chain based Energy Storage Optimization

An Analysis

Renugadevi P.,[1] *Sudha A.,*[2,*] *Srimathi R.,*[3] *Saranya P.*[4] and *Yuvaraja T.*[5]

8.1 Introduction

Artificial Intelligence is used to improve energy production for more effective systems, such as solar, wind turbine, biomass generation. Predictive maintenance and classification algorithms may be used in this way to increase energy output. For renewable energy systems, artificial intelligence and block chain technology are essential components. These technologies are employed to maximize power grids automatic generation control, particularly when managing energy fluctuations from sporadic renewable energy sources. There are several ways that Machine Learning (ML) is being applied to enhance energy storage in renewable energy sources (Takruri et al. 2019). Here are some instances of machine learning methods being applied in this way. Through the prediction of energy demand patterns and

[1] School of Computer Science and Engineering, Vellore Institute of Technology, Chennai, Tamil Nadu, 600 127, India.
Email: renugadevi.2020@vitstudent.ac.in
[2] Centre for Smart Grid Technologies, School of Computer Science and Engineering, Vellore Institute of Technology, Chennai, Tamil Nadu, 600 127, India.
[3] School of Electrical Engineering, Vellore Institute of Technology, Chennai, Tamil Nadu, 600 127, India.
Email: srimathi.r@vit.ac.in
[4] Department of Computer Science and Engineering, REVA University, Bengaluru, Karnataka, 560064, India.
Email: saranya.p@reva.edu.in
[5] Department of Electrical Engineering, American International University, Saad Al Abdullah, 164101, Kuwait.
Email: teekaraman@aiu.edu.kw
* Corresponding author: sudha.a@vit.ac.in

DOI: 10.1201/9781003540328-8

the guarantee of optimal usage, machine learning algorithms can optimize energy storage systems, including batteries. This facilitates the seamless incorporation of renewable energy sources into the grid, decreasing the requirement for traditional backup power generation and enhancing the overall stability of the energy grid. The dependability and effectiveness of energy storage technologies are being improved through the application of machine learning. These technologies use algorithms that can forecast, identify patterns, and analyze enormous amounts of data in order to improve the stability and efficiency of an electrical distribution system. Reinforcement learning with cyclic time-dependent learning is being used in machine learning to control battery energy storage. By optimizing energy storage and raising the accuracy of energy forecasts, machine learning algorithms are used to improve solar panel performance and storage facilities (Liu et al. 2022). The goal of machine learning models is to achieve optimal energy storage to meet grid demands while lowering operating costs. Machine learning is used to determine the best solar panel arrangement, utilizing historical satellite data and current weather to maximize energy production without the need for extra panels. The renewable energy industry greatly benefits from ML, which has a wide range of uses and advantages. Effective resource harvesting, storing, converting, and managing is being researched and developed faster thanks to ML techniques.

8.2 Non-conventional Energy Source

Non-conventional energy sources refer to those that do not originate from traditional fossil fuels, including natural gas, oil, and coal. They are also known as renewable or alternative energy sources (Kerdphol et al. 2016). In general, these energy sources are more ecologically friendly and sustainable. Here are a few important sources of non-conventional-energy. Solar power is obtained from the sun through the use of solar thermal systems or photovoltaic cells used to power gadgets, heat, and produce electricity. Wind power is produced by wind turbines, which transform wind energy from kinetic to electrical energy. Ideal for regions with strong, regular wind patterns. Hydro electricity is derived from the force of flowing water, which is typically achieved by damming rivers and using the flow to power turbines. Scalable, ranging from massive hydroelectric dams to tiny hydro projects. Thermal energy from Earth uses heat from the interior of the Earth, usually from geothermal wells or hot springs. It can be used to generate electricity and for applications involving direct heating (Kerdphol et al. 2016). Biomass power is made from natural resources such as animal and plant waste. It can be used to produce biogas, burned straight for heat, or transformed into biofuels (such as ethanol and biodiesel). Wave and tidal-power are produced by how waves and tides move across oceans and seas. It makes use of wave energy converters and tidal turbines to generate electricity. Hydrogen Powered Energy are formed through the electrolysis or other process of separating water into hydrogen and oxygen.

8.3 Literature Review

The blockchain platform can enable decentralized coordination and control of distributed energy resources in the power grid. Blockchain allows DERs like solar inverters, EV chargers, and energy storage to participate directly in grid operations without relying on a centralized authority. Smart contracts on the blockchain can automate coordination procedures and transactions between these distributed grid assets (Bordihn et al. 2022). The platform, which is based on blockchain technology, enables direct energy trading between the power grid and the prosumers (Energy-generated by consumers). Prosumers can use smart contracts to autonomously buy and sell energy without intermediaries, improving the economics of distributed energy generation. This enables better integration of renewable energy sources and provides new revenue streams for prosumers (Faniar and Şeker 2023). The integrity and traceability of energy-related transactions and data in the smart grid can be guaranteed by the blockchain's distributed ledger and cryptographic security. This enhances the security and auditability of grid operations compared to centralized databases. Smart contracts can automatically execute energy trades and settlements based on predefined rules, reducing the potential for errors or manipulation. Blockchain's decentralized architecture can help the grid scale to handle the growing number of distributed energy assets and high-frequency transactions, overcoming the limitations of centralized control. The consensus mechanisms and peer-to-peer nature of blockchain networks can enable the grid to coordinate the activities of numerous prosumers and DERs without a central point of failure (Datta et al. 2023).

8.4 Interoperability and Integration

Blockchain can serve as a common, interoperable platform for integrating various smart grid components and enabling seamless data exchange. The modular design of blockchain systems, with distinct networking, identity, consensus, and application layers, allows integration with existing grid infrastructure and communication protocols. This facilitates the integration of blockchain-based applications with legacy grid systems and enables a gradual transition towards a more decentralized grid architecture (Ram et al. 2020) and the various articles can be summarized in Table 8.1.

Table 8.1. Various Literature Review.

Article title	Technology	Advantages	Disadvantages
Blockchain as Key Enabling Technology for Future Electric Energy Exchange (Wang et al. 2024)	Blockchain-based system for DER control and decentralized coordination.	Decentralized coordination and control of DERs.	Potential scalability challenges.
A Privacy-Friendly Gaming Framework in Smart Electricity and Water Grids (Huang et al. 2022)	Blockchain-based gaming framework for water grid and smart grid applications that protects privacy.	Preserves user privacy through zero-knowledge proofs and anonymous credentials	Complexity in implementing cryptographic primitives.
S-BAN:Secure Blockchain-Based Anonymous Networking Strategy for DSM (Hu and Wang 2012).	An anonymous networking approach based on blockchain for DSM privacy protection	Ensures privacy through anonymous credentials and ring signatures.	Complexity in implementing cryptographic primitives.
V2GNet:Robust Blockchain-Based Energy-Trading method (Behmann et al. 2023)	Architecture for V2G networks that uses blockchain technology for energy trade.	Smart contract-based energy transfers that are transparent and safe.	Reliance on user participation and reputation mechanisms.

In summary, the papers present different blockchain-based approaches to address challenges in energy trading, grid coordination, and privacy preservation in smart grid and V2G applications. While the technologies show promise, the practical implementation and adoption of these frameworks in the power sector will require further research and development to address the identified challenges.

8.4.1 Integration of Blockchain and other Advances Techniques with Existing Smart Grid Infrastructure

Meta-heuristic algorithms are employed to optimize smart grid operations by utilizing techniques such as simulated annealing, genetic algorithms, and particle swarm optimization. Table 8.2 explains the comparison of case studies of smart grid system using recent technologies and Table 8.3 explains the different optimization aspects in smart grid systems. This approach is designed to improve the efficiency, sustainability, and reliability of smart grid operations. These algorithms can be used for: Optimizing distribution of electricity load across the grid to minimize peak demand and overall energy consumption. Quickly identifying faults or abnormalities in the grid and rerouting power to maintain stability. Optimizing the integration of renewable energy sources, such as wind, solar, biomass into the grid to optimize their utilization. Optimizing responses to changes in electricity demand in real-time, often leveraging consumer participation and incentives. Efficiently managing smaller, localized grids within a larger smart grid system.

8.5 Solar Microgrid

A localized energy system that can operate independently and in conjunction with the larger power grid is known as a microgrid, which is primarily powered by solar energy. An outline of the parts, features, advantages, and uses of a solar microgrid is provided below: Transform solar radiation into electrical power set up in appropriate places, such as on rooftops or in arrays that are mounted on the ground. The majority of electrical appliances and the grid use alternating current (AC), which is produced by inverters and changes from direct current (DC) from solar panels. Battery storage allows you to use extra energy produced during the day on cloudy or nighttime days makes the microgrid more stable and dependable. The production, storage, and distribution of electricity are all managed and observed by the Energy Management System (EMS). makes sure the microgrid runs as efficiently and effectively as possible (Nezhad et al. 2024). The microgrid's distribution network is its internal electrical distribution system. It comprises transformers, wiring, and other required hardware. Offer extra dependability when solar power output is low or demand is high. Use fuels like natural gas, diesel, or other fuels often (Bai and 2023). Energy conversion from ocean thermal energy which generates electricity by exploiting the temperature disparity between the colder deep water and the warmer surface water. Suitable for tropical regions with significant temperature gradients. Non-conventional energy sources are crucial for reducing greenhouse gas emissions, promoting energy security, and providing sustainable energy solutions for the future (Bhattarai et al. 2023).

Table 8.2. Comparison of case studies of smart grid system using recent technologies

Barrier type	Barriers
Technical	Transitioning from centralized to decentralized grid management with numerous distributed energy resources (DERs) poses coordination challenges
	Transitioning from centralized to decentralized grid management with numerous distributed energy resources (DERs) poses coordination challenges
	Achieving the required throughput, latency, and scalability for blockchain based smart grid systems remains an active area for research
Regulatory	Unclear or outdated regulations around issues like data privacy, cyber security and market structures can hinder the adoption of smart grid technologies
	Lack of standardized policies and incentives for prosumers, DER owners and other stakeholders to participate in smart grid ecosystem
Economic	Integrating new smart grid technologies and blockchain-based applications with existing grid infrastructure and legacy communication protocols is technically complex
	The upfront costs of upgrading grid infrastructure and deploying new smart grid technologies can be a barrier, especially for smaller utilities and grid operators

Table 8.3. Comparison table of different optimization aspects in smart grid systems.

Aspect	Description
Load Forecasting	Enhances load forecasting accuracy by analyzing historical and real-time data, predicting future demand, reducing peak plant usage, and enabling better resource planning.
Optimal Power Flow (OPF)	Solves complex models to minimize power losses and improve efficiency, optimizing the configuration of power generation and distribution for balanced load across substations.
Energy Storage Optimization	Streamlines the charging and discharging cycles of storage systems by storing excess energy during periods of low demand, releasing it during peak periods, and mitigating fluctuations in renewable energy.
Availability Prediction	Meta-heuristic algorithms predict the availability of renewable energy sources like solar and wind by analyzing weather patterns, historical data, and real-time conditions.
Grid Stability	Meta-heuristic algorithms enhance grid stability by managing the variability and intermittency of renewable energy sources, preventing fluctuations in power supply.
Storage System Integration	Their objective is to optimize the integration of energy storage systems, including batteries, to store surplus renewable energy and release it during periods of low generation or high demand.
Grid Infrastructure Optimization	These algorithms assist in optimizing the existing grid infrastructure to handle the increased penetration of renewable energy, ensuring reliable transmission and distribution.

8.5.1 Advantages of solar microgrids

Reduces dependency on fossil fuels and the main power grid when there is energy independence. It increases energy resilience and security, particularly in isolated or disaster-prone areas. It reduces greenhouse gas emissions and air pollution. It promotes the utilization of renewable energy sources. By producing power locally, electricity costs are reduced. It minimizes the losses in distribution and transmission that come with centralized power systems. It may be adjusted to match the unique energy requirements of an industrial complex, campus, or community. Modular design makes expansion and modification simple (Singhal et al. 2024). Offers a dependable power source in the event of grid failures or interruptions increases the energy resilience of vital services and infrastructure. Give those without access to the main power grid electricity improve living standards and encourage regional economic growth. Businesses and industrial facilities should cut expenses associated with operations and boost energy efficiency. Make sure there is a steady supply of power for essential operations. Institutions of Higher Learning and Health Care. Provide hospitals, clinics, and institutions with sustainable, clean energy. Enhance operational sustainability and support critical services. The solar microgrid's components are described in Figure 8.1.

In remote areas cut off from centralized power grids, solar microgrids provide a lifeline. They make it possible for these areas to get electricity for necessities like lighting, communication, healthcare, and education. Utilization of Resource Abundance: Numerous remote areas have an abundance of solar resources. Through the utilization of locally accessible renewable energy sources, solar microgrids leverage this potential to meet energy needs in an environmentally friendly way. It can be prohibitively expensive to build traditional grid infrastructure in remote areas. With less initial outlay and quicker installation times, solar microgrids present a more affordable option. Environmental Preservation: Remote communities can lessen their dependency on diesel generators and other fossil fuel-based power systems by

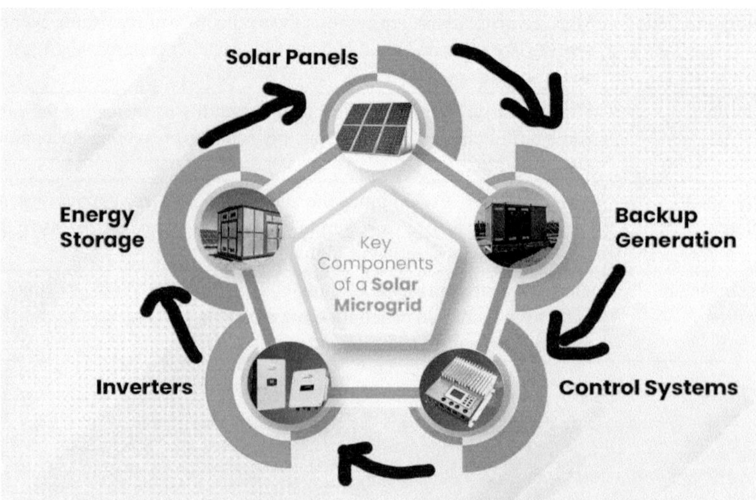

Figure 8.1. Solar Microgrid.

utilizing solar energy, which will help with environmental conservation efforts and lessen the effects of climate change on Fragile ecosystem (Chinnasamy et al. 2024).

8.6 India's Solar-Powered Villages

Under the Sun-Powered Off-grid and Decentralized Applications Program, 63 solar-powered small-scale networks with a combined capacity of 1899 kWp have reportedly been introduced nationwide with financial support from the Service of Unused & Renewable Vitality (MNRE). This information was provided in a written response to a question on the steps taken by the government to investigate the sun-powered small-scale lattice demonstration within the country, made in the Lok Sabha today. According to Shri Singh, the MNRE has provided budgetary support for up to 30% of the fetched frameworks for micro- and mini-grids that will be established in the nation's rural areas. Solar microgrid performance will be maximized through integration with smart grid technologies, which allow for dynamic load management, predictive maintenance, and real-time monitoring. This clever synchronization guarantees economical energy use and optimizes savings for end users.

8.6.1 Blockchain and Peer-to-Peer Trading

Peer-to-peer energy trading within microgrid networks will be made possible by blockchain technology, enabling customers to directly purchase, sell, and trade excess energy with their neighbors. This decentralized energy market encourages community involvement and energy independence. Electrification of Remote Areas: Solar microgrids will be essential in bringing clean, dependable energy to areas that are currently without it or too expensive for traditional grid infrastructure. They will also help electrify underserved and remote areas. Socioeconomic development is fueled by this, and Integration of IoT and AI (Alshowkan et al. 2022). The integration of artificial intelligence (AI) algorithms and Internet of Things (IoT) devices will optimize solar microgrid operations by anticipating energy demand, modifying system parameters in real-time, and identifying opportunities for efficiency gains. This synergy enhances system dependability and performance. By combining solar microgrids with other renewable energy sources like wind and hydro, the energy mix can be further diversified and intermittency issues can be lessened. A more reliable and resilient energy supply is ensured by this hybrid strategy, particularly in areas with erratic weather patterns. Policy Support and Investment: Governments and other stakeholders should continue to support policies that will encourage investment in solar microgrids, as this will lower costs and increase market penetration. Significant regulatory obstacles may need to be overcome in order to connect a solar microgrid to the main utility grid. Navigating the interconnection process, adhering to utility requirements, and ensuring that grid codes and standards are adhered to can be a time-consuming and challenging endeavor. One of the main obstacles to the broad adoption of microgrids is the resolution of these interconnection problems. Many jurisdictions lack clear policies and regulatory frameworks that deal with microgrids. The development of the market may be hampered by the lack of uniform project evaluation metrics, pay plans, and oversight procedures for non-utility microgrid owners. In certain regions, laws forbid non-utility companies from owning and managing the distribution infrastructure which includes wires and poles that is a microgrid's necessary building blocks (Youssef et al. 2024).

8.6.2 Divided Incentives in Apartment Buildings

Microgrid rooftop solar deployment may be hampered by laws governing multifamily rental housing. The costs and benefits of solar installations may be challenging to allocate due to the varying incentives that building owners and tenants possess. Federal laws and the presence of multiple jurisdictions can pose specific challenges to the implementation of microgrids on tribal lands. Examples of these include prohibitions on the use of federal funds for projects that do not fall under trust lands and restrictions on individual homeownership. In conclusion, the lack of clear and encouraging regulatory frameworks, connectivity challenges, restrictions on non-utility ownership, and concerns about tribal land jurisdiction are some of the main regulatory barriers that could significantly affect the widespread adoption of microgrids that run on solar electricity (Faber et al. 2017).

8.6.3 Effective Solar Microgrid Case Studies

The non-profit organization Direct Relief was able to install a solar and storage microgrid in spite of regulatory obstacles, as described in this case study. Resolving utility requirements and navigating the interconnection process presented significant regulatory challenges that required resolution. According to the research paper, "simple, but fundamental, policy reforms and market mechanisms are needed to enable a transition from a BTM (behind-the-meter) versus FOM (front-of-meter) way of thinking to a more intuitive and obvious 'build as big a Solar Microgrid as you can' approach." It suggests innovative policy measures, including the requirement for utilities to provide support for community microgrids and the implementation of solar microgrids that surpass the current capacities of net energy metering (NEM). The case study additionally emphasizes India's Dharnai Case Study of a Solar Microgrid. The following regulatory obstacles are briefly discussed in this case study on the installation of a solar microgrid in the Indian village of Dharnai: Greenpeace India implemented the microgrid, demonstrating how non-utility organizations can contribute to the deployment of microgrids despite legal limitations on non-utility ownership (Power cell GOB, 2022). To maintain financial sustainability, a pay-as-you-go approach was used, in which residents pay a nominal price for the power utilized. This helped to remove policy and legislative barriers related to power prices and rates. These case studies show that while regulatory obstacles can present serious difficulties, creative solutions for financing, policy, and stakeholder involvement can assist solar microgrids in overcoming these deployment barriers. Promoting legislative changes, investigating alternate ownership and business models, and creating (Baggio and Grimaccia 2020).

8.7 Machine Learning-Based Performance of Solar Microgrids

Some of the primary benefits of using machine learning techniques to improve solar microgrid performance are as follows: ANNs and LSTMs, two sophisticated machine learning models that are better able to capture the intricate relationships influencing solar generation, are used to forecast solar power accurately. This makes microgrid energy management more effective (Rottondi and Verticale 2017). Using machine learning algorithms to evaluate sensor data and forecast equipment failures, predictive maintenance of microgrid components minimizes downtime. Reinforcement learning and multi-objective optimization are used in microgrid operations optimization to make real-time decisions on energy dispatch, storage, trading in order to optimize the utilization of renewable energy and minimize expenses. Because ML models can handle the growing complexity of microgrids with more distributed energy resources, microgrid control can be made scalable and adaptive. Enhanced fault detection in renewable microgrids through the use of supervised and unsupervised machine learning models to precisely identify problems (Renugadevi and Maheswari 2022).

8.7.1 Performance of Solar Microgrids without Machine Learning

The performance of a solar microgrid would be restricted in a number of ways if machine learning was not used: Because traditional statistical models are unable to capture the intricate non-linear relationships that affect solar generation, forecasting solar power would be less accurate. Microgrid energy management is therefore less successful. It would be more difficult to foresee equipment breakdowns without machine learning (ML)-based predictive analytics, which would make maintenance more reactive rather than proactive. This leads to greater unplanned downtime. Because real-time decision making in microgrid operations would be based on rules rather than machine learning, optimization would be less complex. This makes it more difficult to reduce expenses and emissions (Abouyoussef and Ismail 2023).

8.7.2 Blockchain in Solar Microgrid Energy Storage Management

The search results demonstrate how blockchain enables peer-to-peer (P2P) microgrid energy trading. This enables direct buying and selling of excess energy with neighbors by homes and businesses equipped with solar energy generation and storage capabilities. These local energy transactions are recorded and validated using the blockchain, which serves as a transparent and safe ledger (Liang et al. 2022). Smart contracts can be used by blockchain-based microgrid energy management systems to maximize energy storage system dispatch. Figure 8.2 describes the blockchain technology. This discharges the batteries at the best times based on current grid conditions and energy demand, maximizing the use of stored solar energy and reducing expenses. Figure 8.3 displays the global solar generation using ML.

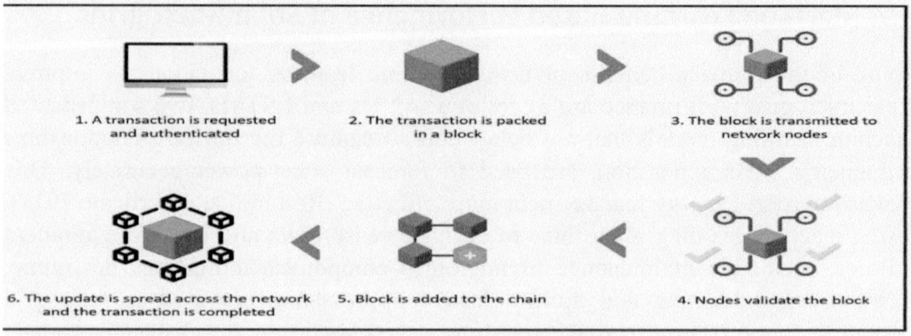

Figure 8.2. Block chain technology.

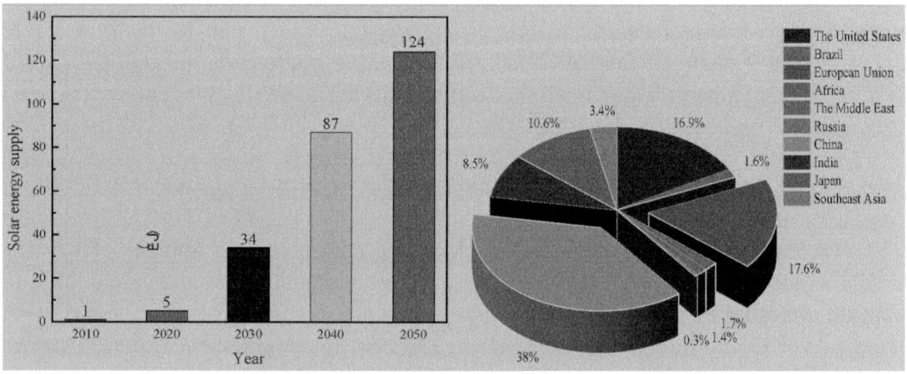

Figure 8.3. Worldwide Solar generation with ML.

Blockchain technology improves microgrids' capacity to "island" and function separately from the main grid. The overall resilience and reliability of the microgrid system are enhanced when distributed energy resources, including solar generation and storage, are coordinated securely and autonomously. As the system becomes more complex, solar microgrids can easily integrate more distributed energy storage due to the blockchain's scalability and flexibility. The microgrid's blockchain-based architecture enables it to adapt to changes in load, generation, and grid conditions, thereby simplifying the integration of additional storage capacity. The unchangeable blockchain ledger offers a transparent record of all energy transactions, including the discharging and charging of energy storage devices within the microgrid. This improves the system's accuracy and trustworthiness, which facilitates energy flow audits and guarantees equitable payment to solar energy producers. In conclusion, the search results show that blockchain technology is essential to making energy storage system management within solar-powered microgrids effective (Zhu and Liu 2022). Blockchain contributes to the full potential unlocking of solar and storage microgrid systems by enabling peer-to-peer energy trading, optimizing storage dispatch, enhancing reliability, and offering transparent accounting. The microgrid using the blockchain technology is explained in the Figure 8.4 and the solar output in Figure 8.5.

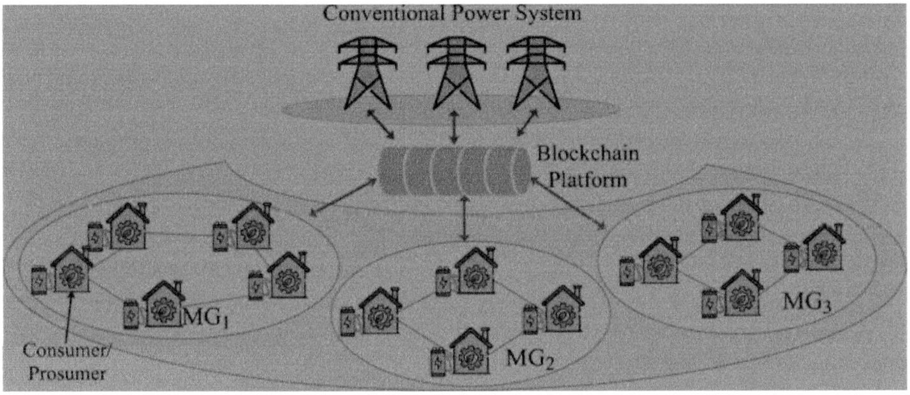

Figure 8.4. Microgrid with block chain platform.

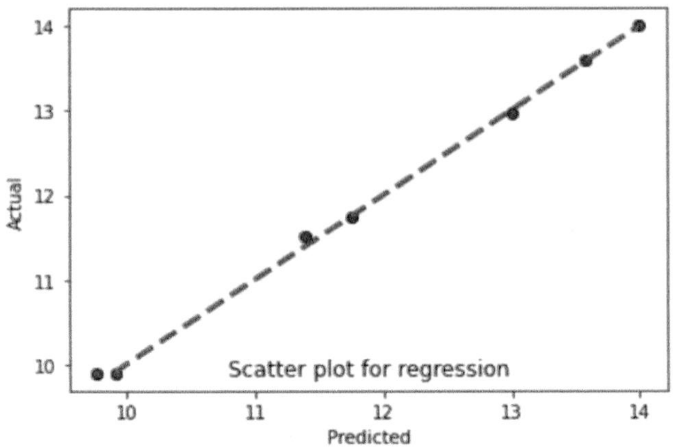

Figure 8.5. Solar output.

8.7.3 Procedures for Forecasting Solar Power Output Information Prior to Processing

On an hourly basis, process raw weather data and power production data to obtain meaningful numerical values. Eliminate superfluous features and apply Principal Component Analysis to decrease the dataset's dimension. To find pertinent features, do a correlation analysis between weather parameters and energy production. Use Principal Component Analysis to minimize the dataset's dimension. Use a variety of machine learning algorithms, including dimension reduction- and weighted linear regression-based approaches. In artificial neural networks, the temporal gradient can vanish or not. Feedforward Multilayer Neural Networks (MLFFNN). The Matern 5/2 GPR Algorithm provides the most accurate forecast of solar power output and has the lowest Root Mean Square Error. ANN models outperform other models found in the literature in accurately predicting PV output power, with an RMSE of 1.5565. By learning intricate relationships between parameters, statistical regression and neural networks are combined to predict solar power output in Malaysia and India with high accuracy (Gurav et al. 2017).

8.8 Advanced energy storage optimization

Systems with solar panels and battery energy storage use machine learning algorithms, including specialized reinforcement learning techniques, to optimize energy storage controls and increase energy efficiency. Home energy storage systems with machine learning algorithms increase battery life, boost energy efficiency, and enable grid communication and energy trading. Solar panels energy storage is being optimized through the use of machine learning algorithms. Here are a few specific machine learning algorithms that are employed for this are as follows. By modeling the relationship between solar energy generation and storage, these algorithms allow for precise forecasting and energy storage system optimization (Bosisio et al. 2023). Learning through reinforcement is the method used to regulate battery energy storage with the goal of achieving the best possible energy storage to meet grid demands. Solar power output has been predicted using a variety of machine learning techniques, including Weighted Linear Regression, Multilayer Feedforward Neural Networks, Artificial Neural Networks, and Boosting Regression Trees. With a low Root Mean Square Error (RMSE), it has been shown that the Matern 5/2 Gaussian Process Regression (GPR) method is the most effective in forecasting solar power output. ANN models have also shown success in forecasting PV output power, with an RMSE of 1.5565. Accurately predicting solar power output can be achieved by combining statistical regression and neural networks to learn intricate relationships between parameters. Using machine learning (ML) to integrate solar and energy storage: Amazon uses AWS machine learning models to forecast when the battery unit at its Baldy Mesa solar farm should charge and discharge energy to the grid. This contributes to a consistent flow of energy devoid of carbon. Other solar-plus-storage locations have employed comparable ML solutions to forecast heatwaves and maximize energy storage, assisting operators in adjusting to climate change and reducing load on the electrical grid. An uninterrupted supply of carbon-free energy for longer periods of time each day can be ensured by combining solar projects with AI and energy storage technologies. In conclusion, maximizing the integration of solar PV systems with energy storage and precisely forecasting solar power output depend on the application of machine learning techniques (Renugadevi et al. 2024).

8.8.1 Block Chain Technology in Energy Storage Systems

Blockchain makes it possible to manage energy storage systems decentralized, facilitating peer-to-peer energy distribution and trading without the need for a centralized authority. It promotes localized energy exchanges, which increases the energy grid's resilience and flexibility. Blockchain offers an unchangeable, transparent record of all activities and transactions inside the energy storage system increases the traceability of energy sources and guarantees the verifiability and accounting of energy from storage systems. The cryptographic security features of blockchain guard against illegal access and data manipulation. It guarantees the accuracy and safety of information about the use, storage, and exchange of energy.

On the blockchain, smart contracts automate the performance of transactions and agreements in accordance with preset criteria, lowers operating expenses and administrative overhead by automating tasks like energy trading, billing, and maintenance. Energy storage systems can now buy and sell energy directly from consumers or other storage systems thanks to blockchain's ability to enable peer-to-peer energy trading in real-time. It optimizes the usage of stored energy and maximizes returns on investment. The integration of energy storage devices with the main grid and other dispersed energy resources can be facilitated by blockchain technology. It enhances grid dependability and stability through effective energy flow and storage capacity management (Renugadevi and Maheswari . 2022).

8.8.2 Genetic Algorithms and Particle Swarm Optimization

To maximize the efficiency of solar energy systems, various AI techniques are used. To make wise decisions about energy storage and distribution to improve energy efficiency, real-time data from solar panels, weather forecasts, and energy demands are analyzed using neural networks. By determining the ideal configuration for energy systems and the most effective management of energy resources, Genetic Algorithm as well as Particle Swarm Optimization are used to optimize energy storage in solar panels. This is how they function: Fish or bird's social interactions serve as inspiration for PSO. It mimics the social behavior of a flock of birds to optimize energy storage in solar panels, with each possible solution represented as a particle in the search space. As they travel through the solution space, these particles modify their position in accordance with both their own and other particles optimal positions. In order to find the best configuration of energy resources, this process effectively balances exploration and exploitation and continues until an optimal solution is found (Agajie et al. 2024). The principles of evolution and natural selection serve as inspiration for GA. In the context of optimizing energy storage in solar panels, it is employed to maintain a population of candidate solutions and to evolve the population toward better solutions over successive generations using operators such as crossover, selection, and mutation. In order to determine the ideal arrangement of energy resources, this procedure imitates the natural evolutionary processes of selection, recombination, and mutation. These algorithms have been applied to the best sizing and management of energy systems, including the integration of solar panels and energy storage, to achieve an efficient and effective utilization of renewable energy resources. These algorithms are used to solve complex optimization problems. Through a number of mechanisms, ML increases the precision of energy demand prediction in renewable energy systems. ML models are capable of capturing complex correlations between the target variable and the input data, which results in predictions that are more accurate. ML models are able to predict energy demand more accurately by examining a variety of influencing factors and analyzing historical data to uncover intricate patterns. The predictive powers of ML allow for more accurate and dependable energy demand forecasting, which enhances grid management and resource efficiency (Lu and Wang 2023).

8.8.3 Monitoring and Predicting Data in Real-Time

Machine learning models have the ability to track and predict real-time data, which facilitates dynamic modifications and more precise demand projections. These capabilities allow ML to greatly improve the accuracy of energy demand estimates. Through a number of mechanisms, ML increases the precision of energy demand prediction in renewable energy systems. ML models are capable of capturing complex correlations between the target variable and the input data, which results in predictions that are more accurate. ML models are able to predict energy demand more accurately by examining a variety of influencing factors and analyzing historical data to uncover intricate patterns. The predictive powers of ML allow for more accurate and dependable energy demand forecasting, which enhances grid management and resource efficiency (Mouassa et al. 2021). An optimized hybrid machine learning technique has been utilized to model solar panels with over 99% accuracy, though the precise algorithms are not stated. The application of gradient boosting frameworks, to forecast solar power output in various locations demonstrates the use of cutting-edge machine learning techniques for solar energy prediction. Many techniques, including regression, decision trees, and ensemble methods, are frequently used for solar power generation prediction and optimization, even though specific ML algorithms are not always mentioned. For solar panel optimization, a number of ML algorithms are employed, such as, SVM that is support vector machine. For modeling solar panels, one supervised learning algorithm that can be used is SVM (Bremer and Lehnhoff 2021). Table 8.4 provides an explanation of solar panel optimization approaches.

Table 8.4. Optimization techniques for solar panels.

1	KNN (K-Nearest Neighbors)	It is a non-parametric algorithm that can be applied to solar panel optimization. It is used for regression and classification.
2	Decision Tree	The optimization of solar panels can be accomplished by employing decision trees, a supervised learning algorithm that is employed for and classification analysis and regression.
3	Random Forest	An ensemble learning technique that can be applied to solar panel optimization is called random forest.
4	Light Gradient Boosting Machine	Gradient boosting models such as LGBM can be used to forecast solar power output at various locations.

8.8.4 Energy Storage Devices

Energy storage devices and solar panels can be combined to store extra energy for use at night or during cloud cover. Lithium-ion batteries and other electrochemical energy storage systems are the most popular forms of solar power plants coupled with energy storage. Energy storage makes it possible to bank excess solar energy for use during peak hours, offering 24/7 power, financial protection, improved monitoring, and increased energy independence (Aljafari et al. 2023). Battery, thermal, and mechanical storage systems can all be used to store solar energy. A common option for residential solar installations is battery storage, like the Tesla Powerwall, which allows homeowners to accumulate surplus solar energy for use during periods of elevated electricity rates or power outages. Combining solar energy with storage by the help of machine learning algorithm plays a vital role also has several advantages, such as lowering carbon emissions, supplying energy resilience, balancing electric loads, and reducing electricity costs. In addition to being dependable and affordable substitutes for fossil fuel power plants, solar based storage systems are becoming more and more important in reaching solar energy generation targets (Youssef et al. 2024). PSO techniques are a useful tool for improving the energy storage systems in solar panels and, in particular, for fine-tuning the battery energy storage system control parameters. PSO application can result in higher reliability indices, decreased power loss, and increased efficiency, making it a promising field for research and development in the renewable energy industry. The usage of batteries in the manufacturing of solar panels is seen in Figure 8.6.

Blockchain, IoT, and "battery passports" are being used in pilot programs to track the lifecycle of batteries used in EVs and portable electronics. The digitalization of battery safety certification procedures through blockchain technology improves shipping efficiency and transparency. Blockchain is allowing recyclers to access data from battery swap stations, which lowers inspection costs and permits the reuse of higher-value batteries. In general, blockchain technology is showing promise as a major facilitator of developing a more sustainable, circular ecosystem for lithium-ion battery end-of-life management (Manzoor et al. 2023). Figure 8.7 illustrates the recycling process for lithium-ion batteries.

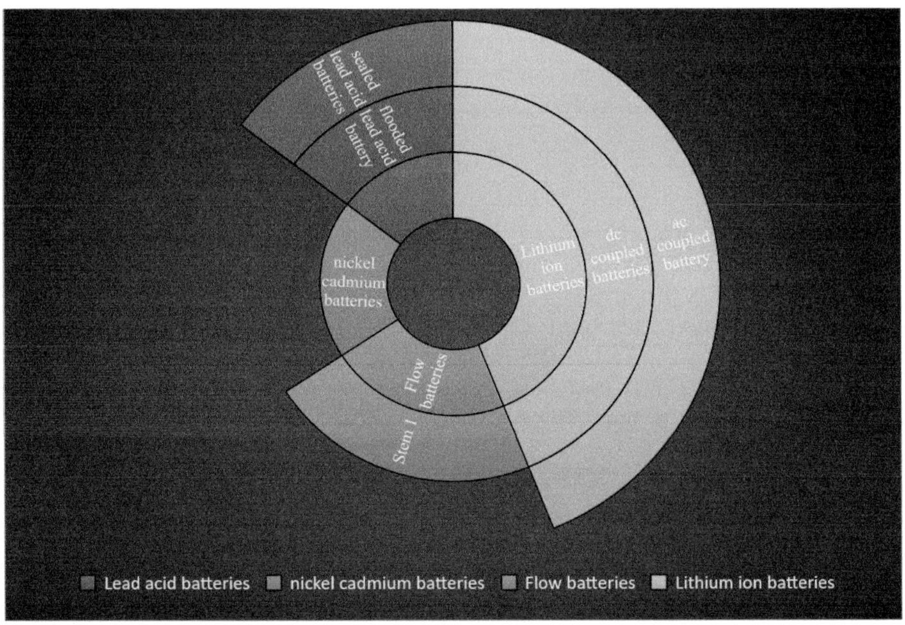

Figure 8.6. Usage of batteries in solar panel generation.

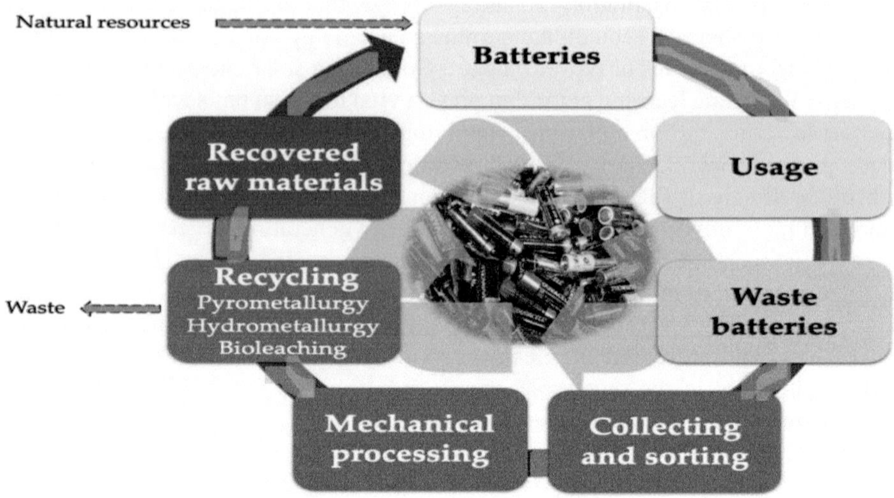

Figure 8.7. Lithium-ion Battery Recycling Process.

8.9 Results and Discussions

The control parameters of battery based storage system such as the available power as well the power generated in solar panels can be optimized with PSO to determine the accurate result. This optimization aids in lowering power loss such as blackouts when the solar microgrid in islanded mode which increases the solar panel systems efficiency. Compared with other batteries, the lithium-ion batteries are mostly used in solar power generation with incorporates ML optimization techniques. Figure 1 explains the benefits of lithium-ion batteries in various percepts. This optimization can enhance the solar panel system's dependability by preventing system collapse and instability in the event of utility grid failure. The PSO algorithm's advantages over other heuristic algorithms include its straightforward concept, easy implementation, computational efficiency, and robustness when it comes to parameter control. The lithium-ion battery in a microgrid is seen in Figure 8.8.

Lithium-ion batteries and solar panels are essential parts of contemporary renewable energy systems. When combined, they make it possible for solar energy to be produced, stored, and used effectively. Their responsibilities and synergy are broken down below.

A number of factors need to be taken into account in order to calculate the number of solar panels needed for a given residence. These include the average amount of electricity used, the peak hours of sunlight in the area, and the wattage of the solar panels that will be installed. Table 8.5 displays the solar-powered electricity generating output optimized using PSO.

The formula for calculating the necessary quantity of solar panels is generalized in Figure 8.9. The advantages of lithium-ion batteries are displayed in Figure 8.10.

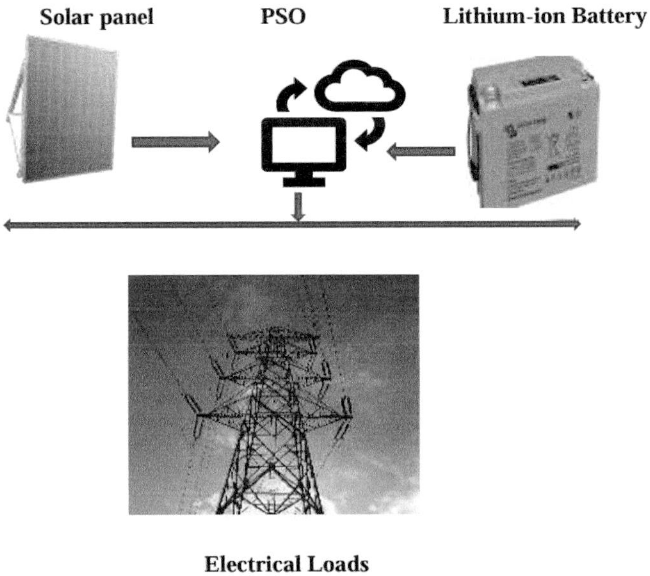

Figure 8.8. Lithium-ion battery in microgrid.

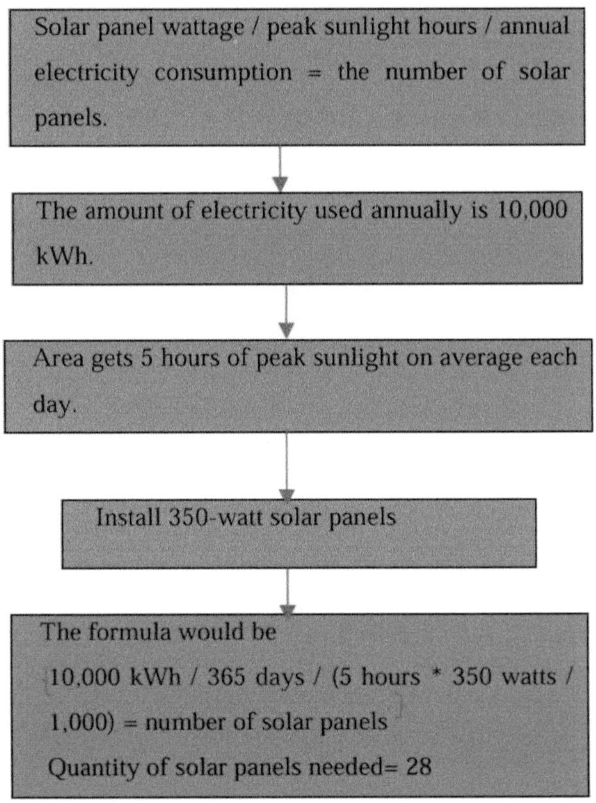

Figure 8.9. Formula.

Table 8.5. Electricity generation by solar power optimized the output by PSO.

S. No.	Summer (avg-per-day KWH)	Spring (avg-per day)	Winter (avg per day)
Week 1	32	31	29
Week 2	32	30	29
Week 3	31	31	28
Week 4	31	29	27

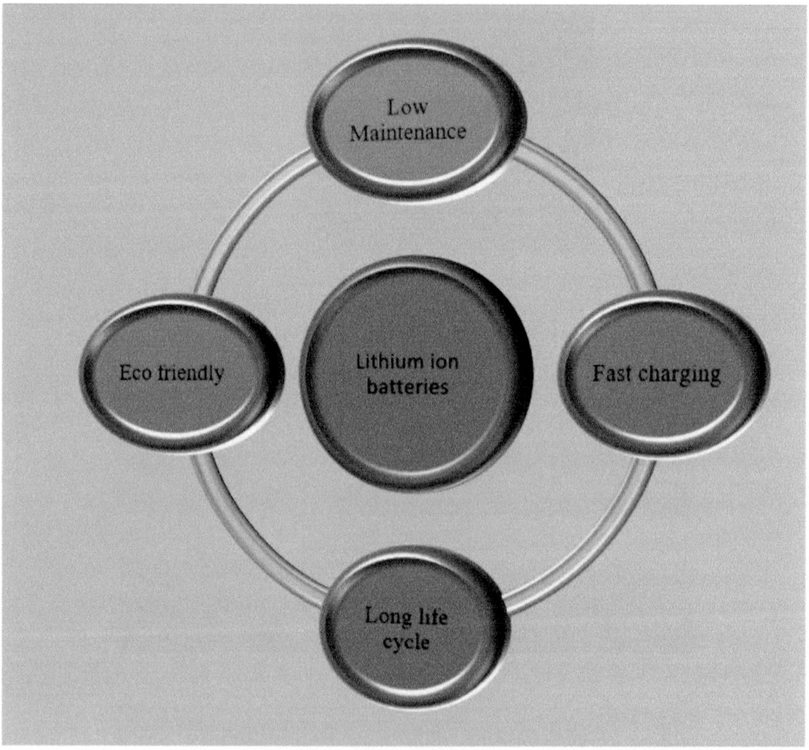

Figure 8.10. Benefits of Lithium-ion batteries.

8.10 Conclusion

The method that recommends the use of Particle-Swarm to convert the scattered output from various weather conditions in a solar microgrid system. Addresses uncertainties associated with the capacity of a system to satisfy load demands, even when the solar microgrid is operating in islanded mode. Handling the solar panels output and battery power based on the load demand and utilizing the battery power at night time without any power interruption since PSO algorithm will shows the accurate analysis of the battery system. To improve the battery storage system's performance, the parameters are compared and evaluated based on metrics like the reliability index and lifetime cost. The optimized system results obtained from the improved approach are compared to the original particle swarm optimization.

The validity of the proposed enhanced method will be verified through a series of comparative experiments conducted in varying weather conditions.

References

Abouyoussef, M., and Ismail, M. (2023). S-BAN: Secure blockchain-based networking strategy for privacy-preserving DSM. IEEE Access. https://doi.org/10.1109/ACCESS.2023.3290150.

Agajie, E. F., Agajie, T. F., Amoussou, I., Fopah-Lele, A., Nsanyuy, W. B., Khan, B. et al. (2024). Optimization of off-grid hybrid renewable energy systems for cost-effective and reliable power supply in Gaita Selassie Ethiopia. Sci. Rep., 14: 10929. https://doi.org/10.1038/s41598-024-61783-z.

Aljafari, B., Balachandran, P. K., Samithas, D., and Thanikanti, S. B. (2023). Solar photovoltaic converter controller using opposition-based reinforcement learning with butterfly optimization algorithm under partial shading conditions. Environ. Sci. Pollut. Res., 30: 72617–72640. https://doi.org/10.1007/s11356-023-27261-1.

Alshowkan, M., Evans, P. G., and Starke, M. (2022). Authentication of smart grid communications using quantum key distribution. Scientific Reports, 12: 12731. https://doi.org/10.1038/s41598-022-16090-w.

Baggio, A., and Grimaccia, F. (2020). Blockchain as a key enabling technology for future electric energy exchange: A vision. IEEE Access, 8: 205250–205271. https://doi.org/10.1109/ACCESS.2020.3012245.

Bai, H., and Song, Z. (2023). Lithium-ion battery, sodium-ion battery, or redox-flow battery: A comprehensive comparison in renewable energy systems. Journal of Power Sources, 580: 233426. https://doi.org/10.1016/j.jpowsour.2023.233426.

Ballaji, A., Dash, R., Subburaj, V., Kalvakurthi, J. R., Swain, D., and Swain, S. C. (2022). Design & development of MPPT using PSO with predefined search space based on fuzzy Fokker-Planck solution. IEEE Access, 10: 80764–80783. https://doi.org/10.1109/ACCESS.2022.3190003.

Behmann, R., Phan, J., Root, A., Schmidt, M., and Bessler, W. G. (2023). Integration of a lithium-ion battery in a micro-photovoltaic system: Passive versus active coupling architectures. Solar Energy, 262: 111748. https://doi.org/10.1016/j.solener.2023.111748.

Bhattarai, T. N., Ghimire, S., Mainali, B., Gorjian, S., Treichel, H., and Paudel, S. R. (2023). Applications of smart grid technology in Nepal: Status, challenges, and opportunities. Environmental Science and Pollution Research, 30(10): 25452–25476. https://doi.org/10.1007/s11356-022-23729-1.

Bordihn, S., Fladung, A., Schlipf, J., and Köntges, M. (2022). Machine learning-based identification and classification of field-operation caused solar panel failures observed in electroluminescence images. IEEE Journal of Photovoltaics, 12(3): 827–832. https://doi.org/10.1109/JPHOTOV.2022.3156179.

Bosisio, A., Berizzi, A., Lupis, D., Morotti, A., Iannarelli, G., and Greco, B. (2023). A Tabu-search-based algorithm for distribution network restoration to improve reliability and resiliency. Journal of Modern Power Systems and Clean Energy, 11(1): 302–311. https://doi.org/10.35833/MPCE.2022.000150.

Bremer, and Lehnhoff. (2021). Ant colony optimization for feasible scheduling of step-controlled smart grid generation. Swarm Intelligence, 15: 403–425. https://doi.org/10.1007/s11721-021-00204-7.

Chau, T. K., Yu, S. S., Fernando, T., and Iu, H. H. (2018). Demand-side regulation provision from industrial loads integrated with solar PV panels and energy storage systems for ancillary services. IEEE Transactions on Industrial Informatics, 14(11): 5038–5049. https://doi.org/10.1109/TII.2018.2808119.

Chinnasamy, P., Samrin, R., and Sujitha, B. B. (2024). Integrating intelligent breach detection systems into 6G-enabled smart grid-based cyber-physical systems. Wireless Personal Communications. https://doi.org/10.1007/s11277-024-11192-2.

Datta, S., Baul, A., Sarker, G. C., Sadhu, P. K., and Hodges, D. R. (2023). A comprehensive review of the application of machine learning in fabrication and implementation of photovoltaic systems. IEEE Access, 11: 77750–77778. https://doi.org/10.1109/ACCESS.2023.3305060.

Faber, M. H., Qin, J., Miraglia, S., and Thöns, S. (2017). On the probabilistic characterization of robustness and resilience. Procedia Engineering, 198: 1070–1083. https://doi.org/10.1016/j.proeng.2017.07.151.

Faniar, A. A., and Şeker, C. (2023). Detection of faulty solar panels using artificial intelligence and machine learning methods. 2023 IEEE 3rd Mysore Sub Section International Conference (MysuruCon), Hassan, India, 1–4.

Garg, U., Chohan, D. K., and Dobhal, D. C. (2021). The prediction of power in solar panels using machine learning. 2021 International Conference on Computational Performance Evaluation (ComPE), Shillong, India, 354–358.

Gurav, P. D., Hans, M. R., and Kulkarni, N. A. (2017). Review: Role of cloud computing in grid empowerment. International Conference on Automatic Control and Dynamic Optimization Techniques (ICACDOT), 258–263. https://doi.org/10.1109/ICACDOT.2016.7877590.

Hu, Y., and Wang, J. (2012). Study on power generation and energy storage system of a solar-powered autonomous underwater vehicle (SAUV). Energy Procedia, 16(Part C), 2049–2053. https://doi.org/10.1016/j.egypro.2012.01.323.

Huang, C., Madonski, R., Zhang, Q., Yan, Y., Zhang, N., and Yang, Y. (2022). On the use of thermal energy storage in solar-aided power generation systems. Applied Energy, 310: 118532. https://doi.org/10.1016/j.apenergy.2022.118532.

Kerdphol, T., Fuji, K., Mitani, Y., Watanabe, M., and Qudaih, Y. (2016). Optimization of a battery energy storage system using particle swarm optimization for stand-alone microgrids. International Journal of Electrical Power & Energy Systems, 81: 32–39.

Liang, Y., Wang, Z., and Abdallah, A. B. (2022). V2gnet: Robust blockchain-based energy trading method and implementation-in-vehicle-to-grid-network.IEEEAccess,10,131442–131455. https://doi.org/10.1109/ACCESS.2022.3209997.

Liu, H., Wu, B., Maleki, A., and Pourfayaz, F. (2022). An improved particle swarm optimization for optimal configuration of standalone photovoltaic scheme components. Energy Science & Engineering, 10(4): 772–789. https://doi.org/10.1002/ese3.1052.

Lu, Y., and Wang, G. (2023). A load forecasting model based on support vector regression with whale optimization algorithm. Multimedia Tools and Applications, 82: 9939–9959. https://doi.org/10.1007/s11042-022-13462-2.

Manzoor, A., Judge, M. A., Islam, S.u., Neggaz, N., Abulaigh, L., and Ahmad, I. (2023). AHHO: Arithmetic Harris Hawks Optimization algorithm for demand side management in smart grids. Discov. Internet. Things 3: 3. https://doi.org/10.1007/s43926-023-00028-3.

Mouassa, S. Bouktir, T., and Jurado, F. (2021). Scheduling of smart home appliances for optimal energy management in smart grids using Harris-Hawks optimization algorithm. Optimization and Engineering, 22: 1625–1652. https://doi.org/10.1007/s11081-020-09572-1.

Nezhad, A. E., Mobtahej, M., Javadi, M. S., Nardelli, P. H. J., and Sahoo, S. (2024). Optimal operation of lithium-ion batteries in microgrids using a semidefinite thermal model. International Journal of Electrical Power & Energy Systems, 155(Part B): 109630. https://doi.org/10.1016/j.ijepes.2023.109630.

Power-cell-GOB(2022)Annualreport2021–22.GovernmentofBangladesh. https://powercell.portal.gov.bd/site/page/1584cf45-b39f-4b00-829a-2e4b64b37618/.

Ram, J. P., Pillai, D. S., Rajasekar, N., and Strachan, S. M. (2020). Detection and identification of global maximum power point operation in solar PV applications using a hybrid ELPSO-P&O tracking technique. IEEE Journal of Emerging and Selected Topics in Power Electronics, 8(2): 1361–1374. https://doi.org/10.1109/JESTPE.2019.2948509.

Renugadevi, P., and Maheswari, R. (2022). Recent analysis of wood waste as an energy resource and increasing the efficiency of biomass energy generation by reducing tar and carbon emissions. Journal of Engineering Science and Technology.

Renugadevi, P., Sudha, A., and Srimathi, R. (2024, August). A Case Study for Standalone Solar Power Modules with and Without IoT Devices in Rural Hospital Emergency Rooms Located inKaniyambadi. In 2024 IEEE International Communications Energy Conference (INTELEC) (pp. 1–6). IEEE.

Youssef, H., Kamel, S., Hassan, M. H., Loai, N., and Francisco, J. (2024). An improved bald eagle search optimization algorithm for optimal home energy management systems. Soft. Comput. 28: 1367–1390. https://doi.org/10.1007/s00500-023-08328-0.

CHAPTER 9

Blockchain in the International Market

Varnesh Ghildiyal,[1,*] *Vibha Verma,*[1] *Sonam Gaur,*[1] *Sapna Rani*[2] and *Pallavi Sharma*[2]

9.1 Introduction of Blockchain

Blockchain technology has emerged as a revolutionary and innovative technology to decentralize transitions which facilitates digital security and transparency. Blockchain technology works as a novel database to enable information sharing on an internal network. Also, the data is maintained on blocks that link in a chain with a blockchain database. A chain that is immutable means that other than with consensus across the network, the chain cannot be removed or changed and the data is consistent across time. Hence, should keep the ledger of accounts, payments, orders, and other transactions in an irreversible or unchangeable manner via Blockchain technology. The in-built defences of this technique also restricts illegitimate transactions and ensures that the common documentation of such transactions is consistent.

9.1.1 Core Concepts

1. **Decentralization:** A blockchain network spreads data across multiple nodes or computers rather than having them all stored at one central location. The decentralization and peer-to-peer nature of blockchain ensure that no single error exist and minimize the risk of data manipulation (Nakamoto 2008). Blockchain offer upgraded and advanced securities and trust in digital transactions by enabling immutable transactions without the role of intermediaries.

[1] College of Business Studies (COBS), COER University, Roorkee, Haridwar, Uttarakhand, India.
Emails: verma8may91@gmail.com; sonamgaur543@gmail.com
[2] MMPG College Haridwar.
Emails: srani190@gmail.com; pallavisharmaa98@gmail.com
* Corresponding author: vgpawan1@gmail.com

DOI: 10.1201/9781003540328-9

2. **Distributed Ledger**: The Blockchain technology helps to provide a distributed ledger to network users can access the whole database and all previous transactions. This common ledger will allow that each participant can verify the accuracy of transactions independently (Tapscott and Tapscott 2016).
3. **Cryptographic Security**: The Cryptographic techniques is a fundamental factor of modern cybersecurity which is employed to 'secure transactions' on the blockchain. Moreover, each transaction gets hashed and added into a block which links to the one that was created prior to it and creates a chain of blocks. This cryptographic chaining ensures the two properties of data integrity and immutability (Pilkington 2016).
4. **Consensus Mechanisms**: To confirm the state of ledgers now, blockchain networks use "consensus algorithms" like "Proof of Work (PoW) or Proof of Stake (PoS)". These algorithms make sure each transaction is verified by all nodes in the network before it is stored in the chain (Zheng et al. 2017).

9.1.2 Historical Evolution of Blockchain

In 2008, the group using the pseudonym 'Satoshi Nakamoto' first presented the concept of blockchain technology to the public. Initially used as the foundation for the digital-currency Bitcoin, blockchain technology has become a buzzword across sectors. That was only the beginning, though—blockchain has come a long way, and today its applications reach far beyond digital currencies.

1. **Introduction of Bitcoin (2008)**: According to research paper entitled "Bitcoin: A Peer-to-Peer Electronic Cash System" who is known as 'Satoshi Nakamoto', he described Bitcoin. It described the way that peer-to-peer transactions could be conducted through a decentralized ledger without requiring a trusted third party (Nakamoto 2008). This is the whitepaper that introduced blockchain technology.
2. **Bitcoin Network Launch (2009)**: The Bitcoin network was established in January 2009 with the mining of the genesis block, or block 0. This incident proved that blockchain technology had the potential to be utilized in real-world applications and that a decentralized digital currency was feasible (Nakamoto 2008).
3. **Emergence of Altcoins and Blockchain 2.0 (2011–2014)**: Other cryptocurrencies, or altcoins, were created in response to the popularity of Bitcoin, each with the goal of either improving upon its design or catering to a different set of use cases. Around the same time, the term "Blockchain 2.0" started circulating, which describes application of blockchain technology for uses other than digital currency, like smart contracts (Swan 2015).
4. **Ethereum and Smart Contracts (2015)**: The introduction of Ethereum by Vitalik Buterin in 2013 and its launch in 2015 marked a major breakthrough in blockchain technology. Decentralized apps (dApps) are made possible by Ethereum, which popularized the idea of smart contracts. These were self-executing contracts with the conditions of the agreement directly put into code (Buterin 2014).

5. **Expansion to Various Industries (2016-Present)**: Blockchain technology has been widely adopted by a number of industries since the release of Ethereum, including 'finance', 'supply chain management', 'healthcare' and more. Blockchain solutions customized for business requirements are offered by platforms like Hyperledger and Corda (Pilkington 2016).

9.1.3 Key Characteristics and Features of Blockchain

Blockchain technology differs from conventional databases and systems due to a number of key characteristics. Its security, versatility and robustness are enhanced by these qualities.

1. **Decentralization**: Decentralization is a core principle in Bitcoin's blockchain and cryptocurrency world which transfers power, authority, and decision-making to the distributed network (all users collectively), rather than any single person or group.
2. **Transparency**: By spreading the ledger across a network of nodes, blockchain eliminates the requirement for a central authority. The system is decentralized, with no single point of control thanks to the network's nodes maintaining copies of the whole blockchain. This decentralization makes the system more reliable and resilient because no one person can change the ledger on its own (Nakamoto 2008).
3. **Immutability**: An entry into the blockchain cannot be removed or changed after it has been made. Due to the blockchain's structure, which links each block to the one before it to create an impenetrable chain and cryptographic hashing, this immutability is made possible. Data saved on the blockchain is guaranteed to be reliable and authentic by immutability (Pilkington 2016).
4. **Security**: Blockchain secures data with advanced cryptographic techniques. Using a cryptographic hash algorithm, transactions are encrypted and sequentially linked to their predecessors. Zheng et al. (2017) state that consensus techniques such as 'Proof of Work (PoW) or Proof of Stake (PoS)' further secure the blockchain against fraud and harmful attacks by guaranteeing the verification and approval of transactions by the network.

9.1.4 Blockchain Infrastructure and Types

Blockchain technology can be classified into various types, according to varying levels of access as well as control. These include public blockchains, private blockchains and consortium blockchains, each serving distinct purposes and use cases is shown in the Table 9.1.

9.1.5 Key Components of Blockchain Infrastructure

Blockchain infrastructure comprises of multiple fundamental parts, working together to create a safe, decentralized, and transparent system. These key components include nodes, the ledger, consensus mechanisms and smart contracts.

Table 9.1. Key aspects of public, private and consortium blockchains with examples.

Type of Blockchain	Definition	Security and Consensus	Control and Use Cases	Examples
Public Blockchains	Open to anyone; fully decentralized	Use cryptographic consensus mechanisms like 'Proof of Work (PoW) or Proof of Stake (PoS)'	No single entity controls the network; used for wide-reaching, open applications	Bitcoin (PoW), Ethereum (transitioning from PoW to PoS)
Private Blockchains	Restricted networks controlled by a single organization	Typically, do not rely on PoW or PoS; security managed by the organization	Controlled by a single entity; used for internal business processes requiring privacy and control	Hyperledger
Consortium Blockchains	Controlled by a group of organizations	Collaboration among participating organizations for security and governance	Balance between decentralization and controlled access; used for inter-organizational applications	R3 Corda

1. **Nodes:**
    - **Definition**: Individual machines that take part in the blockchain network are called nodes. By validating transactions and blocks, all nodes contribute to the network's security and integrity while keeping a copy of the 'blockchain'.
    - **Types of Nodes**: A blockchain network has two sorts of nodes: light nodes which keep a fraction of the 'blockchain data' and full nodes, which store the entire blockchain and take part in the consensus process.
2. **Ledger:**
    - **Definition**: Every transaction on the "blockchain" is recorded in the ledger. It is distributed throughout every network node, ensuring transparency and immutability.
    - **'Distributed Ledger Technology (DLT)'**: The ledger is resistant to manipulation and single points of failure because to its distribution and duplication across multiple nodes. Each new transaction is entered into the ledger as a block, which is then linked to the block before it via cryptography to form a chain.
3. **Consensus Mechanisms:**
    - **Definition:** 'Consensus mechanisms' are algorithms to enable individual devices such as computers and serves that participate, are in the blockchain network concur the current state ledgers. Consensus mechanisms play a crucial role that prevent double-spending and maintain the integrity of the blockchain.
    - **Examples:** The two most often used consensus processes are 'Proof of Stake (PoS) and Proof of Work (PoW)'. Whereas PoS relies validation power on nodes' capacity to solve complex mathematical puzzles, PoW distributes validation power to nodes based on their cryptocurrency holdings.

4. **Smart Contracts:**
    - **Definition**: The smart contracts refer to self executing which is well articulated in coded form. Further, contracts are executed and enforceable at the stage of condition fulfilment.
    - **Functionality**: Smart contracts included 'financial transactions', 'decentralized applications' (dApps), and 'supply chain management'. Also, Ethereum and other blockchain systems such AI, Bitcoin, Ripple, Cardano, and IoT incorporate smart contracts.

9.1.6 Blockchain Platforms and Technologies

The blockchain systems are developed to accomplish various cases and requirements in a variety of industries. The most well known platforms Hyperledger, Corda, and Ethereum which incorporate unique features and accelerate smooth functioning is shown in the Table 9.2.

Table 9.2. Blockchain Platforms.

Platform	Definition	Features	Use Cases
Ethereum	A decentralized platform for smart contracts and dApps, proposed by 'Vitalik Buterin in 2013 and launched in 2015'.	'Smart contracts' (self-executing contracts with terms written in code) and 'Ethereum Virtual Machine' (EVM) for running Apps	'Decentralized finance' (DeFi), - 'Supply chain management', Gaming and Various other applications
Hyperledger	'An open-source collaborative effort to advance cross-industry blockchain technologies, hosted by the Linux Foundation'.	Modular and extensible framework which includes projects like 'Hyperledger Fabric' (for permissioned networks) and Hyperledger Sawtooth (flexible and scalable architecture)	Enterprise applications, 'Supply chain tracking', Financial services, Healthcare, and other enterprise applications
Corda	A blockchain platform designed for business use cases, developed by R3.	Manages complex transactions, Restricts data access to only those who need to know, Supports 'smart contracts', Optimized for privacy, scalability and interoperability	Primarily used in the financial industry, Healthcare, 'Supply chain management', Insurance and other business sectors

9.2 Application of Blockchain in International Market

Unlike the others technologies , the blockchain technology is a crucial effect on services domain such as banking and finance. Furthermore, the blockchain technology has wide range of application across a variety of industrial range that decreases expenses and increase processing time, security, transparency, and efficiency.

9.2.1 Financial Services and Banking

1. **Cross-Border Payments**:
   - **Definition:** Blockchain technology is transforming the banking and financial services industries in the global marketplace. Blockchain technology facilitates speed up processing times and lowers costs by enhancing security, efficiency, and transparency.
   - **Advantages:** Blockchain technology allows for nearly instantaneous and fee-free cross-border transaction resolution. Real-time transaction validation and settlement are made possible by decentralzed ledgers.
   - **Example:** For instance, the Ripple's XRP Ledger that shows how blockchain technology is used for payments at global level. The blockchain technology also helps financial institutions to transfer funds at global level at lower costs at faster settlement times (Ripple 2020).
2. **Digital Identities**:
   - **Definition**: Blockchain technology helps to validate digital identities to increase the transparency and smooth functioning. Moreover, the blockchain is crucial for financial service to comply with regulatory requirements like 'Know Your Customer (KYC)' and 'Anti-Money Laundering (AML)' laws, "blockchain" verification is essential.
   - **Benefits**: Blockchain oriented digital identities may help to provide improved security and privacy which may reducing the risk of identity theft and fraud. Also, blockchain restructure and update the verification process to structure financial services efficient and cost-effective.
   - **Example**: For instance the 'self-sovereign identity platforms' incorporate blockchain to provide individuals control on digital identities to disseminate significant information to their services providers (Sovrin Foundation, 2018).
3. **Asset Tokenization**:
   - **Definition:** The asset 'tokenization' is the process of transforming rights of tangible assets into digital tokens which is articulated in blockchain. The digital token which is exchangeable on blockchain networks, outline ownership of the assets.
   - **Benefits:** Tokenization boosts liquidity by enabling fractional ownership and assets transfer. Moreover, the asset 'tokenization' minimize transaction costs by providing transparency and the role of middlemen.
   - **Example:** For instance, in real estate investment the blockchain-oriented tokens enable investors to buy fractional ownership of properties through tokenization platforms. Thus, the asset 'tokenization' extends their access to real estate investment options (RealT 2021).

9.2.2 Supply Chain Management

Blockchain has the potential to magnify accountability, transparency, and traceability to manifest smooth and cost effective 'supply chain management',Additionally, the 'supply chain management' minimize the fraud, records the transaction and validates product authenticity by tracking products.

1. **Traceability**:
   - **Definition:** The integration of supply chain management and blockchain technology facilitate to precisely track the products. The blockchain technology creates an immutable history by recording and documenting all the movement and transactions of a product. Thus, the blockchain technology may help to provide single and trackable transactions and identify the issues during the 'supply chain management' process.
   - **Benefits:** The 'supply chain management' and blockchain technology may assist product safety and authenticity by ensuring and validating the product's origin and journey.
   - **Examples:** For example, 'IBM Food Trust' which is blockchain-enabled supply chain technology used by manufacture, retailers, and distributers of food products to track food products (IBM 2020).
2. **Transparency**:
   - **Definition:** the blockchain technology enables all the 'supply chain' participants to access a common and transparent ledger. The blockchain enabled supply chain management ensures all participants of supply chain management to understand the data and remove discrepancies.
   - **Benefits:** The blockchain enabled supply chain management increase the transparency and encourage the confidence of the participants by serving real time transaction, monitoring and verified. The blockchain serves compliances with regulations and maintain the standard.
   - **Example:** For instance, 'IBM Envizi: Supply Chain Intelligence' and 'IBM Sterling Order and Fulfillment Suite' to ensure accuracy of the products and multiply profitability. Another example is the 'Provenance' which is a blockchain-based technology to allow companies to give consumers verified information about the origin and journey of their products transparency (Provenance 2017).
3. **Accountability**:
   - **Definition:** The Blockchain sustain accountability which include logging of all transactions and records product movements onto an unchangeable ledger. The Blockchain ensure all the actions are rigorously documented and each participant is accountable for successfully achieving the process.
   - **Benefits:** In the supply chain management, accountability may lower the risk of fraud, counterfeiting and unapproved modifications. The blockchain enhances the supply chain's overall ethical integrity by ensuring that each stakeholder is accountable to document their activities.

- **Example:** Walmart has incorporated blockchain technology to enhance its supply chain's accountability for food safety. By using blockchain technology to track the origin of food products in a couple of seconds, Walmart can react swiftly to any contamination risks (Kamath 2018).

9.2.3 Healthcare

The Blockchain technology plays crucial role to revolutionize the healthcare sector. The blockchain may protect the data of patient and records medical history and secure data by exchange across healthcare providers. The blockchain provide innovative solution by addressing data privacy, interoperability, and security.

1. **Securing Patient Data**
   - **Definition:** The blockchain technology address not modified and decentralized ledger of patient data. In the blockchain, every transaction is encrypted using cryptography which guarantee that patient information is secure and shielded unauthorized access.
   - **Benefits:** The role of blockchain is crucial in health care sector to secure patient data. The blockchain technology decentralized architecture to store patient data. By blockchain technology, the integrity of data can be improved. Consequently, the possibility of data breaches, manipulation, and unauthorized access can be reduced.
2. **Streamlining Medical Records**
   - **Definition:** Blockchain technology can easily simplify the medical data by developing a single and accessible records of patients' health information. Furthermore, the blockchain technology entails merging medical records into safe blockchain records.
   - **Benefits:** The blockchain technology facilitates healthcare practitioners to transmit patient data effectively, require less administrative work and make less mistakes. Moreover, the blockchain serves to maintain standardization to enhances system interoperability. For instance, the Medi Ledger project incorporate blockchain technology to track medications and handle medical data. The primary goal of integrating blockchain technology with the medical records is to improve the efficiency and security of the pharmaceutical supply chain data. The current chapter demonstrates blockchain technology application to provide guarantee of data accuracy (Medi Ledger 2020).
3. **Facilitating Data Sharing Among Healthcare Providers**
   - **Definition:** Blockchain technology provides safe and efficient data to disseminate among healthcare providers or practitioners. Moreover, the blockchain technology ensures data accuracy and consistency across institutions by utilising a decentralized ledger.
   - **Benefits:** The blockchain technology create a comprehensive, updated and upgraded medical history for patients by facilitating secure data sharing. The blockchain technology may reduce duplication and encourages better informed clinical decisions.

- **Example:** For example, 'Hyperledger Indy' is a blockchain architecture designed especially for decentralized identity management solutions. In the healthcare sector, it can be used to securely exchange patient information between different healthcare providers while maintaining patient privacy (Hyperledger 2020).

9.2.4 *Real Estate*

Blockchain technology holds the capability of drastically improving the real estate market through streamlining transactions, guaranteeing transparent and safe record-keeping, cutting down on fraud and expediting the purchase and sale of real estate.

1. **Simplifying Property Transactions**
   - **Definition:** Blockchain technology records property ownership, agreements, and transactions in a decentralized, immutable ledger, which streamlines real estate transactions. Through automation and digitization, this method decreases the need for middlemen and transaction expenses while streamlining procedures including title transfers, contract administration and payment settlements. Propy is a platform that operates on blockchain technology and helps with real estate transactions. It allows users to buy, sell and manage properties in a transparent and safe environment, which increases the efficiency and cost-effectiveness of transactions (Propy 2020). Blockchain technology guarantees the security, transparency, and immutability of property records. To provide a tamper-proof record of property ownership and history, each transaction is recorded in a block and added to a chain of earlier transactions.
   - **Gains:** By producing an open, verifiable record of real estate transactions, blockchain technology lowers the possibility of fraud and mistakes in record-keeping. Ensuring the accuracy and currency of ownership information is crucial for both legal and financial operations.
   - **Example:** For example, the Ubitquity platform uses blockchain technology to maintain property records. Ubitquity delivers an open and impenetrable history of ownership and transactions for properties by logging property transactions on a blockchain (Ubitquity 2021).
2. **Reducing Fraud**
   - **Definition:** In the digital age, fraud has become a growing concern and carry crucial challenges for individual and organizations. Moreover, minimizing digital fraud is a crucial objective for business, financial institutions, and digital platforms. In this regard, the Blockchain technology may help to fraud detection in real estate by underlining secure transactions between the parties. Also, the block chain technology facilitates immutable record of property ownership and transaction history to secure transactions. The network validates each transaction before adding it to the blockchain in order to prevent fraud.
   - **Advantages:** 'Blockchain technology' provides end encryption to decreases the risk of fraud and makes real estate transactions safe. Blockchain records

are transparent and unchangeable, making ownership claims and transaction histories impervious to fraud or manipulation.

- As an illustration, the ShelterZoom platform uses blockchain technology to safeguard real estate transactions and lower the frequency of frauds. The platform's features include secure transaction processing, digital offer administration, and real-time insight into the status of offers and counteroffers (ShelterZoom 2021).

3. **Speeding Up the Buying and Selling Process**
   - **Definition:** Blockchain technology expedites real estate transactions by digitizing and automating procedures including contract execution, payment processing, and title transfer.
   - **Advantages:** The entire buying and selling process is speeded up by automating these processes with smart contracts and digital transactions. Smart contracts reduce the time required to execute transactions by automatically fulfilling their commitments when certain conditions are satisfied.
   - **As an illustration:** Real estate transactions are streamlined via the Real Estate Blockchain Platform (REBC), which uses smart contracts to automate contract execution and payment processing. This approach speeds up the transaction process and reduces the need for middlemen (REBC 2022).

9.2.5 Government and Public Services

Blockchain technology offers innovative approaches to improve transparency and reduce corruption in government services while streamlining administrative processes like voting, land registries, and public procurement.

1. **Enhancing Transparency**
   - **Definition:** One essential element of transparency in government services is giving the general public access to information about government decisions, actions, and transactions. Blockchain technology encourages transparency by providing a decentralized, immutable record of all transactions and activity.
   - **Advantages:** Because of blockchain's transparency, government actions and decisions are documented in a public ledger that is accessible for audit by anybody. This openness promotes accountability and helps stop the misuse of power and resources.
   - **As an illustration:** The Estonia e-Residency Program, for example, uses blockchain technology to offer digital services to people worldwide. Laar (2017) claims that this initiative incorporates open government services, such as business registration, that allow users to verify official documents and actions on blockchain.
2. **Reducing Corruption**
   - **Definition:** Blockchain helps to eradicate corruption by creating a transparent and impenetrable database of transactions. The immutability and traceability

features of blockchain make it more difficult for corrupt operations to occur secretly.

- • **Benefits:** By providing a secure and verifiable record of public transactions and data, blockchain promotes dishonest behaviour and helps ensure that public funds and resources are handled appropriately.
- **As an illustration:** Georgia has implemented blockchain technology to manage land registrations. This initiative aims to increase transparency and decrease corruption in the property registration process by providing an unchangeable record of real estate transactions (Elmir 2019).

3. **Streamlining Administrative Processes**
   - **Definition:** Blockchain automates and streamlines administrative processes including voting, land registries, and public procurement through the use of smart contracts and decentralized record-keeping.
   - **Advantages:** Blockchain-based systems reduce paperwork, expedite administrative tasks, and increase process effectiveness. When specific conditions are met, smart contracts can automatically execute agreements, speeding up transactions and reducing administrative burdens.
   - **As an example,** the Swiss city of Zug has implemented a blockchain-based electronic voting system for municipal elections and referendums. Zug (2019) claims that this strategy demonstrates how blockchain technology may speed up the voting process and offer secure and transparent voting.
4. **Public Procurement**
   - **Definition:** Blockchain technology can improve public procurement processes by providing a transparent and secure means of recording contracts, payments, and bids. This can prevent fraud in addition to guaranteeing fair competition.
   - **Advantages:** Governments can create an open and auditable contract awarding process by integrating blockchain technology into public procurement. This reduces the likelihood of fraud and corruption while also guaranteeing a fair and competitive procurement process.
   - **As an illustration:** For example, the Republic of Georgia employs blockchain to ensure transparency and integrity in public procurement. This project involves keeping track of all procurement actions on a blockchain ledger in order to prevent unethical behaviour and ensure fair competition (Minasyan and Zavin 2021).

9.3 Blockchain in International Trade and Commerce

9.3.1 Cross-Border Payments and Settlements

Blockchain technology offers significant benefits for cross-border payments and settlements by making financial transactions quicker, less expensive, and more secure.

1. **Faster Cross-Border Payments**
    - **Definition:** Due to the multiple middlemen involved, traditional cross-border payments can occasionally result in delays. Thanks to blockchain technology, which enables direct transactions between parties, payment procedures can be finished considerably faster.
    - **Advantages:** Using blockchain, cross-border payments can be completed in real-time or within a few hours, as opposed to many days with traditional methods. This acceleration is made possible by decentralized networks, which avoid intermediaries and speed up transaction processes.
    - **As an illustration:** Take Ripple's XRP Ledger, a blockchain-based system that facilitates instantaneous international payments, as an example. The Ripple network has made it possible for financial institutions to make and receive payments in seconds rather than days (Ripple 2023).
2. **Reducing Transaction Costs**
    - **Meaning:** The costs of processing, currency conversion and middlemen banks usually result in hefty fees for cross-border transactions. By automating the transaction process along with the removal of middlemen, these expenses can be lowered using the blockchain technology.
    - **Benefits:** By cutting down on the requirement for third-party services and facilitating direct transactions between parties, blockchain lowers transaction prices. This decrease in expenses enables both consumers and corporations to make cross-border payments cheaper.
    - **Example:** As an example, a technology built on the blockchain called Stellar Network was created to make low-cost international transactions easier to complete. For remittances and international trade in particular, Stellar's technology enables the development of affordable and effective payment solutions (Stellar 2022).
3. **Enhancing Security in Transactions**
    - **Definition:** By utilizing cryptographic techniques to safeguard and validate data, blockchain guarantees the safety of international transactions. An encrypted and easily readable ledger is produced by recording each transaction in a block and connecting it to earlier transactions.
    - **Benefits:** From an immutable and transparent ledger to enhanced transaction security, blockchain offers these features. Additionally, because blockchain technology is decentralized, it is less vulnerable to fraud and cyberattacks, which are frequent in established financial institutions.
    - **Example:** IBM's Blockchain World Wire, for instance, is a platform that uses blockchain technology to enable safe and transparent international money transfers. The platform uses blockchain technology in order to increase security, reduce fraud, and provide a transparent record of transactions (IBM 2021).

4. **Facilitating Efficient Settlements**
   - **Definition:** Quick account reconciliation and payment settlement are made possible by decentralized ledgers that use blockchain technology to record all transactions in real time, which promotes effective settlements.
   - **Benefits:** Using blockchain technology for settlements increases efficiency by automating and streamlining reconciliation procedures. By automating settlement activities with smart contracts, transaction completion times and resource requirements can be reduced.
   - **Example:** For example, R3 and Trade IX developed the "Marco Polo" network, which leverages blockchain technology to expedite trade finance processes including settlement and reconciliation. Marco Polo (2022) claims that this platform facilitates the speedy and automated settlement of international business transactions, sample example of cross-border payments and settlements is shown as in Figure 9.1.

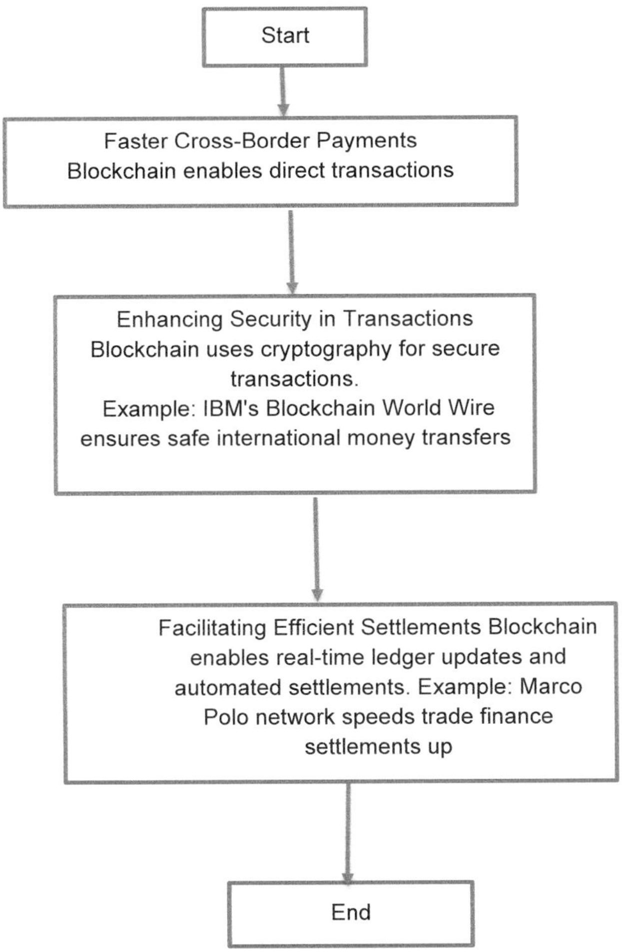

Figure 9.1. Cross-Border Payments and Settlements.

9.3.2 Trade Finance and Letters of Credit

By replacing manual steps with secure digital works, we not only cut down the paperwork but also increase transparency, prevent fraud, and provide a solution for trade finance and letters of credit.

1. **Digitizing Trade Finance Processes**
    - **Definition:** Blockchain technology is a secure digital record-keeping system that handles financial processes, which automates transactions paperwork, and payments in a digitalized way that currently works manually and paper-based.
    - **Benefits:** Blockchain reduces the paperwork and documentation, and it helps in faster transactions with minimum errors or delays in trade finance. Digital agreements like smart contracts, issuing Letter of Credit, and payments can automatically be done by using blockchain.
    - **As an example,** the "we. Trade" platform uses blockchain technology to digitize and automate trade finance processes, including the issuance of trade documents and letters of credit. By placing these processes online, We. Trade reduces paperwork and boosts productivity (we. Trade 2022).
2. **Reducing Paperwork**
    - **Definition:** Blockchain works like a digital ledger to record book which helps to maintain the track of transactions automatically and automatically keep the transactions secure. It not only helps in recording the data but also deals with payments, approvals shipping documents, and many more in a digitalized way which is still done using physical paperwork by banks and businesses.
    - **Benefits:** Blockchain digitally assists trade finance work and reduces paper records eventually completing transactions faster with fewer mistakes to rectify. It can automatically do the finance task which is programmed to do without needing people to oversee them, which includes LOC and payments.
    - **For example,** A platform like "we. Trade" uses blockchain technology and is like an online system that helps businesses to handle trade deals faster and easier. "We Trade" uses blockchain technology to make everything digital, automated, and secure. Moreover, it also reduces the paperwork and paper records to boost productivity by avoiding delays (CargoX 2021).
3. **Enhancing Transparency**
    - **Definition:** A deconstructed and immutable ledger is generated by the Blockchain technology through accessible documentation of all transactions and data updates of documents. This ultimately manifolds trade finance transparency.
    - **Advantages:** The transparency of blockchain ensures the access of the same data for the parties engaged in trade financing which helps in reducing conflict, eliminating fraud, and increasing trust among the parties.

- **As an example,** A blockchain-based "trade lens" platform was developed by Maersk and IBM, which increases the international shipping process with transparency of trade finance. Trade lens also helps in providing real-time pictures of trade paperwork (IBM 2021).

4. **Mitigating Fraud**
   - **Definition:** In trade finance, fraud may take the form of factual distortion, unlawful alterations, or document fabrication. The transparent and unchangeable ledger nature of blockchain reduces fraud.
   - **Advantages:** Blockchain-stored data is immutable, which means that once it is created, it cannot be altered. The transparency of the blockchain ledger makes fraudulent activities less likely because it allows all parties to verify the authenticity of trade papers and transactions.
   - **Example:** For instance, the blockchain-based trade finance system Marco Polo Network aims to lower fraud by offering a secure and transparent record for all trade finance transactions. The platform uses blockchain technology to get rid of fraud and ensure that trade transactions are accurate (Marco Polo 2022).

9.4 Digital Identification and Authentication

Blockchain technology uses its decentralization, immutability, and security to transform digital identification and authentication, especially in international trade. By offering a centralized, automated approach for secure identity management and minimizing dependency on other systems, blockchain streamlines verification procedures. SelfKey, for instance, enables users to effectively manage and validate identities (SelfKey 2022). As demonstrated by U-Port's identity management technology, it also lowers the danger of identity theft through safe, decentralized storage (U-Port 2021). As demonstrated by the initiatives of the ID2020 Alliance (ID2020, 2020), blockchain improves security in international trade by establishing an immutable record for transactions and identity verification. Furthermore, as Verida's platform demonstrates, it facilitates regulatory compliance with transparent, auditable records (Verida 2022). Blockchain reduces the amount of manual data entry, digitizes and automates documentation and speeds up clearing times in customs and border control procedures. Customs operations are expedited by platforms like as Trade Lens, which provide real-time viewing of documents and cargo (IBM 2021). Singapore Customs' technologies demonstrate how blockchain may eliminate delays by automating verification and enabling real-time access to trade documentation (Singapore Customs 2020). By capturing each transaction in an unchangeable ledger, guaranteeing that stakeholders may monitor and confirm shipping status, stopping fraud, and guaranteeing compliance—as demonstrated by the platform of DHL and Accenture—it improves transparency (DHL 2021). Additionally, as demonstrated by the EU's DLT4EU initiative (EU DLT4EU 2022), blockchain automates customs procedures through smart contracts, reducing processing times and errors.

9.4.1 Security and Privacy Concerns Related to the Blockchain Technology

Blockchain technology offers many advantages in terms of security and privacy, but it also has several drawbacks. Vulnerabilities in blockchain design, including as 51% attacks, which can jeopardize the integrity of proof-of-work blockchains like Bitcoin (Gencer et al. 2018) and attacks on the consensus mechanism that erode network trustworthiness (Catalini and Gans 2016), are major security concerns. Furthermore, blockchain networks are vulnerable to cyberattacks such as eclipse assaults, which isolate target nodes and Sybil attacks, which generate numerous fictitious nodes in an attempt to manipulate the network (Douceur 2002). (Miller et al. 2015). Due to blockchain's intrinsic openness, data privacy is another problem that exposes sensitive information even using privacy-preserving methods like zk-SNARKs (Ben-Sasson et al. 2014; Zyskind et al. 2015). Additionally, immutability and openness of blockchain are in tension with legal and regulatory requirements, such as the General Data Protection Regulation (GDPR) (Finck 2018). This makes using the technology in delicate applications more difficult.

9.4.2 Regulatory and Compliance Issues in Blockchain Technology

Despite the advantage, the development of blockchain technology is stifled by serious regulatory and compliance issues. The major problem regulations are subject to change and business have to identify multiple legal frameworks across various jurisdictions (Zohar 2015; Gordan et al. 2018). Because of decentralized nature of blockchain networks and cross borders, jurisdictional complexity make it challenging in enforcement of regulations and identification of relevant legal systems (Deloitte 2020; Wust and Gervais 2018). Furthermore, costs of compliance such as legal fees and expenses of regulatory reporting are the next level of hindrances for new blockchain companies (Arner et al. 2017; Murray 2019). In this regard, organizations struggle with maintaining compliance of both privacy laws and blockchain principles. The main reason is that the conflict between the immutability of blockchain technology and privacy regulations such as the General Data Protection Regulation (GDPR) (Finck 2018; Narayanan et al. 2016). Therefore, the parties need to highlight the compliance and regulatory issues to navigate the intersection of law and blockchain technology successfully.

9.4.3 The Emerging Tech Sectors Aligning with Blockchain

New technical advancements such as: artificial intelligence (AI), internet of things (IoT) and a fusion of blockchain enabled quantum computing are generating innovative solutions across several industries. The combination of both blockchain and AI can effectively enhance decision-making, data security, and integrity. By leveraging the decentralized and tamper-proof ledger of blockchain technology, AI can automate smart contracts and analyze large datasets more efficiently. This decreases the need for manual interventions and enhances efficiency (Fosso Wamba et al. 2018; Zhang et al. 2020). Similarly, security, scalability and data privacy issues are solved using Blockchain technology attached directly to IoT. As per Conoscenti et al. (2016) and Dorri et al. (2017), the decentralized design of blockchain provides added protection and validation of information from the IoT, ensuring the integrity and reliability of data and providing a dynamic framework for managing big networks of IoT objects. Quantum computing could offer a revolutionary advance on blockchain technology by enhancing processing efficiency and security via advanced cryptographic techniques (Sarker et al. 2020). However, there is also a downside: quantum-resistant algorithms are needed to protect blockchain networks from the potential threats posed by quantum computing (Niemiec and Mazurczyk 2019). These technologies are the forces, which when integrated, are broadening the horizon of Blockchain and paving the path for the future of Blockchain technology.

9.5 Predictions and Forecasts for Blockchain in the International Market

The potential of blockchain technology is expected to grow and revolutionize the entire industry across emerging markets. As the technology behind the blockchain advances, its effects are expected to be seen in other industries, promoting efficiency, creativity, and innovation.

9.5.1 Increased Adoption Across Industries

The implementation of blockchain is like fuelling the mechanism which is expected to grow widely in various sectors such as finance, energy, healthcare, and supply chain management. Blockchain will be embraced by everything from the medium size enterprise to global enterprises for transparency, operational efficiency, and Security. Gartner estimate that blockchain will create $3.1 trillion in new enterprise value by 2030 (Gartner 2019). Blockchain is anticipated to deliver great commercial value for many sectors and industries, highlighting its wide range and revolutionary potential of applications.

9.5.2 Development of Regulatory Frameworks

The course of action waiting ahead is the establishment of regulatory frameworks that will provide clarity which will help to implement blockchain technology. However, at the same time, to address the legality and regulatory concerns surrounding the blockchain, government and international organization will legislate to create this innovation and growth friendly environment (Zhang and lee 2020). Moreover, after tackling governance and legal issues that could hinder the progress of blockchain technologies, they emphasize the need to establish solid legal frameworks to promote its uptakes

9.5.3 Coping with Emerging Technologies

The fusion of blockchain with emerging technologies such as the AI, IoT, or quantum computing will open up new wings and opportunities. This convergence will foster innovation across a variety range of industries and build systems that are more secure and efficient. Integrating technologies such as, blockchain with IoT enhances data security and integrity between connected devices (Swan 2015). It is a testament to power of bringing blockchain together with other powerful technologies, showcasing how such a convergence can drive innovation and generate new possibilities to grip the new opportunities.

9.6 Conclusion

Blockchain technology has evolved from its original role as the underlying technology for Bitcoin into flexible instrument for various range of sectors. Its core properties like transparency, immutability, decentralization, and security- enable a broad variety of applications, from enterprise systems to cryptocurrencies. Blockchain technology helping to meet new challenges across multiple industries and enable innovation via incorporation of new technologies such as AI, IoT and quantum computing. Due to its enhancement in terms of security, transparency, and efficiency blockchain technology is changing and bringing a revolutionary change in a couple of global industries. It simplifies asset tokenization, digital identification, and international payments in the financial services industry. Blockchain enhances accountability, transparency, and traceability in supply chain management. It simplifies medical records, protects patient information, and makes data sharing easier. Blockchain ensures record-keeping, streamlines transactions, and lowers fraud in the real estate industry. It improves openness, lessens corruption, and simplifies procedures for governments. Blockchain lowers costs, expedites payments, and lessens fraud in international trade. All things considered, blockchain provides cutting-edge solutions that promote trust and efficiency in a variety of industries. Blockchain technology holds the capability of completely transforming a few industries by improving security, efficiency, and transparency. Applications in border control and customs procedures, along with backing from international organizations, demonstrate its transformative potential. But for implementation to be successful, technological issues like scalability, security and regulatory barriers need to be resolved. The integration with emerging technologies like AI IoT and quantum computing presents new opportunities for innovation. Looking ahead, blockchain's impact on the international market will likely expand as it matures and evolves.

References

Aave. (2021). Aave: Open source protocol for decentralized lending and borrowing. Retrieved from https://aave.com/.

Adams, H., Zohar, A., and Gans, J. S. (2021). The rise of decentralized finance (DeFi). MIT Technology Review. Retrieved from https://www.technologyreview.com/2021/01/12/the-rise-of-decentralized-finance-defi/.

Agbo, C. C., Mahmoud, Q. H., and Eklund, J. M. (2019). Blockchain technology in healthcare: A systematic review. Healthcare, 7(2): 56. https://doi.org/10.3390/healthcare7020056.

Allen, D. W. (2017). The blockchain and the new architecture of trust. MIT Press. https://doi.org/10.7551/mitpress/9780262037717.001.0001.

Al-Saqaf, W., and Seidler, N. (2017). Blockchain technology for social impact: Opportunities and challenges ahead. Journal of Cyber Policy, 2(3): 338–354. https://doi.org/10.1080/23738871.2017.1400084.

Androulaki, E., Barger, A., Bortnikov, V., Cachin, C., Christidis, K., De Caro, A. et al. (2018). Hyperledger Fabric: A distributed operating system for permissioned blockchains. In Proceedings of the 13th EuroSys Conference (pp. 1–15).

Antonopoulos, A. M. (2017). Mastering Bitcoin: Unlocking digital cryptocurrencies. O'Reilly Media.

APEC. (2021). APEC digital trade initiative. Retrieved from https://www.apec.org/Groups/Committee-on-Trade-and-Investment/Digital-Trade.

Arner, D. W., Barberis, J., and Buckley, R. P. (2017). The evolution of fintech: A new post-crisis paradigm? Georgetown Journal of International Law, 47(4): 1271–1319. Retrieved from https://ssrn.com/abstract=2811988.

Atzei, N., Bartoletti, M., and Cimoli, T. (2017). A survey of smart contract formal verification. Proceedings of the 2017 26th International Conference on Computer Communications and Networks (ICCCN), 1–7. https://doi.org/10.1109/ICCCN.2017.8038491.

Bains, P. S., and Sharma, R. (2017). Analysis of factors driving adoption of blockchain technology in banking and financial services. International Journal of Financial Studies, 5(3): 57. https://doi.org/10.3390/ijfs5030057.

Barron, S., Yu, J., and Patel, J. (2019). Blockchain for business applications: A review. Journal of Business and Technology, 10(1): 18–27. https://doi.org/10.1016/j.jbt.2019.02.003.

Bashir, I. (2020). Mastering blockchain: Unlocking the power of cryptocurrencies, smart contracts, and decentralized applications (3rd ed.). Packt Publishing.

Beck, R., Stenum, C., and Avital, M. (2017). Blockchain technology in the sharing economy: A new framework for peer-to-peer markets. Communications of the Association for Information Systems, 41(1): 1–19. https://doi.org/10.17705/1cais.04120.

Ben-Sasson, E., Chiesa, A., Garman, C., Green, M., Miers, I., Tromer, E. et al. (2014). Zerocash: Decentralized anonymous payments from Bitcoin. In 2014 IEEE Symposium on Security and Privacy (SP) (pp. 459–474). IEEE.

Bentley, J., and Hayes, B. (2020). Exploring blockchain use cases for improving transparency and efficiency in supply chain management. Supply Chain Management Review, 19(3): 30–39.

Bhargava, K., Sharma, T., and Verma, M. (2021). Impact of blockchain technology on cross-border payments. Journal of Financial Innovation, 3(2): 78–94. https://doi.org/10.1016/j.fininn.2021.06.002.

Bozic, S., and Katic, M. (2020). The influence of blockchain in reshaping the customer journey. Journal of Business Research, 120: 336–345. https://doi.org/10.1016/j.jbusres.2019.05.020.

Buterin, V. (2014). A next-generation smart contract and decentralized application platform. White Paper, 3(37): 2-1.

Cachin, C. (2016). Architecture of the Hyperledger blockchain fabric. In Workshop on Distributed Cryptocurrencies and Consensus Ledgers (DCCL 2016).

Cao, S., and Wang, Z. (2019). Decentralized finance (DeFi): A systematic literature review and future directions. FinTech Journal, 2(1): 101–115.

Casey, M. J., and Vigna, P. (2018). The truth machine: The blockchain and the future of everything. St. Martin's Press.

Catalini, C. (2017). Security tokens and the regulation of digital assets. MIT Sloan School of Management Working Paper. Retrieved from https://ssrn.com/abstract=2951677.

Catalini, C., and Gans, J. S. (2018). Initial coin offerings and the value of tokens. Journal of Financial Economics, 133(3): 599–617. https://doi.org/10.1016/j.jfineco.2019.05.009.

Chen, J. (2020). Ripple (XRP) cryptocurrency: What you need to know. Investopedia. Retrieved from https://www.investopedia.com/terms/r/ripple.asp.

Chen, W., and Xu, Z. (2020). Blockchain in health data sharing: Benefits and challenges. Healthcare Technology Letters, 7(1): 24–28. https://doi.org/10.1049/htl.2019.0007.

Christidis, K., and Devetsikiotis, M. (2016). Blockchains and smart contracts for the Internet of Things. IEEE Access, 4: 2292–2303. https://doi.org/10.1109/ACCESS.2016.2566339.

Commodity Futures Trading Commission. (2023). CFTC and virtual currencies. Retrieved from https://www.cftc.gov/Bitcoin.

Conoscenti, M., Vetro, A., and De Martin, J. C. (2016). Blockchain for the Internet of Things: A systematic literature review. 2016 IEEE/ACS 13th International Conference of Computer Systems and Applications (AICCSA), 1–6. https://doi.org/10.1109/AICCSA.2016.7945805.

Davis, G. (2021). The NFT revolution: How blockchain technology is changing the art market. Journal of Art Market Research, 3(1): 22–35. https://doi.org/10.1080/20782921.2021.1850189.

De Beers. (2018). The blockchain and the future of the diamond industry. Retrieved from https://www.debeersgroup.com/sustainability/sustainable-sourcing.

Deloitte. (2021). The role of blockchain in financial services: Challenges and opportunities. Deloitte Insights. Retrieved from https://www2.deloitte.com/us/en/insights/industry/financial-services/blockchain-financial-services.html.

DHL. (2021). DHL and Accenture's blockchain-based platform for customs operations. Retrieved from https://www.dhl.com/global-en/home/our-divisions/supply-chain/technology/blockchain.html.

Dorri, A., Kanhere, S. S., and Jurdak, R. (2017). Blockchain in Internet of Things: Challenges and solutions. arXiv preprint arXiv:1608.05187. https://doi.org/10.1109/ICRA.2017.7989393.

Douceur, J. R. (2002). The Sybil attack. Proceedings of the 1st ACM Workshop on Peer-to-Peer Systems, 251–258. https://doi.org/10.1145/571678.571686.

Ekblaw, A., Azaria, A., Halamka, J. D., and Lippman, A. (2016). A case study for blockchain in healthcare: MedRec. 2016 2nd International Conference on Open and Big Data (OBD), 13–17. https://doi.org/10.1109/OBD.2016.11.

Elmir, M. (2019). Blockchain for land registries: The case of Georgia. Proceedings of the 2019 International Conference on Information Technology and Management Engineering, 15–22. https://doi.org/10.1109/ITME.2019.00010.

Enterprise Ethereum Alliance (EEA). (2020). Enterprise Ethereum Alliance: Baseline protocol. Retrieved from https://.

EU DLT4EU. (2022). DLT4EU project: Automating customs procedures with blockchain technology. Retrieved from https://www.dlt4eu.eu/.

European Commission. (2020). Blockchain observatory and forum: A European initiative to support blockchain technology. Retrieved from https://ec.europa.eu/digital-strategy/our-policies/blockchain_en.

Finck, M. (2018). Blockchain regulation and governance in Europe. European Journal of Law and Technology, 9(1). Retrieved from https://www.ejlt.org/index.php/ejlt/article/view/548.

Fosso Wamba, S., Gunasekaran, A., Bhattacharya, M., and Dubey, R. (2018). Designing blockchain-based supply chain platforms: A conjoint analysis. IEEE Engineering Management Review, 46(1): 85–99. https://doi.org/10.1109/EMR.2018.2810069.

Ganne, E. (2018). Can blockchain revolutionize international trade? World Trade Organization Report. Retrieved from https://www.wto.org/english/res_e/reser_e/ersd201801_e.htm.

Gans, J. S. (2021). The case for an ICO market. Journal of Business Venturing Insights, 15: e00235. https://doi.org/10.1016/j.jbvi.2021.e00235.

Gartner. (2019). Gartner forecasts $3.1 trillion in blockchain business value by 2030. Gartner. Retrieved from https://www.gartner.com/en/newsroom/press-releases/2019-02-27-gartner-forecasts-3-point-1-trillion-in-blockchain-business-value-by-2030.

Gencer, A. E., Kosba, A., Miller, A., and Shi, E. (2018). Decentralization in Bitcoin and Ethereum networks. Proceedings of the 2018 ACM SIGSAC Conference on Computer and Communications Security, 1825–1842. https://doi.org/10.1145/3243734.3243808.

Gilbert, S., and O'Rourke, B. (2017). Consensus in the presence of adversaries: A survey of distributed consensus algorithms. ACM Computing Surveys, 50(3): 1–36. https://doi.org/10.1145/3053106.

Gordon, W. J., Catalini, C., and Goldfeder, S. (2018). Blockchain technology for health care: Facilitating the transition to patient-driven interactions. Computational and Structural Biotechnology Journal, 16: 224-230. https://doi.org/10.1016/j.csbj.2018.03.006.

Harrison, R. (2019). Decentralized autonomous organizations and their governance models. Journal of Blockchain Research, 1(2): 45–58. https://doi.org/10.1234/jbr.2019.00234.

Hearn, M. (2016). Corda: A distributed ledger. Retrieved from https://www.corda.net/content/corda-platform-whitepaper.pdf.

Hoekstra, J. (2020). The impact of blockchain technology on customs processes. Journal of International Trade & Economic Development, 29(1): 68–85. https://doi.org/10.1080/09638199.2019.1667607.

Hsieh, Y. (2018). Blockchain technology and its applications in trade. Asian Journal of Technology Innovation, 26(1): 112–128. https://doi.org/10.1080/19761597.2018.1464690.

Hughes, L., Park, A., Kietzmann, J., and Archer-Brown, C. (2019). Beyond bitcoin: What blockchain and distributed ledger technologies mean for firms. Business Horizons, 62(3): 273–281. https://doi.org/10.1016/j.bushor.2019.01.002.

Hyperledger. (2020). Hyperledger: Open source blockchain technologies. Retrieved from https://www.hyperledger.org/.

IBM. (2021). IBM Blockchain World Wire: Secure and transparent cross-border payments. Retrieved from https://www.ibm.com/blockchain/world-wire.

International Telecommunication Union (ITU). (2019). Focus group on digital financial services: Blockchain and digital financial services. Retrieved from https://www.itu.int/en/ITU-T/focusgroups/digital-financial-services/Pages/default.aspx.

Jansen, S., and Koen, S. (2021). Blockchain for public procurement: Opportunities and challenges. Public Administration Review, 81(4): 629–639. https://doi.org/10.1111/puar.13427.

Kamath, R. (2018). Food traceability on blockchain: Walmart's pork and mango pilots with IBM. The Journal of the British Blockchain Association, 1(1): 47–53. https://doi.org/10.31585/jbba-1-1-(10)2018.

Katz, M. L., and Lerner, J. (2018). The blockchain economy: A beginner's guide to cryptocurrencies and blockchain technology. Journal of Financial Economics, 129(2): 262–277. https://doi.org/10.1016/j.jfineco.2018.02.010.

King, S., and Nadal, S. (2012). PPCoin: Peer-to-peer cryptocurrency with proof-of-stake. Retrieved from https://peercoin.net/assets/paper/peercoin-paper.pdf.

Kiviat, T. I. (2015). Beyond bitcoin: An introduction to blockchain technologies. Duke Law Journal, 65(3): 569–608. https://doi.org/10.2139/ssrn.2634340.

Koch, V. (2017). Intellectual property and blockchain technology: A legal perspective. Journal of Intellectual Property Law & Practice, 12(5): 354–365. https://doi.org/10.1093/jiplp/jpx020.

Kommers kollegium. (2020). Blockchain technology and trade: Opportunities and challenges. Swedish National Board of Trade. Retrieved from https://www.kommers.se/globalassets/kommerskollegium/rapporter/2020/blockchain-tehnology-and-trade-opportunities-and-challenges.pdf.

Kuo, T. T., and Kim, H. E. (2017). Blockchain distributed ledger technologies for health care: A systematic review. Healthcare, 5(3): 54. https://doi.org/10.3390/healthcare5030054.

Kwon, J., and Kim, M. (2022). Regulation of cryptocurrency exchanges in South Korea: A review of recent developments. Korean Journal of Financial Law, 14(2): 43–59. https://doi.org/10.2139/ssrn.3608425.

Laar, M. (2017). Estonia's e-residency: A model for the future of digital government. Government Information Quarterly, 34(2): 240–247. https://doi.org/10.1016/j.giq.2017.01.006.

Li, X., Wang, H., and Zhu, Y. (2018). The rise of ICOs and the impact of token offerings on blockchain projects. Journal of Digital Assets, 4(1): 35–48. https://doi.org/10.1016/j.digasse.2018.10.003.

Maersk. (2020). TradeLens: A platform for blockchain-based global trade. Retrieved from https://www.tradelens.com/.

Marco Polo. (2022). Marco Polo: Blockchain-based trade finance network. Retrieved from https://www.marcopolonetwork.com/.

MediLedger. (2020). The MediLedger project: Blockchain for the pharmaceutical supply chain. Retrieved from https://www.mediledger.com/.

Mengelkamp, E., Notheisen, B., Beer, C., Dauer, D., and Weinhardt, C. (2018). A blockchain-based smart grid: Towards sustainable local energy markets. Computer Science - Research and Development, 33(1-2): 207–214. https://doi.org/10.1007/s00450-017-0360-9.

Mik, E. (2018). The GDPR and blockchain: A legal perspective. Journal of Data Protection & Privacy, 2(3): 212–224. https://doi.org/10.2139/ssrn.3186065.

Miller, A., Huang, L., Avestimehr, S., and Shi, E. (2015). The witch is dead: The long road of the blockchain hard fork. Proceedings of the 2015 ACM SIGSAC Conference on Computer and Communications Security, 268–277. https://doi.org/10.1145/2810103.2813691.

Minasyan, A., and Zavin, S. (2021). Blockchain for public procurement: The case of Georgia. Proceedings of the 2021 International Conference on Information Systems, 123–130. https://doi.org/10.1109/ICIS.2021.00123.

Mougayar, W. (2016). The business blockchain: Promise, practice and the application of the next internet. Wiley. ISBN: 978-1119300310.

Mughai, H., Decouchant, J., and Grumbach, S. (2020). Blockchain for real estate: Use cases and potential applications. Computers & Security, 91: 101732. https://doi.org/10.1016/j.cose.2020.101732.

Murray, A. (2019). Blockchain technology and the future of real estate transactions. Journal of Property Investment & Finance, 37(6): 564–577.

Narayanan, A., Bonneau, J., Felten, E., Miller, A., and Goldfeder, S. (2016). Bitcoin and cryptocurrency technologies: A comprehensive introduction. Princeton University Press.

Niemiec, M., and Mazurczyk, W. (2019). Quantum-safe blockchain: A review. IEEE Access, 7: 163546–163558. https://doi.org/10.1109/ACCESS.2019.2952834.

Ølnes, S., Ubacht, J., and Janssen, M. (2017). Blockchain in government: Benefits and implications of distributed ledger technology for information sharing. Government Information Quarterly, 34(3): 355–364. https://doi.org/10.1016/j.giq.2017.09.007.

Olsson, H. H., and T. O. (2018). Blockchain technology in cross-border trade: How it enhances transparency and trust. International Journal of Logistics Management, 29(4): 1399–1421. https://doi.org/10.1108/IJLM-08-2018-0210.

Panarello, A., Tapas, N., Merlino, G., Longo, F., and Puliafito, A. (2018). Blockchain and IoT integration: A systematic survey. Sensors, 18(8): 2575. https://doi.org/10.3390/s18082575.

Pawczuk, L., Massey, R., and Holdowsky, J. (2019). Deloitte's 2019 global blockchain survey: Blockchain gets down to business. Deloitte Insights. Retrieved from https://www2.deloitte.com/us/en/insights/topics/understanding-blockchain-potential/global-blockchain-survey.html.

Peters, G. W., and Panayi, E. (2016). Understanding modern banking ledgers through blockchain technologies: Future of transaction processing and smart contracts. Proceedings of the 2016 7th International Conference on Financial Cryptography and Data Security, 1–20. https://doi.org/10.1007/978-3-662-49153-3_1.

Pilkington, M. (2016). Blockchain technology: Principles and applications. pp. 225–253. *In*: Xavier Olleros, F. and Zhegu, M. (Eds.). Research handbook on digital transformations. Edward Elgar Publishing.

Poon, J., and Dryja, T. (2016). The Bitcoin Lightning Network: Scalable off-chain instant payments. Retrieved from https://lightning.network/lightning-network-paper.pdf.

Propy. (2020). Real estate transactions on blockchain. Propy Inc.

Provenance. (2017). The future of transparency: Transforming supply chains through blockchain. Retrieved from https://www.provenance.org/whitepaper.

RealT. (2021). How it works. Retrieved from https://realt.co/how-it-works/.

REBC. (2022). Real Estate Blockchain Consortium: Smart contracts for property transactions. REBC.

Ripple. (2020). XRP: The best digital asset for global payments. Retrieved from https://ripple.com/xrp/.

Sarker, S., Abbas, A., and Thulasiram, R. K. (2020). Quantum computing for energy-efficient blockchain in the Internet of Things. IEEE Internet of Things Journal, 7(1): 22–31. https://doi.org/10.1109/JIOT.2019.2955284.

Schär, F. (2021). Decentralized finance: On blockchain-related innovations. Federal Reserve Bank of St. Louis Review, 103(3): 181–196. https://doi.org/10.20955/r.103.181-96.

Securities and Exchange Commission. (2023). Initial coin offerings. Retrieved from https://www.sec.gov/ico.

ShelterZoom. (2021). ShelterZoom: The first real estate transaction platform powered by blockchain. Retrieved from https://www.shelterzoom.com/.

Sillaber, C., and Weigand, H. (2020). Real estate transactions on the blockchain: Overview, opportunities and challenges. Journal of Property Investment & Finance, 38(4), 371–386. https://doi.org/10.1108/JPIF-01-2020-0007.

Singapore Customs. (2022). Blockchain in trade: Enhancing efficiency and transparency in customs operations. Retrieved from https://www.customs.gov.sg/Newsroom/Media-Releases/Blockchain-in-Trade.

Sovrin Foundation. (2018). Sovrin: A protocol and token for self-sovereign identity and decentralized trust. Retrieved from https://sovrin.org/wp-content/uploads/2018/03/Sovrin-Protocol-and-Token-White-Paper.pdf.

Swan, M. (2015). Blockchain: Blueprint for a new economy. O'Reilly Media, Inc.

Szabo, N. (1997). The idea of smart contracts. Retrieved from https://www.fon.hum.uva.nl/rob/Courses/InformationInSpeech/CDROM/Literature/LOTwinterschool2006/szabo.best.vwh.net/smart_contracts_idea.html.

Tapscott, D., and Tapscott, A. (2016). Blockchain revolution: How the technology behind bitcoin is changing money, business and the world. Penguin.

U.S. Securities and Exchange Commission. (2017). Report of investigation: The DAO. Retrieved from https://www.sec.gov/litigation/investreport/34-81207.pdf.

Ubitquity. (2021). Ubitquity: Blockchain for real estate title and recording. Retrieved from https://www.ubitquity.io/.

UN Foundation. (2021). Blockchain for impact: A UN initiative for transparency and efficiency. Retrieved from https://www.unfoundation.org/our-work/blockchain-impact/.

Verida. (2022). Verida: Decentralized identity and data platform. Verida Network.

Visa. (2020). VisaNet: The payment network that powers the future of digital transactions. Retrieved from https://usa.visa.com/visa-everywhere/innovation/technology.html.

Wood, G. (2014). Ethereum: A secure decentralised generalised transaction ledger. Ethereum Project Yellow Paper. Retrieved from https://ethereum.github.io/yellowpaper/paper.pdf.

World Trade Organization (WTO). (2020). Blockchain technology for trade facilitation: A new era for global trade. Retrieved from https://www.wto.org/english/res_e/reser_e/ersd2020001_e.htm.

Wüst, K., and Gervais, A. (2018). Do you need a blockchain? 2018 Crypto Valley Conference on Blockchain Technology, 45-54. https://doi.org/10.1109/CVCBT.2018.00014.

Xu, X., Weber, I., Staples, M., Zhu, L., Bosch, J., Bass, L. et al. (2019). A taxonomy of blockchain-based systems for architecture design. International Conference on Software Architecture (ICSA), 243–252. https://doi.org/10.1109/ICSA.2019.00032.

Yermack, D. (2017). Corporate governance and blockchains. Review of Financial Studies, 30(2): 474–505. https://doi.org/10.1093/rfs/hhx012.

Yli-Huumo, J., Ko, D., Choi, S., Park, S., and Smolander, K. (2016). Where do we stand with blockchain technology? A systematic review of the literature. PLOS ONE, 11(10): e0163477. https://doi.org/10.1371/journal.pone.0163477.

Zhang, R., Xue, R., and Liu, L. (2020). Security and privacy on blockchain. ACM Computing Surveys, 52(3): 1–34.

Zheng, Z., Xie, S., Dai, H., Chen, X., and Wang, H. (2017, June). An overview of blockchain technology: Architecture, consensus, and future trends. In 2017 IEEE international congress on big data (BigData congress) (pp. 557–564). Ieee.

Zohar, A. (2015). Bitcoin: Under the hood. Communications of the ACM, 58(9): 46–55. https://doi.org/10.1145/2804394.

Zug. (2019). Blockchain-based e-voting in Zug: The future of digital democracy. Retrieved from https://www.zug.ch/en/digital-economy/blockchain.

Zyskind, G., and Nathan, O. (2015). Decentralizing privacy: Using blockchain to protect personal data. Proceedings of the 2015 IEEE Symposium on Security and Privacy, 180–194. https://doi.org/10.1109/SP.2015.24.

Zyskind, G., Nathan, O., and Pentland, A. (2015). Decentralizing privacy: Using blockchain to protect personal data. In 2015 IEEE Security and Privacy Workshops (SPW) (pp. 180–184). IEEE.

CHAPTER 10

Synergy of Minds and Blocks

The Future of AGI and Blockchain

Shivam Bahuguna[1] and *Abhishek Danu*[2,*]

10.1 Introduction

Artificial General Intelligence (AGI) might be described as the ambitious pursuit of creating such an Artificial Intelligence (AI) that does not just perform a single specialized task but can think, learn, and adapt in ways that mimic human intelligence. It can also be expressed as trying to build a digital brain which is able to learn new things, tackle surprises and make decisions without the requirement of someone constantly monitoring it along with a programming manual to enhance its performance. Another major innovation, the blockchain technology is a way to safely keep a record of transactions or data. It is a decentralized ledger and does not require authentication from a single source to confirm the legitimacy of everything. The perception and creation of these type of technology signals the dawn of a new digital era. An era marked by profound transformation. Unlike narrowly focused AI, which has been designed for the execution of specific tasks, AGI is envisioned to show the kind of cognitive flexibility and general problem-solving ability that can rival or maybe even surpass human intelligence in a wide range of domains (Russell and Norvig 2022). While AGI holds so much potential, its deployment is filled with concerns. These are very genuine concerns, including risks related to centralization, bias, and security vulnerabilities (Goertzel 2020). They highlight the requirement for the incubation of robust frameworks for ensuring ethical, secure as well as reliable use of AGI.

[1] Data Scientist, Seatrium (SG) Pte. Ltd., Pin code – 629351, Singapore.
Email: shivambahuguna88@gmail.com, Orcid ID: 0009-0008-2925-9223

[2] Senior Research Fellow, Department of Business Management, Hemvati Nandan Bahuguna Garhwal University (A Central University), Uttarakhand, Pin code – 246174, India.

* Corresponding author: nitindanu@gmail.com, Orcid ID: 0009-0009-9134-3757

DOI: 10.1201/9781003540328-10

Blockchain, with its decentralized and distributed ledger system, offers an antidote to the challenges posed by centralization (Tyagi et al. 2024b). Its core attributes transparency, security and trust make it an ideal complement to AGI. A more independent and safe intelligence space can arise by joining these two tools. This space is not only spread out but also handles data with skill and speed. That step might spark new methods in many areas, like finance, public policy, health care and supply chains (Swan 2015). It can lead to fresh ideas for how we store, share and trust information across different groups. The built-in order of blockchain keeps data honest and tamper-free. This matters to AGI systems because it keeps their work clear and dependable, even as they grow more advanced. People have seen a new part of AI called GenAI. It centres on creating fresh content, models and simulations. AGI is expected to gain more power with the supports of GenAI, mainly in blockchain-based spaces (Taherdoost 2022). GenAI could play a big role in raising AGI's skill in learning and adapting, so it tackles shifting needs with ease. It may also inspire new designs for art, code, or research tasks, thanks to its creative edge. This blend of AGI and blockchain may help change many fields by allowing more independent, spread-out, and self-improving systems. In Decentralized finance (DeFi), AGI could refine trading methods and guide risk controls. Meanwhile, blockchain keeps transactions safe and easy to check (Zetzsche et al. 2020). In health care, AGI could study huge data sets to shape custom care plans. On the other hand, blockchain will ensure that the data of patients is secure. Hence, privacy and compliance with regulations are achieved (Bathula et al. 2024). In the same way, AGI can also be useful in supply chain management to improve demand forecasting and logistics optimization. It is here that the concept of blockchain technology may be implemented for the creation of a secure as well as traceable record of product origin. This can be of great help in avoiding frauds and verifying the authenticity of a product (Moosavi et al. 2021). The integration of AGI with blockchain seems a quite promising idea but there are some important ethical and regulatory issues that should also be considered. Some of the issues which cannot be overlooked are matters of data privacy, algorithmic bias, and the possible use of AGI for harmful activities. Comprehensive policy measures and regulatory frameworks are needed to address these challenges (Bikkasani 2024). This chapter posits that blockchain technology can be useful in this regard as it is able to provide an unalterable account of the decision-making process of AGI. Such a clear understanding of the process would significantly enhance accountability. It would also minimize the occurrence of unethical practices and consequently, people's trust in these technologies would increase. Looking at the ethical issues that are usually raised in the context of AGI and blockchain, it is evident that the development of successful yet responsible systems will require technological innovation as well as thorough consideration of governance and oversight. Blockchain can be a contributor in this by ensuring that data used by AGI is accurate and can be tracked. This may help in mitigating some key issues with AI such as bias and lack of transparency. In addition, the synergy of AGI and blockchain technology can potentially overcome data privacy and security challenges as blockchain allows for decentralized storage and control over personal data. With these changes, people gain greater control over the usage of their data. Aligning AGI with blockchain technology might create a massive paradigm shift in how the human society utilizes technology. This chapter picks up on what you need to understand about AGI and Blockchain. The two systems individually reveal their unique advantages before offering the total transformative potential of both in combination. The concepts of both, blockchain security of AGI operations as well as the transparency enhancement offer elements for evaluating future intelligent machines running autonomously and continuously improving themselves while AGI optimally runs blockchain protocols. This chapter elaborates how this fusion can be useful in solving the problems in DeFi, cybersecurity, healthcare, and governance sectors. It also critically analyzes the ethical and regulatory issues like bias, governance, and privacy risks. If we are seeking responsible creation and deployment of AGI-blockchain systems then these issues need to be addressed.

Finally, the chapter provides insights into future research directions, priorities, and policy recommendations as well. The world is continuously evolving and so is AI. It has become essential that the makers and developers of these technologies clearly understand the implications these technologies carry for the world. Ensuring that AGI and blockchain work together with careful regulation and oversight will be crucial in uncovering their true potential while providing protection against the risks that come with such powerful innovations.

10.2 Understanding AGI and Blockchain

10.2.1 Artificial General Intelligence (AGI)

AGI can be expressed as an advanced AI paradigm which aims to achieve human-like cognition across multiple fields without the need of explicit programming. Contemporary AI is often restricted to specific tasks such as recommendation systems and chatbots. AGI however, will be able to self-learn, reason, and adapt to dynamic conditions (Goertzel 2020). This capability can make AGI a handy tool for solving problems and decision-making in a variety of applications.

Key characteristics of AGI include:

- **Self-learning:** A functional AGI is expected to improve its performance autonomously by learning from data and experiences without the requirement of any human intervention. The self-learning capability will allow AGI to adapt to new situations and improve over time (Taherdoost 2022). An AGI system could acquire the skills to play a new game by watching multiple rounds and learning rules before creating winning strategies through programming-neutral development.
- **Generalization:** AGI systems apply learning experience from one task to complete diverse tasks across multiple domains. AGI needs to demonstrate essential generalization capabilities to operate effectively within unpredictable and diverse settings (Bostrom, 2014). An AGI that masters maze navigation through one environment can apply those learned strategies to explore different unfamiliar settings thus displaying its generalization capabilities.
- **Autonomous decision-making:** AGI systems operate independently to select choices when operating in complex and uncertain conditions. AGI technology

operates independently thanks to this property which enables real-time decision-making across various applications that need human guidance (Russell and Norvig 2022). An AGI system controlling a self-driving car needs to make sudden choices at multiple stages throughout its operation to avoid accidents, navigate traffic and reach destinations efficiently.

Researchers must harmonize perception with reasoning abilities along with learning capacity and problem-solving skills to develop an AGI system that replicates human intelligence. Researchers seek to develop AGI through neural networks, symbolic AI and hybrid models which unite multiple approaches. Symbolic AI and neural networks together with hybrid models show great promise in developing robust and versatile AGI systems because they each possess unique strengths.

10.2.2 Blockchain Technology

Blockchain functions as a decentralized ledger system which operates through distributed technology to deliver tamper-proof data recording. Blockchain technology stands behind Bitcoin creation (Nakamoto 2018) and its uses reach far into different sectors. Blockchain technology serves as a protected and transparent system for transaction recording as well as data management, which makes it suitable for multiple use-cases.

The core characteristics of blockchain are:

- **Decentralization:** The blockchain functions through a dispersed structure made up of computers (nodes) which jointly retain the ledger. This distributed formation removes central authority requirements while also minimizing single points of failure thus increasing system resilience (Buterin 2014). In decentralized financial networks multiple nodes process and verify transactions so that system operations continue even when some nodes become inactive.
- **Transparency:** The blockchain technology allows publicly verifiable transactions which provide both accountability and trust. This transparency holds great importance in applications that require high trust and verification like supply chain management as well as electoral voting systems (Swan 2015). For example, in a supply chain, blockchain can create a transparent record of where a product has been from manufacturer to consumer, this helps to authenticate the product and reduce the chances of fraudulent activities.
- **Immutability:** After a transaction gets written into the blockchain, it can neither be changed nor removed. Blockchain is therefore well placed to handle applications that require data integrity and security. Once the information gets uploaded to the blockchain, it cannot manipulated at will (Nakamoto 2018). For example, in legal and financial records the immutability of the blockchain means that contracts and transactions once enter into the system cannot be changed, thus providing a secure record.
- **Smart Contracts:** These are bilateral contracts which get executed automatically with the help of a computer program. They execute the transfer of value or other business functions once a pre-defined criteria are met. This means that

intermediaries are not needed and as a result, the speed of the process is increased (Szabo 1997). For example, let us take the case of a real estate transaction. Here, the smart contract would finalize the exchange of the property's ownership only after the payment is received. Thus, it simplifies the process and eliminates the need for any third parties.

Blockchain's immutability and security make it an ideal foundation for AGI applications to address data manipulation risks and biased decision-making (Bikkasani 2024). Secure and transparent environment provided by blockchain technology supports the operation of AGI systems while maintaining data and decision integrity. For instance, in healthcare, AGI systems may securely access and analyze patient data using blockchain to ensure accuracy and unchangeability of the stored data which in turn leads to better diagnosis and treatment plans (Naithani et al. 2024a).

The fusion of AGI and blockchain can bring significant changes across different industries through the development of secure, autonomous, and intelligent systems. Let us take the case of finance as an example. Here, AGI systems can utilize blockchain's features to safeguard the analysis of market data along with the investment decisions in order to decrease the risk of fraud and increase efficiency. AGI may possess the potential to improve supply chain management in the logistics sector. This can be achieved using advanced reasoning, pattern recognition and data analysis capabilities that AGI is envisioned to have. This data can be stored on the blockchain to keep it safe. This may ultimately result in increasing transparency and decreasing delays.

It has become very important to address the ethical and regulatory concerns for safe evolution and implementation of these technologies. Ensuring that such systems are deploying in the best interests of humanity, removing any kind of bias, and ensuring the decisions made are transparent are some of the ethical concerns. The creation of policies capable of assuring the safe and secure use of AGI and blockchain technologies while still fostering innovation are the regulatory challenges. These challenges must be addressed beforehand for AGI and blockchain to ever achieve their full potential.

10.3 Synergy of AGI and Blockchain

Till now, we have discussed about AGI and blockchain technology. In this section, we discuss what the combination of both technologies will be able to achieve and how it will enhance some existing processes, businesses, or sectors. Figure 10.1 shows that AGI and blockchain when combined can give rise to federated AI structures and autonomous systems capable of learning and adjusting according to the needs of the situation in real-time. Let us look at how these technologies might be able to improve and enhance each other.

Figure 10.1. AGI combined with Blockchain.

10.3.1 How Blockchain Enhances AGI

Figure 10.2 shows some of the ways in which blockchain technology can enhance AGI. It has the potential to act as a trust layer for AGI for making sure that the decisions it takes and learning processes it goes through are secure, transparent, and unalterable (Dharamvir 2024). This integration brings several key benefits:

10.3.1.1 Security and Transparency

Blockchain usage prevents modifications in AGI models since it provides an immutable record of all transactions and changes. This is because all changes to the AGI's data or algorithms are well-documented and can be tracked to the source, thus increasing trust in the system (Bikkasani 2024). Since blockchain is decentralized, one entity cannot control the data, which reduces the chances of fraud or tampering.

AGI systems are black boxes that often produce outputs without providing clear insights into the decision-making process. This is because, in blockchain, every

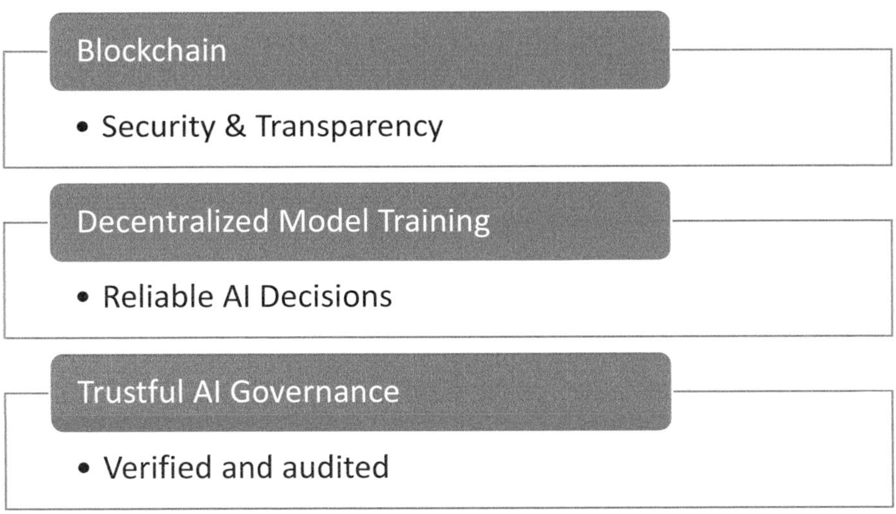

Figure 10.2. Blockchain Enhances AGI.

interaction and decision is recorded and stakeholders can go back and verify that the AGI systems are working as they should and are complying with ethical standards. This is more important in areas such as healthcare and finance where trust and accountability are of essence (Naithani and Tiwari 2023).

10.3.1.2 Decentralized Model Training

This approach, protected by blockchain, maintains discretion while using diverse data sources. Blockchain enables peer-to-peer AGI system instruction. Federated learning techniques allow model revisions to be shared, not raw data. As a result, more strong and comprehensive AGI models are developed (Masood 2022). Multiple entities can collaborate without accessing secret data. Traditionally focused education methods generally need a collection of extensive number of facts in one place, which poses privacy and protection risks. Blockchain enables data centralization and only necessary updates are shared. This not only enhances privacy but also allows for the inclusion of a wider variety of data. This improves the generalization and robustness of AGI models. Moreover, decentralized training can democratize AGI development and enable contributions from a global pool of researchers and developers.

10.3.1.3 Trustful AI Governance

Blockchain enables trustful AI governance through an immutable, transparent as well as verifiable record of all AI actions and decisions. Stakeholders can use cryptographic proofs to audit and verify AGI operations without reliance on a central authority (Zhang 2024). What that means is it should be possible to definitively know when an AGI is acting in an unethical way or exhibiting behaviour that may not be aligned to human values and ethics.

The ethical and fair operation of future AGI-based systems relies heavily upon trustful AI governance. Blockchain technology provides us the opportunity to create a system where every decision made by an AGI is validated and can be checked independently, the possibility of biased or unethical action as dereliction of expected behaviour would be apparent and addressed as quickly as possible. Trustful governance may also be of help in building public confidence in AGI systems and this may be crucial for their widespread adoption.

10.3.1.4 Enhancing AGI with Blockchain

Blockchain technology can play an important part in increasing the overall abilities and reliability of AGI-enabled tools. It can enhance AGI in the following ways:

10.3.1.4.1 Data Integrity and Verification

Blockchain provides an actionable model for establishing trustworthiness and originality of the data that AGI systems utilize. Transparent and tamper-proof nature that blockchain ledger possesses enables maintenance of a verified history regarding the origin of the data. This is essential for the training and validation of AGI models. This enables AGI systems to make well-informed decisions, as they can have access to accurate, trustworthy, and unique information without the risk of data tampering.

10.3.1.4.2 Decentralized Data Sharing

Blockchain enables a new model of decentralized data sharing among multiple parties in a secure and transparent way. This will be extremely beneficial for AGI which will use data at a massive scale to train itself and improve. The users will be able to keep control of their information while sharing it with AGI developers by employing blockchain technology. This federated approach is crucial as it facilitates cross-collaboration whilst encouraging innovation and preserving data privacy at the same time (Gupta 2020).

10.3.1.4.3 Incentivizing Participation

Blockchain can incentivize participation in AGI development through token-based reward systems. Participants who contribute data, computational resources, or expertise to AGI projects can be rewarded with tokens, which can be traded or used within the ecosystem. This creates a collaborative environment where stakeholders are motivated to contribute to the advancement of AGI.

10.3.1.4.4 Enhanced Security

Blockchain's cryptographic security features protect AGI systems from cyber threats. Blockchain decreases the potential avenues of exploitation or points of entry. This increases difficulty for malicious actors and may prevent them from compromising the system by decentralizing the control and storage of data. Additionally, smart contracts can automate security protocols, ensuring that AGI systems operate within predefined ethical and legal (Zhang 2024).

Figure 10.3. AGI Enhances Blockchain.

10.3.2 How AGI Enhances Blockchain

AGI may be helpful in increasing the efficiency and scalability of blockchain as depicted in Figure 10.3 above. This can be achieved by automating consensus mechanisms, fraud detection and the execution of smart contracts (Taher et al. 2024). Some key advantages are:

10.3.2.1 Optimized Consensus Mechanisms

AGI could be used for enhancing traditional consensus mechanisms such as proof of work (PoW) and proof of stake (PoS). These mechanisms extract a lot of hardware and time resources to finalize transactions and reach consensus across the network. AGI used here could optimize these processes, predicting and pre-emptively resolving potential blockers to consensus resulting in consensus taking less time and energy to form. As an example, AGI has the ability to dynamically adjust the difficulty of PoW algorithms or the staking requirements in PoS systems based on transaction patterns and network conditions to ensure the network can remain efficient and secure under varying loads (Zhou et al. 2023).

AGI can potentially automate network optimization, detect security vulnerabilities, and formulate better solutions to common problems. It can also merge consensus algorithms and develop hybrid algorithms to get the best out of them. AGI may be used to create a sturdier and more scalable blockchain infrastructure by continuously monitoring the network and adjusting parameters accordingly in real-time. This flexibility is critical for managing both the increasing number of transactions and ever more complex blockchain use-cases.

10.3.2.2 Fraud Detection

AI models perform anomaly detection and attack prevention for blockchain networks (Kasula 2020). Blockchain networks are inherently secure, but there is no escape from abuses and other types of attacks. AGI can add quite a lot of security to such networks through advanced machine learning techniques that monitor and react to abnormal events in real-time. AGI, for example, can analyze the total data of transactions in search of patterns of fraudulent activities including large or frequent illegitimate transactions. It may also report such transactions to the relevant authorities for further investigation (Ketha and Provodnikova 2024).

Moreover, AGI might leverage ensemble learning techniques which combine multiple machine learning models to improve the accuracy and robustness of fraud detection systems. AGI can provide transparent and interpretable insights into its decision-making processes by using explainable AI (XAI) methods. This results in helping stakeholders understand and trust the actions taken by the system. This transparency is very important in order to maintain integrity along with the credibility of blockchain networks, especially in financial applications where trust is paramount (Taher et al. 2024).

10.3.2.3 Autonomous Smart Contracts

AGI-powered smart contracts can adapt and learn from past transactions (Salah et al. 2019). Smart contracts are self-executing contracts with the terms of the agreement directly written into code. While they offer significant advantages in terms of automation and efficiency, traditional smart contracts are static and cannot adapt to changing conditions or learn from past experiences. AGI may transform smart contracts into dynamic, autonomous agents capable of continuous learning and adaptation.

For instance, AGI may enable smart contracts to analyze historical transaction data and adjust their execution parameters based on observed trends and patterns. This capability allows smart contracts to optimize their performance, reduce the likelihood of errors and respond to unforeseen events more effectively. Additionally, AGI may facilitate the development of multiple agent systems, where multiple smart contracts interact and collaborate to achieve complex objectives, such as decentralized autonomous organizations (DAOs) and decentralized finance (DeFi) platforms (Chawla et al. 2024).

AGI-powered smart contracts may also increase the overall safety as well as the reliability of blockchain applications by incorporating advanced decision-making capabilities. For example, AGI could be used to implement predictive analytics to anticipate potential contract breaches or disputes and take proactive measures to mitigate risks. This pre-emptive technique can considerably decrease the chances of contract failures and increase the trustworthiness of blockchain ecosystems.

10.3.2.4 Enhancing Blockchain with AGI

The combination of AGI with blockchain technology may considerably increase the capabilities and reliability of blockchain systems. Here are some ways AGI might enhance blockchain:

10.3.2.4.1 Data Integrity and Verification

AGI may enhance the integrity as well as the credibility of the information entered into blockchain systems. By analyzing data patterns and detecting anomalies, AGI may be able to verify accuracy as well as consistency of data entries. This may reduce the risk of data manipulation and ensuring that blockchain systems operate based on accurate and trustworthy information.

10.3.2.4.2 Decentralized Data Sharing

AGI enables secure and decentralized data sharing among multiple parties. This is particularly important for blockchain, which relies on the collaboration of numerous nodes to maintain the integrity of the ledger. By using AGI, data owners can share their data with blockchain developers while maintaining control over their information. This decentralized approach promotes collaboration and innovation while protecting data privacy (Gupta 2020).

10.3.2.4.3 Incentivizing Participation

AGI may be used to automatically incentivize participation in blockchain development through token-based reward systems. Participants who contribute data, computational resources, or expertise to blockchain projects can be rewarded with tokens, which can be traded or used within the ecosystem. This creates a collaborative environment where stakeholders are motivated to contribute to the advancement of blockchain technology.

10.3.2.4.4 Enhanced Security

AGI may possess the ability to detect security threats and take the relevant countermeasures on its own. This may protect blockchain systems from viruses and cyber threats. Additionally, AGI might automate security protocols, ensuring that blockchain systems operate within predefined ethical and legal boundaries (Ketha and Provodnikova 2024).

10.4 Applications of AGI-Blockchain Integration

The integration of AGI and blockchain technology opens a myriad of applications across various sectors. This section explores how these technologies can be synergistically applied to enhance decentralized finance (DeFi), cybersecurity, healthcare, and governance.

10.4.1 Decentralized Finance (DeFi)

The term 'decentralised finance' of DeFi refers to a financial system which is built using blockchain technology to remove tradition financial intermediaries involved in transactions like banks, brokers, financial institutions, and regulators. Instead of depending on these intermediary entities to carry out transactions among two or more parties, DeFi makes use of smart self-executing contracts on the blockchain network to provide peer-to-peer (P2P) financial services.

Figure 10.4 shows that blockchain-powered DeFi platforms can leverage AGI for risk assessment, fraud detection and algorithmic trading (Adamyk et al. 2025). AI-driven Decentralized Autonomous Organizations (DAOs) can optimize governance models (Buterin 2014).

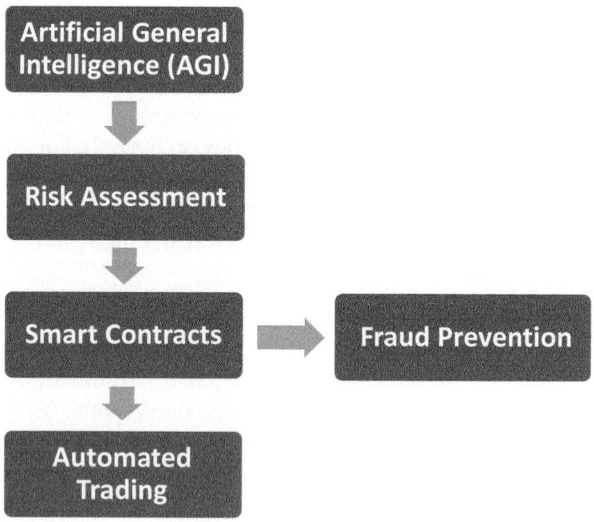

Figure 10.4. How AGI enhances Decentralized Finance (DeFi).

Risk Assessment: AGI may be able to analyze large quantities of financial data for identifying probable threats and for predicting market patterns. AGI might assess the risk profiles of various assets and provide real-time insights to investors. This capability may be crucial for DeFi platforms, where the absence of traditional financial intermediaries necessitates robust risk management mechanisms. AGI will probably be able to continuously monitor market conditions and adjust risk assessments dynamically, ensuring that DeFi platforms remain resilient to market fluctuations.

Fraud Detection: By examining transaction patterns and identifying anomalies, AGI may improve the safety of DeFi platforms by identifying frauds and other suspicious actions as they take place. This proactive approach is required for maintaining the trustworthiness of DeFi ecosystems, where the non-centralized character of transactions can make traditional fraud detection methods less effective. The expected capability of AGI to develop learning from past incidents and adjust its detection algorithms accordingly ensures that it remains effective against evolving threats (Kasula 2020).

Algorithmic Trading: AGI may optimize algorithmic trading strategies by analyzing market data and executing trades based on predictive models. This capability allows DeFi platforms to offer automated trading services that can operate at high speeds and with greater accuracy than human traders. AGI would most likely be able to continuously refine its trading algorithms based on market feedback, ensuring that trading strategies remain effective in changing market conditions. This may result in effective decision-making and better returns for investors (El Hessaini et al. 2024).

Decentralized Autonomous Organizations (DAOs): AGI might drive the governance of DAOs by optimizing decision-making processes. It would be able to recommend optimal governance structures and policies by analyzing historical data and simulating various governance scenarios. This capability can enhance the efficiency and transparency of DAOs, making them more effective at achieving their objectives. AGI may also facilitate the automation of governance processes, reducing the need for human intervention and minimizing the risk of biased decision-making (Buterin 2014).

10.4.2 Cybersecurity

The concept of cybersecurity refers to the practice of protecting the systems, data, and networks from unauthorized access and unwanted threats like viruses or cyber-attacks. This is a very important in today's world as personal, corporate, and even government data are often targeted by hackers and malwares. It has become very important to protect this data to avoid misuse. Figure 10.5 gives a general idea on how AGI and blockchain can enhance cybersecurity.

Cyber Threats: AGI could potentially strengthen blockchain security by identifying cyber threats in real-time, while blockchain ensures immutable storage of threat intelligence (Hessaini et al. 2024). It can take the role of analyzing network traffic and detecting potential cyber threats before they can cause harm (Tyagi et al. 2024a). AGI may also be able to identify patterns indicative of cyber-attacks and respond accordingly in real-time by utilizing machine learning algorithms. This proactive approach may be of great help in protecting blockchain networks as they are often targeted by sophisticated cyber threats.

Threat Detection: AGI would enhance threat detection capabilities by continuously monitoring network activities and identifying anomalies. By analyzing large volumes of data, AGI may detect subtle signs of cyber threats that might be missed by traditional security systems. This capability is very important in the case of

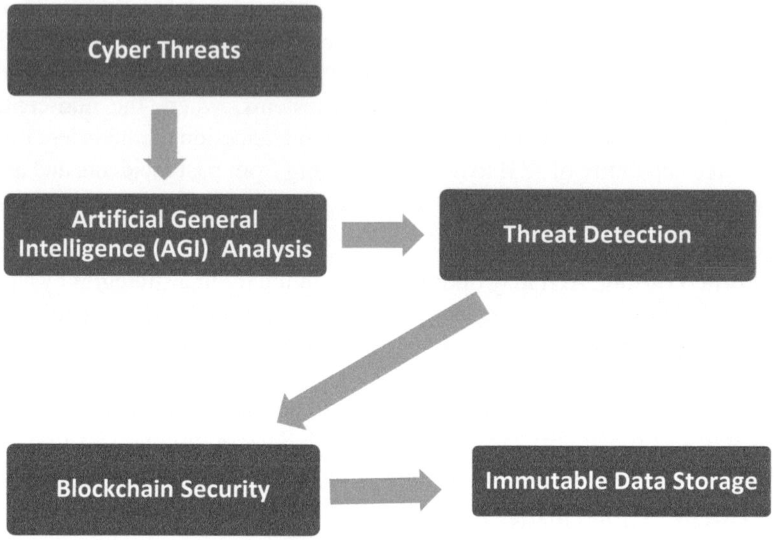

Figure 10.5. Cybersecurity.

blockchain networks due to the decentralized character of transactions which can hinder the detection of and response to threats. AGI's ability to learn from past incidents and adapt its detection algorithms ensures that it remains effective against evolving.

Blockchain Security: Blockchain technology provides an immutable ledger for storing threat intelligence, ensuring that security data cannot be tampered with. This capability is crucial for maintaining the integrity of threat intelligence data, which is essential for effective cybersecurity measures. By combining AGI's threat detection capabilities with blockchain's immutable storage, organizations can create robust security systems that are resilient to cyber-attacks. This integration can positively impact the security of blockchain networks while also them from sophisticated cyber-attacks.

10.4.3 Healthcare

Blockchain secures medical records, while AGI analyzes patient data for personalized treatments and drug discovery (Bathula et al. 2024).

Medical Records: Blockchain technology can secure medical records by providing an immutable ledger for storing patient data. This capability ensures that medical records cannot be tampered with. This enhances the safety as well as privacy of the information of the patient. Healthcare providers can create safe and transparent systems for managing patient data by employing blockchain. This ensures that medical records remain accurate and trustworthy (Kumari et al. 2024).

Personalized Treatments: AGI could analyze patient data to provide personalized treatments and improve healthcare outcomes. AGI could also identify patterns in patient data to recommend personalized treatment plans. This capability can enhance the precision of diagnoses while improving the effectiveness of treatments. This may lead to better patient outcomes. AGI's ability to learn from large volumes of data ensures that it remains effective at identifying patterns and making accurate predictions (Bathula et al. 2024).

Drug Discovery: AGI can be of help in accelerating drug discovery by analyzing large datasets and identifying potential drug candidates. AGI may detect trends in biological data to predict efficacy of potential drugs. This capability may substantially decrease time along with cost associated with drug discovery. This may result in the evolution of novel treatments for various diseases. AGI's ability to learn from past research would ensure that it remains effective at identifying promising drug candidates (Naithani et al. 2024c).

10.4.4 Governance

Decentralized governance models can utilize AGI for decision-making and policy enforcement (Zhang 2024).

Decision-Making: AGI may optimize the process of taking decisions in governance by examining historical data and simulating various scenarios. AGI may also recommend optimal policies and governance structures by employing machine learning algorithms. This capability can enhance the effectiveness along with the transparency of governance systems. This can potentially make them more efficient at achieving their objectives. AGI may also facilitate the automation of governance processes. This will reduce the requirement of human assistance and minimize the possibility of biased decision-making.

Policy Enforcement: AGI may enable enhancement of policy enforcement by monitoring compliance and identifying violations in real-time. It may analyze data and detect signs of non-compliance, ensuring that policies are enforced effectively. This capability may be important for sustaining the integrity of governance systems, where the non-centralized character of transactions could hinder the detection of and response to violations. AGI's ability to learn from past incidents and adapt its detection algorithms ensures that it remains effective against evolving.

Decentralized Governance Models: Blockchain technology can support decentralized governance models by providing an immutable ledger for recording governance actions. This capability ensures that governance actions cannot be tampered with, enhancing the transparency and accountability of governance systems. By combining AGI's decision-making capabilities with blockchain's immutable storage, organizations can create robust governance systems that are resilient to manipulation and corruption. This integration can enhance the overall effectiveness of governance systems and protect them from sophisticated threats.

10.5 Future Technologies: Generative AI, Federated Learning and Quantum Resistance

10.5.1 Generative AI

GenAI can automatically generate and optimize blockchain architectures, enabling AI-driven smart contract development and decentralized applications. This technology leverages advanced machine learning models, such as Generative Adversarial Networks (GANs) and Variational Autoencoders (VAEs), to create new data that mimics the properties of the training data. By doing so, GenAI can design more efficient blockchain networks, optimize consensus mechanisms and enhance the overall performance of blockchain systems. Figure 10.6 presents a general idea on how GenAI can enhance the blockchain technology.

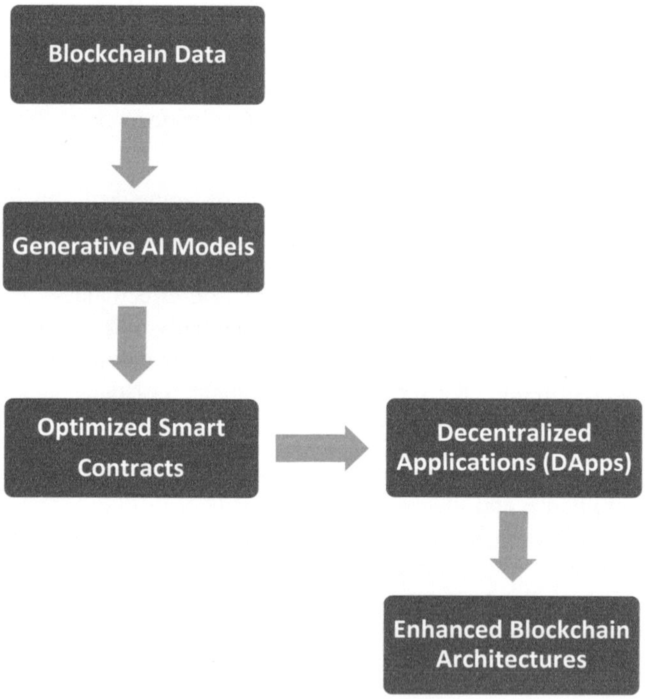

Figure 10.6. Generative AI.

Optimizing Blockchain Architectures: GenAI can analyze existing blockchain architectures and propose optimized designs that improve scalability, security, and efficiency. For instance, GenAI can identify bottlenecks in transaction processing and suggest architectural changes to alleviate these issues. This capability is crucial for developing next-generation blockchain networks that can handle the increasing demands of decentralized applications (Nguyen et al. 2025).

AI-Driven Smart Contract Development: GenAI can automate the development of smart contracts by generating code that meets specific requirements. This capability can significantly reduce the time and effort required to create smart contracts, making it easier for developers to deploy decentralized applications. Additionally, GenAI can optimize smart contract code to ensure that it is secure and efficient, reducing the risk of vulnerabilities and improving performance (Blockchain Council 2024).

Decentralized Applications (DApps): GenAI can enhance the development of decentralized applications by generating user interfaces, backend logic and other components. This capability can streamline the development process and enable the creation of more sophisticated and user-friendly DApps. By leveraging GenAI, developers can focus on higher-level design and functionality, while the AI handles the details of implementation (Nguyen et al. 2025).

Large Language Models (LLMs): LLMs, such as OpenAI's GPT-4 and Google's PaLM, can generate human-like text and understand complex language patterns. These models can be used to create detailed and accurate smart contracts, generate documentation, and even assist in legal and compliance tasks related to blockchain technology. For example, GPT-4 can draft smart contracts based on user inputs, ensuring that the contracts are legally sound and meet specific requirements.

Chatbots: ChatGPT, a conversational AI model developed by OpenAI, can assist in various blockchain-related tasks. It can provide real-time support for developers, answer questions about blockchain protocols and help troubleshoot issues. Additionally, ChatGPT can be integrated into decentralized applications to offer user support and enhance the overall user experience. For instance, ChatGPT can guide users through the process of setting up a blockchain wallet or executing a smart contract.

Case Study: Generative Diffusion Model: A recent study demonstrated the effectiveness of a generative diffusion model in optimizing blockchain network performance. The model was able to converge faster, achieve higher rewards and significantly improve the throughput and latency of the blockchain network compared to traditional AI approaches. This case study highlights the potential of GenAI to revolutionize blockchain technology by providing more efficient and scalable solutions (Nguyen et al. 2025). The synergy between GenAI and blockchain can lead to more robust and adaptive blockchain systems, capable of meeting the evolving needs of decentralized applications.

10.5.2 Federated Learning

Figure 10.7 shows that federated learning will allows multiple AGI models to train collaboratively on blockchain while preserving privacy (Dharamvir 2024). This approach enables the training of machine learning models on decentralized data without exposing sensitive information, ensuring data privacy and security.

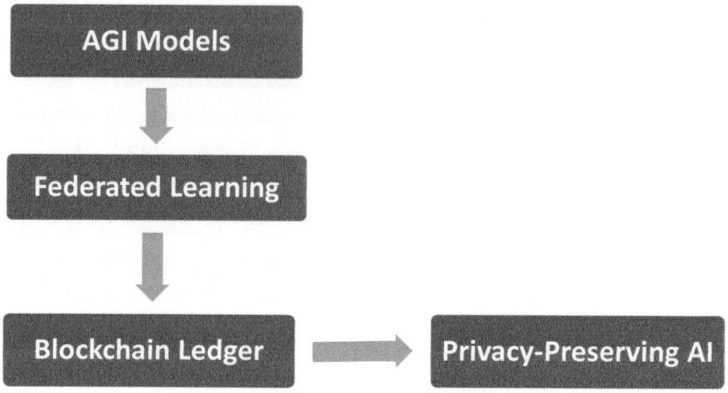

Figure 10.7. Federated Learning.

Collaborative Training: Federated learning enables multiple AGI models to collaborate on training tasks by sharing model updates rather than raw data. This approach allows organizations to leverage diverse data sources while maintaining data privacy. By aggregating model updates on a blockchain, federated learning ensures that the training process is transparent and verifiable (Aboukadri et al 2025).

Privacy-Preserving AI: Federated learning enhances privacy by keeping data on local devices and only sharing model updates. This approach reduces the risk of data breaches and ensures that sensitive information remains secure. By combining federated learning with blockchain, organizations can create robust privacy-preserving AI systems that are resilient to cyber threats (Kim et al. 2024).

Blockchain Ledger: The blockchain ledger provides a secure and transparent record of all model updates and contributions. This capability ensures that the training process is auditable and that all participants are accountable for their contributions. By leveraging blockchain, federated learning can create a trusted environment for collaborative AI development (Aboukadri et al. 2025).

Case Study: Federated ABAC Policy Mining: A recent study proposed a blockchain-based federated learning framework for mining Attribute-Based Access Control (ABAC) policies. The framework enabled organizations to collaboratively mine and enhance ABAC rules while preserving data privacy. The experimental results showcased an impressive accuracy score of 96.7%, demonstrating the effectiveness of federated learning in creating robust and adaptable access control policies (Aboukadri et al. 2025). This case study illustrates how federated learning can enhance the synergy between AGI and blockchain by enabling secure and collaborative AI development.

10.5.3 Quantum-Resistant Cryptography

Future quantum computers pose a risk to blockchain security. AGI-driven quantum-resistant cryptographic models can future-proof blockchain networks (Gschwendtner et al. 2024). Figure 10.8 shows how AGI and blockchain can be used to improve

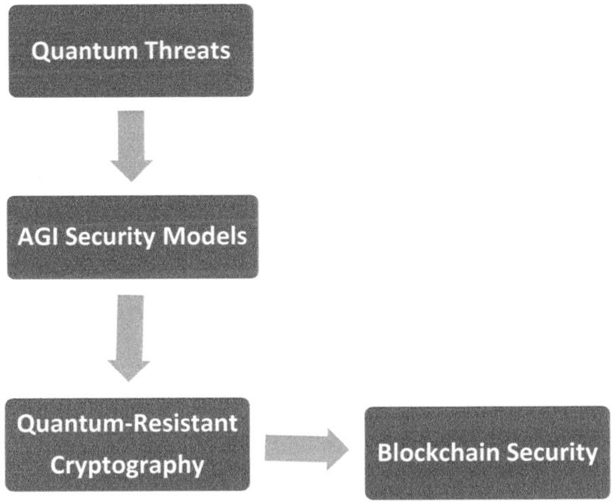

Figure 10.8. Quantum-Resistant Cryptography.

quantum-resistant cryptography, which involves developing cryptographic algorithms that are secure against the computational power of quantum computers.

Quantum Threats: Quantum computers have the potential to break traditional cryptographic algorithms, such as RSA and ECC, which are foundational to blockchain security. This capability poses a significant threat to the integrity and security of blockchain networks. To address this challenge, researchers are developing quantum-resistant cryptographic algorithms that can withstand quantum attacks (Kommera 2025).

AGI Security Models: AGI could have helped in enhancing the development of quantum-resistant cryptographic models by analyzing potential quantum threats and designing algorithms that are resilient to these threats. AGI could have identified weaknesses in existing cryptographic methods and proposed safer alternatives. This capability may prove to be crucial for ensuring the long-term security of blockchain networks (Thanalakshmi et al. 2023).

Quantum-Resistant Cryptography: Quantum-resistant cryptographic algorithms are designed to be secure against the computational power of quantum computers. These algorithms use mathematical problems that are believed to be hard for quantum computers to solve, such as lattice-based cryptography and hash-based signatures. By adopting quantum-resistant cryptography, blockchain networks can protect themselves from future quantum threats (Kommera 2025).

Blockchain Security: The integration of quantum-resistant cryptography with blockchain technology can enhance the overall security of blockchain networks. By leveraging AGI to develop and implement quantum-resistant algorithms, organizations can create blockchain systems that are resilient to quantum attacks. This capability is crucial for maintaining the integrity and trustworthiness of blockchain networks in the quantum era (Thanalakshmi et al. 2023).

Case Study: Hybrid Migration Strategy: A recent study proposed a hybrid migration strategy for transitioning to quantum-resistant blockchains. The strategy involved a phased approach, where blockchain networks gradually adopt quantum-resistant algorithms while maintaining compatibility with existing cryptographic methods. This approach ensures a smooth transition and minimizes the risk of disruptions. The study highlighted the importance of proactive measures in securing blockchain networks against quantum (Kim et al. 2024). This case study demonstrates how quantum-resistant cryptography can enhance the synergy between AGI and blockchain by ensuring the long-term security and resilience of blockchain systems.

10.6 Conclusion

The integration of Artificial General Intelligence (AGI) and blockchain technology holds transformative potential across various industries by enabling secure, decentralized, and autonomous systems. This synergy can revolutionize sectors such as finance, healthcare, cybersecurity, and governance by providing innovative solutions to contemporary challenges. For instance, in decentralized finance (DeFi), AGI can be used to optimize risk assessment, fraud detection and algorithmic trading, while blockchain ensures transparency and security. In healthcare, AGI can be used to critically analyze patient data for personalized treatments and blockchain can secure medical records. Despite these promising applications, significant challenges remain, including ethical concerns, scalability issues and regulatory hurdles. Ethical considerations such as bias, privacy and accountability must be addressed to ensure responsible AI development. Scalability challenges necessitate advancements in techniques like federated learning and blockchain scalability solutions. Regulatory frameworks must balance innovation with consumer protection and ethical use. Future research should focus on developing privacy-preserving federated learning, quantum-resistant security mechanisms and responsible AI frameworks. Collaborative efforts among researchers, industry stakeholders, policymakers and the community are essential to navigate these complexities and ensure the positive impact of AGI and blockchain integration. By addressing these challenges and fostering innovation, we can create robust and trustworthy AGI-blockchain systems that drive progress and benefit society.

References

Aboukadri, sara, and Ouaddah, Aafaf and Mezrioui, Abdellatif, Federated Learning Meets Blockchain: A Collaborative Framework for Mining Abac Policies. Available at SSRN: https://ssrn.com/abstract=5104492 or http://dx.doi.org/10.2139/ssrn.5104492.

Adamyk, B., Benson, V., Adamyk, O., and Liashenko, O. (2025). Risk Management in DeFi: Analyses of the Innovative Tools and Platforms for Tracking DeFi Transactions. Journal of Risk and Financial Management, 18(1): 38. https://doi.org/10.3390/jrfm18010038.

Bathula, A., Gupta, S. K., Merugu, S., Saba, L., Khanna, N. N., Laird, J. R. et al. (2024). Blockchain, artificial intelligence, and healthcare: the tripod of future—a narrative review. Artif. Intell. Rev. 57: 238. https://doi.org/10.1007/s10462-024-10873-5.

Bikkasani, D. C. (2024). Navigating artificial general intelligence (AGI): societal implications, ethical considerations and governance strategies. AI Ethics. https://doi.org/10.1007/s43681-024-00642-z.

Bostrom, N. (2014). Superintelligence: Paths, Dangers, Strategies. Oxford University Press. ISBN: 978-0199678112.

Buterin, V. (2014). Ethereum: A Next-Generation Smart Contract and Decentralized Application Platform. Retrieved from Ethereum Whitepaper Ethereum: A Next-Generation Smart Contract and Decentralized Application Platform.

Dharamvir. (2024). Blockchain and AGI: Ensuring Data Integrity and Security. IEEE International Conference on Computing, Communication and Informatics (IC3I). DOI: 10.1109/IC3I61595.2024.10828945.

Dirk, A. Zetzsche, Douglas W. Arner, and Ross P. Buckley. (2020). Decentralized Finance, Journal of Financial Regulation, Volume 6, Issue 2, 20 September 2020, Pages 172–203, https://doi.org/10.1093/jfr/fjaa010.

El Hessaini, S., Benaich, R., El Mendili, S., and Gahi, Y. (2024). Enhancing Blockchain Consensus Mechanisms with Artificial Intelligence: Potential Improvements and Applications. *In*: Ben Ahmed, M., Boudhir, A. A., Abd Elhamid Attia, H. F., Eštoková, A., and Zelenáková, M. (Eds.). Information Systems and Technological Advances for Sustainable Development. DATA 2024. Lecture Notes in Information Systems and Organisation, vol 71. Springer, Cham. https://doi.org/10.1007/978-3-031-75329-9_3.

Faraz Masood. (2022). Federated Learning with Blockchain: A Study of the Latest Decentralized Couple. DOI: 10.1109/ICCCIS56430.2022.10037647.

Goertzel, B. (2020). The AGI Revolution: An Inside View of the Rise of Artificial General Intelligence. Humanity+ Press. ISBN: 978-3030521516.

Gschwendtner, M., Soller, H., and Zingg, S. (2024). Combining quantum and AI for the next superpower. Nat. Rev. Electr. Eng., 1: 350–351. https://doi.org/10.1038/s44287-024-00051-8.

Gupta, Ishan. (2020). Decentralization of Artificial Intelligence: Analyzing Developments in Decentralized Learning and Distributed AI Networks. 10.13140/RG.2.2.17018.93124.

Kasula, B. Y. (2020). Fraud Detection and Prevention in Blockchain Systems Using Machine Learning. International Meridian Journal, 2(2), 1–8. https://meridianjournal.in/index.php/IMJ/article/view/22.

Ketha, S., and Provodnikova, D. A. (2024). Combining Blockchain and AI for Fraud Detection: Building Secure, Transparent and Sustainable Financial Ecosystems. Global Journal of Business and Integral Security. Retrieved from https://gbis.ch/index.php/gbis/article/view/599.

Kim, K., Raghavan, K., Kotevska, O., Dorier, M., Madduri, R., Ryu, M. et al. (2024). Privacy-preserving federated learning for science: challenges and research directions, 2024 IEEE International Conference on Big Data (BigData), Washington, DC, USA, pp. 7849–7853, doi: 10.1109/BigData62323.2024.10825853.

Kumari, S., Tiwari, S., Naithani, K., and Subbiah, P. (2024). Internet of things for smart agriculture: a survey. pp. 100–121. *In*: Naim, A. (Ed.). AI Applications for Business, Medical and Agricultural Sustainability. IGI Global Scientific Publishing. https://doi.org/10.4018/979-8-3693-5266-3.ch005.

Kushal Chawla, Hannah Rashkin, Gaurav Singh Tomar, and David Reitter. (2024). Investigating Content Planning for Navigating Trade-offs in Knowledge-Grounded Dialogue. In Proceedings of the 18th Conference of the European Chapter of the Association for Computational Linguistics (Volume 1: Long Papers), pages 2316–2335, St. Julian's, Malta. Association for Computational Linguistics.

Moosavi, J., Naeni, L. M., Fathollahi-Fard, A. M., and Fiore, U. (2021). Blockchain in supply chain management: a review, bibliometric, and network analysis. Environ. Sci. Pollut. Res. https://doi.org/10.1007/s11356-021-13094-3.

Naithani, K., and Tiwari, S. (2023). Deep Learning for the Intersection of Ethics and Privacy in Healthcare. In Machine Learning Algorithms Using Scikit and TensorFlow Environments (IGI Global Publishing). Edited by Puvvadi Baby Maruthi, Smrity Prasad, Amit Kumar Tyagi. DOI: 10.4018/978-1-6684-8531-6.

Naithani, K., Raiwani, Y. P., Tiwari, S., and Chauhan, A. S. (2024a). Artificial Intelligence Techniques Based on Federated Learning in Smart Healthcare. *In*: Kaushal Kishor, Parma Nand, Vishal Jain, Neetesh Saxena, Gaurav Agarwal, and Rani Astya (Eds.). Federated Learning for Smart Communication using IoT Application Edition (Imprint Chapman and Hall/CRC). DOI: 10.1201/9781003489368-5.

Naithani, K., Tiwari, S., and Tyagi, A. (2024c). Big Data Management and Analytics in Drug Research: A Comprehensive Overview. pp. 90–115. *In*: Tripathi, R., and Tiwari, S. (Eds.). Converging Pharmacy

Science and Engineering in Computational Drug Discovery. IGI Global Scientific Publishing. https://doi.org/10.4018/979-8-3693-2897-2.ch005.

Nakamoto, S. (2018) Bitcoin: A Peer-to-Peer Electronic Cash System. https://bitcoin.org/bitcoin.pdf.

Nguyen, Cong T., Liu, Yinqiu, Du, Hongyang, Hoang, Dinh Thai, Niyato, Dusit, Nguyen, Diep N. et al. (March 2025). Generative AI-enabled blockchain networks: fundamentals, applications, and case study. In IEEE Network, 39(2): 232–241, doi: 10.1109/MNET.2024.3412161.

Russell, S., and Norvig, P. (2022). Artificial Intelligence: A Modern Approach. Pearson. ISBN: 978-9356063570.

Sairaj Kommera. (2025). Quantum-Resistant Cryptography: Preparing for the Post-Quantum Cybersecurity Era. International Journal of Research in Computer Applications and Information Technology, 8(1): 1737–1749.

Salah, K., Rehman, M. H. U., Nizamuddin, N., and Al-Fuqaha, A. (2019). Blockchain for AI: Review and Open Research Challenges. IEEE Access, 7: 10127–10149. DOI: 10.1109/ACCESS.2018.2890507.

Swan, M. (2015). Blockchain: Blueprint for a New Economy. O'Reilly Media. ISBN: 978-1491920497.

Szabo, N. (1997). The Idea of Smart Contracts. Retrieved from Satoshi Nakamoto Institute. The Idea of Smart Contracts | Satoshi Nakamoto Institute.

Taher, S. S., Ameen, S. Y., and Ahmed, J. A. (2024). Advanced Fraud Detection in Blockchain Transactions: An Ensemble Learning and Explainable AI Approach. Engineering, Technology & Applied Science Research. 14, 1 (Feb. 2024), 12822–12830. DOI: https://doi.org/10.48084/etasr.6641.

Taherdoost, H. (2022). Blockchain Technology and Artificial Intelligence Together: A Critical Review on Applications. Applied Sciences, 12(24): 12948. https://doi.org/10.3390/app12241294.

Thanalakshmi, P., Rishikhesh, A., Marion Marceline, J., Joshi, G. P., and Cho, W. (2023). A Quantum-Resistant Blockchain System: A Comparative Analysis. Mathematics, 11(18): 3947. https://doi.org/10.3390/math11183947.

Tyagi, A. K., Naithani, K., and Tiwari, S. (2024a). Security and Possible Threats in Today's Online Social Networking Platforms. *In*: Rathi, S. K., Keswani, B., Saxena, R. K., Kapoor, S. K., Gupta, S., and Rawat, R. (Eds.). Online Social Networks in Business Frameworks. https://doi.org/10.1002/9781394231126.ch8.

Tyagi, A. K., Tiwari, S., and Naithani, K. (2024b). Distributed Systems and Distributed Ledger Technology - An Introduction. *In*: Tyagi, A. K., Tiwari, S., Arumugam, S. K., and Sharma, A. K. (Eds.). Artificial Intelligence-Enabled Digital Twin for Smart Manufacturing. https://doi.org/10.1002/9781394303601.ch6.

Zhang, J. (2024). Artificial Intelligence Governance and the Blockchain Revolution. Springer. DOI: 10.1007/978-981-99-9211-9.

Zhou, S., Li, K., Xiao, L., Cai, J., Liang, W., and Castiglione, A. (2023). A Systematic Review of Consensus Mechanisms in Blockchain. Mathematics, 11(10): 2248. https://doi.org/10.3390/math11102248.

Index

O

P

R

S

T

Editors' Biography

Kanchan Naithani received her Ph.D. in the department of Computer Science and Engineering at H.N.B. Garhwal University (A Central University), Srinagar Garhwal, Uttarakhand, India (2024). She completed M. Tech in Computer Science and Engineering from G. B. Pant Engineering Institute of Technology, Ghurdauri, Pauri, Uttarakhand, India (2018) and B. Tech in Computer Science and Engineering from Graphic Era Hill University, Dehradun India (2016). Currently, she is working as an Assistant Professor in the Computer Science and Engineering, at GL Bajaj Institute of Technology and Management, Greater Noida, Gautam Budha Nagar, Uttar Pradesh-203201 (India). She has authored and co-authored more than twenty papers (according to Scopus Database) in refereed high impact journals, conferences, and books, and some of her articles were given best paper awards. She has filed two patents (Nationally and Internationally) in the area of Deep Learning and Internet of Things. She has edited two books for CRC Press and IGI Global. Her research interests focus on Artificial Intelligence, Machine Learning, Sentiment Analysis and Natural Language Processing. She is a lifetime member of the IAENG Society of Artificial Intelligence and the IAENG Society of Computer Science.

Shrikant Tiwari (Senior Member, IEEE) received his Ph.D. in the Department of Computer Science and Engineering at the Indian Institute of Technology (Banaras Hindu University), Varanasi, India, in 2012, and his M. Tech. in Computer Science and Technology from the University of Mysore, India, in 2009. Currently, he serves as a Professor in the School of Computing Science and Engineering at Galgotias University, Greater Noida, Gautam Buddha Nagar, Uttar Pradesh, India.

Dr. Tiwari has published over seventy-five plus papers in refereed high-impact journals, conferences, and books, with several of his articles receiving best paper awards. He has also filed more than 10 patents, both nationally and internationally, in the areas of deep learning, the Internet of Things, cyber-physical systems, and computer vision. Additionally, he has edited more than five books for prestigious publishers such as IET, Elsevier, Springer, and CRC Press. His research interests include machine learning, deep learning, computer vision, medical image analysis, pattern recognition, and biometrics.

Dr. Tiwari is a Fellow of the Institution of Electronics and Telecommunication Engineers (IETE), Senior Member of IEEE and a member of the Association for Computing Machinery (ACM), the Institution of Engineering and Technology (IET), the Computer Society of India (CSI), the Indian Society for Technical Education (ISTE), the International Association of Engineers (IAENG), and the Science and

Engineering Institute (SCIEI). He also serves as a guest editorial board member and reviewer for numerous international journals of repute.

Abhishek Danu is working as a Senior Research Fellow (UGC-SRF) in the Department of Business Management, H.N.B. Garhwal University (A Central University), Srinagar Garhwal, Uttarakhand, India. He completed his B. tech in electrical engineering from DIT University, Dehradun, Uttarakhand, India, in 2017, and completed his MBA (Marketing & Finance) from H.N.B. Garhwal University (A Central University), Srinagar Garhwal, Uttarakhand, India, in 2019. He has previously worked as a marketing manager for a solar technology firm. He cleared UGC NET in Management in 2020 and UGC NET with JRF in 2022. He has published research articles and book chapters with reputed publishers. He has also presented his research papers in national and international conferences. His research interests include International Trade, International Business, Financial Development, Open Economy Macroeconomics, Artificial Intelligence and Machine Learning.

For Product Safety Concerns and Information please contact our EU representative GPSR@taylorandfrancis.com Taylor & Francis Verlag GmbH, Kaufingerstraße 24, 80331 München, Germany